Caveat Emptor

Reading Virtual Minds Volume I: Science and History is a "Let's explore the possibilities" book, not a "How to do it" book. As such, it deals with how NextStage did it (not to mention things that happened along the way). It does not explain how you can do it. This book's purpose is to open a new territory to you and give you some basic tools for exploration.

There are no magic bullets, quick fixes, simple demonstrations, et cetera, that will turn you into jedis, gurus, kings, queens, samurai, rock stars, mavens, heroes, thought leaders, so on and so forth.

How to Do It starts with **Volume II: Experience and Expectation** and continues through future volumes in this series. We've included a **Volume II: Experience and Expectation** preview with a *How to Do It* example on page 302 so you can peek if that's your interest.

That noted, I'm quite sure that you won't get the full benefit of future volumes without reading this one because unless you've read this one you won't understand the territory you're exploring in those future volumes.

- Joseph

Comments on NextStage and Reading Virtual Minds

This is the closest thing to a crystal ball I've ever seen.– *Rob Graham, ClickZ columnist and Director, LearningCraft.com*

I wouldn't be surprised if the techniques suggested by Joseph Carrabis don't become standard ways of increasing traffic to websites. – *Theresa Quantinilla, qViews.com*

Companies need to start utilizing the ethnographic and sociologic research that NextStage is doing. – *Annette Priest, Dell Usability Research Manager*

You can trust me to give it to you the way I see it. NextStage's ideas and methods are important to website success and indeed, to marketing success. If you are involved in marketing on any level, NextStage is important to you. It can help you be a better marketer, a more successful marketer, with much higher customer satisfaction scores than you are experiencing today. – *Jim Sterne, Target Marketing, Emetrics Summit Organizer, WAA Founder*

NextStage has had capabilities for more than 10 years that are a generation beyond "bits and bytes". If you'd prefer to make investment decisions by knowing investors' preferences moment-by-moment rather than use last quarter's earnings reports, NextStage is your go-to. You could compare NextStage's Evolution Technology to Big Data but it would be like putting a Lamborghini next to a tricycle. The tricycle's cute but the Lamborghini's for grownups. – *Catherine McQuaid, International Trade and Development Entrepreneur*

NextStage's insights and views are something that a web analyst, marketing managers, site designers and anybody who has anything to do with site layout should be aware of. – *Anil Batra on Web Analysis, Behavioral Targeting and Advertising*

...exactly the type of thought leadership that's important... – *Brian Merrill, FamaPR*

What a concept: designing websites to work with human beings the way humans interact naturally with the world about them! – *Mark DeYoung, Principal Systems Engineer, Performance Engineering Specialist, HP*

NextStage has come up with a new and definite success metric for the online economy. We will be taking their findings and working with partners to help them improve the overall effectiveness of their websites. – *David Ireland, President OpenEdge Division, SVP Progress Software*

I am enthralled by the level of insight Joseph brings to understanding the difference between how men and women react to marketing. – *Susan Bratton, CEO, Personal Life Media*

NextStage's patented technology uses mouse tracking techniques to collect subconscious behavior, which is mapped to 70+ different personality types derived from traditional psycho and emotional cognitive behaviors from a 100k+ behaviors database. The technology also eliminates the need for first- or third-party cookies, giving a much more accurate read on unique visitors. It can even tell unique visitors apart on shared computers because the subconscious behavior is different by user. ... [NextStage's Sentiment Mining technology] can be used in place of traditional qualitative research techniques and quantitative surveys, especially in the area of product development and response to design and communications. – *Shaina Boone, Marketing Science Director, Critical Mass*

I have never read a book where the mind of the author is laid out there like this and the personality/brilliance shines. – *Laureen Martel, Business Development Manager - Application Partner Alliances, Progress Software*

What you do and the experience you have is invaluable. – *Slava Sambu, E-Business Analytics Manager, Vance Publishing Corp*

In a haze of numbers generated by the technology advances in marketing and information delivery, people too often forget that their website visitors are human beings. *Reading Virtual Minds* is a fascinating journey into how years of research about human learning, behaviors, expectations, and interests in the offline world molds their behavior online. *– Angie Brown, Strategic Services Consultant, Coremetrics*

NextStage Evolution is doing things that months ago, we could not dream of ... and doing them REALLY well. 'Innovative' is not a strong enough term for what NextStage Evolution has done to the field of Internet marketing research. The ideas are revolutionary; the implications staggering. *– Dave McCullough II, Marketing Analyst, WincoID*

Joseph Carrabis is one of the century's most innovative thinkers. He links bodies of knowledge as different as anthropology and statistics to create a whole new body of learning. The result is logical induction on a level unheard of — he can take the words in the document you just wrote and tell you the age and gender of the people you admire. *– Robbin Steif, CEO, Lunametrics*

A word of thanks to Joseph for conducting a site review on www.metricks.org yesterday. Unlike the nefarious SEO companies who tell me my site is performing badly and has a ton of things wrong with it, Joseph's review was positive, insightful and extremely helpful. It was also fun! We had many a good laugh.
Joseph's reasoning included how people use sites based on their prior experiences in life, culture, gender and a myriad of other factors, rather than limited to purely digital experience.
Joseph also explained some of his techniques after he'd used them on me, which was fascinating and a very valuable learning experience.
I highly recommend using the service - you will get a lot out of it and if your site is anything like mine, i.e., slightly neglected, a lengthy to do list! *- Jon Whitehead, Director of Data Insights and Analytics*

Marketing research methodologies that rely on questionnaires and standard surveys are inherently loaded with biases and errors related to the sampling frame, the survey instruments, the interviewers and the fact that the respondents know that they are being evaluated. NextStage is truly a non-biasing research tool with a lot of validity and reliability because it is based on non-conscious responses to information. This methodology offers a lot of advantages over traditional methods to evaluate the appeal and the benefits of a website. – *Eric Drouart, Former VP, International Operations, Bristol-Myers Squibb*

NextStage has developed a capability for measuring user thought patterns and responses. Using their technology, two users can access the same file and the information could be presented in formats uniquely tailored to suit each user. That means the computer no longer treats all users in the same way, but can distinguish and adapt to user Bob versus user Sue dynamically. No longer do we have to learn how to use the computer, but the computer will have to start learning how to be used by us. – *Jayson Lee, Sr. Developer, Mitre Corp*

Joseph is one of those guys I wish I had more time with because I always glean something new from every conversation. His no-nonsense approach and ability to help better understand and meet the needs of users/visitors online has been very valuable and provides a unique view on the success/failure of your online efforts. – *Scott Baldwin, Manager, Web Services at North Shore Credit Union*

[NextStage has] developed a technology that is able to evaluate if a product, a site, a brochure etc.. will work without doing any focus group, testing or anything. How? They have compiled bazillion of data points on the behavior, attitudes, emotions, tastes, preferences of millions of Western educated people and have derived a statistical model that allows to do predictive modeling for specific behavior. This is the type of technology that will make marketing leapfrog to neuromarketing. – *Pierre Guillaume Wielezynski, Corporate Communications – Online Outreach, The World Bank Group*

I think it is always interesting to watch how humans walk around a large space like a college campus. While sidewalks define the space in some ways, it is the paths worn in the grass that tell how people really walk around. Traditional analytic tools are most comfortable measuring what's happening on the sidewalks. They measure force loads on predefined spaces. Your tools don't really care about that. Your tools really are measuring the intersection of the visitor and the true space they are navigating. You tickled my thinky bone once again. Thanks! – *Matt Van Wagner, CEO, FindMeFaster*

Reading Virtual Minds
Volume I: Science and History

Understanding and Using
Evolution Technology
4th Edition

Joseph Carrabis
CRO & Founder
The NextStage Companies

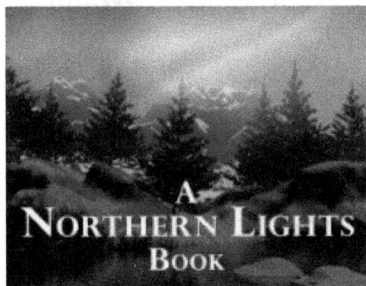

First Edition Publication Sept 2009
Second Edition Publication Oct 2009
Third Edition Publication Dec 2010
Fourth Edition Publication Jul 2015
Northern Lights Publishing
Nashua, NH, USA

Reading Virtual Minds Volume 1: Science and History,
4th Edition
all material copyright © 1999-2015 Joseph Carrabis.
All rights reserved.

Sections of this book were previously published on
The Hungry Peasant, http://www.hungrypeasant.com

ISBN: 978-0-9841403-4-3

Le coeur a ses raisons que la raison ne connait pas
– Pascal

Dedication

First for Susan
(because everything should be),

Second to AJ
(because in The End you'll see that it was his idea in the beginning)

Acknowledgements

Many people took part in the work on this book. My thanks to those who read through the chapters and offered critical comment and review:

Andy Black, Business Marketing Consultant, New Hampshire Business Review
Tom Connors, Consulting Economist, Ridma
Jack Carroll, PhD, Principal, VOC Partners
Greg Jarboe, Owner, SEO-PR
Laureen Martel, Senior Product Marketing Consultant, Progress Software
Susan O'Neil, CEO, WebSitePublicity
Todd A. Sullivan, Managing Attorney, Hayes Soloway PC
David Van Wie, Chairman, Palo Alto Software
Brian Merrill
Dan Hill, CEO, Sensory Logic,
David J. McCullough
David R. McCullough, President, WincoID
David Nelson
Derek Ross
Dmitri Eronshenko, CEO, ClickLab,

John Robinson, PhD, PIC, MRC-Delphi,
Marie Wemett
Marie White, CEO, WincoID
Paul McNulty
Stan Buchin, PhD
Theresa Craig, CEO, SunCoast Systems

To those who put up with questions and research,

To those who listened and debated,

And in beloved memory of those who got me out
from behind the keyboard,

Fenris and Merlin,

Rest well, dear ones.

Thanks to you all.

Special 4th edition thanks to

Jennifer "The Editress" Day
&
Dolores "HawkEye" Fallon

*If you don't ask the right questions
every answer seems wrong.
- Ani Di Franco*

Table of Contents

Digital Resources for the Reading Virtual Minds *Series*

Some of the images in the **Reading Virtual Minds** series print editions are dark and difficult to read due to grayscaling and sizing issues. You can find high resolution, full color images of most charts and graphs used in this series at http://nlb.pub/rvm

Evolution Technology™ (ET), the technology described in this book and the external demonstration of much described in this series, is the foundation of several tools used for a variety of purposes by people ranging from lovers to politicians to business people to researchers and more. You can watch a video explaining and using many of the tools developed from ET at http://nlb.pub/3

Please note that case matters ("A" isn't the same as "a") with all nlb.pub urls.

Preface to the Fourth Edition

I'm actually writing *Reading Virtual Minds Volume II: Experience and Expectation* right now. In the process of doing that, we realized we needed to add an index to this book. We also wanted to make a full color ebook version available to NextStage Members[a].

In the process of making a full color version, we realized we'd misplaced some of the original slides and, of course, the charting software had changed since we originally published this volume (same information, different charting system). Also Susan and Jennifer "The Editress" Day wanted the images standardized as much as possible.

We included an *Appendix B – Proofs* (starting on page 187) for the curious, updated *Appendix C – Further Readings* (starting on page 236). We migrated a blog used for reference purposes so there may be more or less reference sources and modified some sections with more recent information.

So this edition has a few more pages and a few different pages. It may have an extra quote or two floating around.

Enjoy.

---

[a] – And you should be one if you're not already! http://nlb.pub/4

About the Cover

The cover illustration is based on a class I've given in both academic and business settings since September 2000. It demonstrates how information in an individual's environment can both help and hurt a company's messaging, communication and marketing efforts and is a stylized version of the image below.

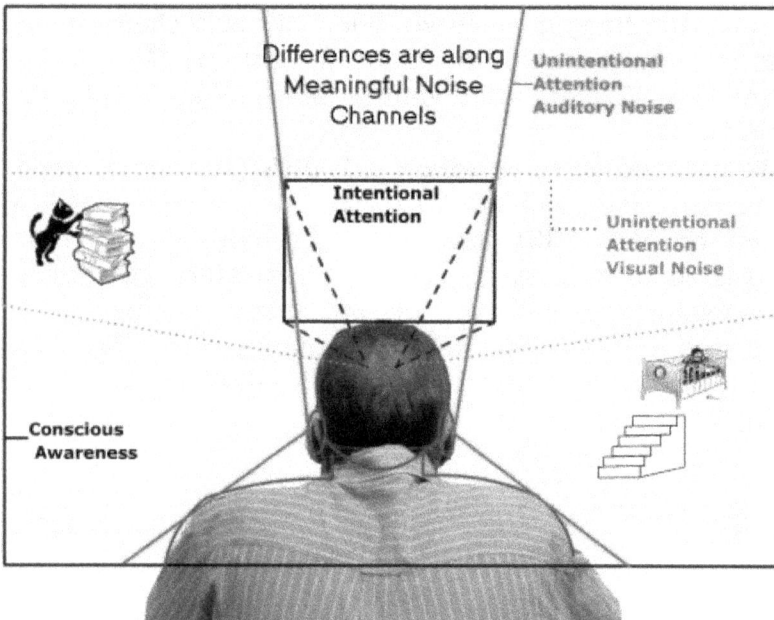

The neural effort required to focus our attention on any one information source is proportional to the amount and intensity of all information sources in our immediate internal and external environments.

An individual will intentionally direct their attention to an information source. It can be a picture, a movie, a music source, print, a scene outside their window, someone's voice, someone's touch, a taste or smell. Willingly focusing our attention on something is called *intentional attention*. What many don't recognize is that the information source doesn't have to be external. A memory can and often does focus our attention along these and other sensory channels. When we're wanting to remember something, our internal attention is intentional.

Whether we're intentionally internally or externally focused, our eyes are constantly sending information to the visual centers of the brain. The brain monitors this visual information and we're constantly non-consciously deciding if something in our visual field is more important than what we're intentionally focusing our eyes on. When our brain determines some visual information is sufficiently important to get our attention, our focus shifts to the new information in the visual field. When this shift in awareness happens, it's called *unintentional attention* — we don't mean to shift our attention from what originally interested us to something else, it just happens and is a hold over from our evolutionary history. Intrusive information in our visual field is called *visual noise*.

For example, we may be watching some video and notice out of the corner of our eye that the cat is about to knock over a stack of books. Our attention goes from the video to the cat and we react to this new information source. Our unintentional attention has shifted our focus and we miss something in the video.

The concept of unintentional attention is true for all our senses. The cover illustrates *auditory noise* as another source of unintentional attention. Again, we could be watching a video or reading and we hear the child cry or something falling down the stairs. Our attention goes from the book or video to the new information source.

The trick presented here is to present information that focuses your audience's senses where you want them when you want them. This is done by introducing differences in the information stream along *meaningful noise channels*. Meaningful noise channels are the things culture and society train us are important and deserve our attention, hence they are different for different cultural, social and economic groups.

And the only things we can recognize as having meaning are things that already exist in our *conscious awareness* and this is where personal beliefs and ideas come into play. Many studies have shown that what an individual recognizes as real — as in "existing in reality" — is really nothing more than what their culture and life experience has trained them to accept as real. The atheist, for example, has no belief in a deity while the fundamentalist believes that a deity intervenes in their life daily.

They will fear what you can do unless you give it the guise of a service they can understand. They won't attempt it, it will be enough that they believe they can do it if they wanted to. And the few who attempt it will fail because they can't understand the true science. The true science, to them, will be magic.
— Nunpa Sunkawakan

Foreword

by Dan Linton
Group Director, Analytics, MRM//McCann

I've been working with Joseph and his tools now for several years. As a digital marketing analytics professional, there are several phrases I can use to describe the man and the technology he creates related to my field of work: game-changing, mind-blowing, visionary.

I don't use those words lightly. We experienced significant lift in results at my previous company, typically double digit, anytime we used NextStage Technology across a variety of projects. I've seen the future of advanced analytics, and it's the next generation technology Joseph has invented and continues to develop.

How do you measure website engagement? Page depth? Time on site? Top viewed content? Satisfaction surveys? Content scoring? These are proxies for what we in digital analytics think reflects visitor engagement. Now imagine a tool that you could put on your website that silently and anonymously watches user behavior like mouse movements and typing patterns, and measures engagement by actually determining how visitors feel about content, without having to ask them.

Then imagine that the same tool can then alter visitor website experience on-the-fly and present more engaging content, learning as it goes. Then imagine watching your conversion rates go through the roof.

It's not fiction or magic. It is a real tool, it is real science, and you can use it on your website to drive real extraordinary business results. It measures more than just engagement, it determines mood, authority and a huge variety of other psychological, behavioral and motivational drivers. Imagine what you could do with that. Companies who choose to engage these tools will instantly be light years ahead of their competition.

And that's just the tip of Joseph's iceberg. He's continually creating new tools, new technology, and new thinking to enable marketers to measure and enhance the effectiveness of their work in ways that haven't even been thought possible before.

I consider myself lucky to have met Joseph, and I am continually awed and humbled by the man. If you're in business and want to do better, I'd suggest you get to know him and his marketing toolbox as well.

If nothing else, you'll at least get a few good jokes out him.

Author's Foreword

Howdy.

My name is Joseph, I'm the author, and this is my foreword. Let me tell you some things about myself that might help you decide if this book is for you.

First, I'm not your standard business executive and this is not your standard business executive's book. I couldn't write a popular business book if I tried. It's not in my nature. I spent an afternoon at a Barnes&Noble™ looking at popular business books before I started writing this one. Between 250 to 350 pages to talk about a single idea nebulously? With no action items? Definitely not my style. This book (this whole series, in fact) is going to cover a very rich topic — how people interact with information (software interfaces, websites, emails, brochures, flyers, other people, etc.) in their environment — and it's going to cover that topic in detail. Be prepared for footnotes and references. And be prepared to lose out if you don't make use of them.

And I hated textbooks which had "...is left to the reader" or "...the derivation is left as an exercise for the student" or some such hobnobble. To me, these were examples of "poof, and then a miracle happened" and "...it's intuitively obvious to the casual observer", neither of which were true. I have a habit of going over things in excruciating detail, explaining something then explaining the explanation.

My feeling is this: if the reader can't follow something from the roots to the treetop then the author is leaving something out[a]. If you're going to read this book, be prepared to take part in the discussion. Let me give you an example...

Once upon a time I was a presenter at an MIT Enterprise Forum. I was there to introduce people to a technology we were

---

[a] – From NextStage's Principles, "What is a Dark Mystery to you is Perfectly Obvious to someone else (and vice versa). So when you explain something to somebody, explain the obvious. When you leave something out and they don't get it, you're the fool, not them." - http://nlb.pub/5

patenting[b]. I started my presentation by walking to the podium and staring at the laptop there. It wasn't my laptop but it did have my presentation on it. I said into the microphone, "Oh-oh. Not Joseph's laptop. Joseph not familiar. Very scary. Ooh."

There were about 200 people in the audience and, as they say, you could have heard a pin drop. I looked up at them and said, "Folks, trust me. I'm not like anybody else you've ever seen."

Some nervous laughter.

"Are you ready?"

More nervous laughter. A few polite nods.

And so I started. I was allowed only twenty minutes for my presentation and follow-up. Half an hour later people were standing up, waving their hands for me to call on them to answer questions or to share their comments. By that time I'd left the podium and was walking through the audience, a Phil Donahue of Technology, handing people the mike so their questions and comments could be heard. An hour later we were still talking back and forth. One fellow, an MD-PhD in neurology, kept shouting out, "That's right! That's exactly how you'd do it!" every time I explained some facet of how our technology worked. After the forum there was a line of people waiting to talk with me. Most of them started with, "That was great" or "That was a riot" or "That was one of the most enjoyable presentations I've ever seen." People were still coming up to me with comments, thoughts and suggestions as I walked to my car. That was in 2003 and people still talk to me about it.

That experience, to me, was fun. It was also a great learning experience for me and, I'm guessing, for most of the people in the audience. Fun and learning. They should go hand-in-hand, I think.

---

[b] – I started writing this book in 2003. We've received the patent since then. You can find out about it at http://nlb.pub/6. You can learn about the journey from 2003 to receiving the patent to publication of this book in *Chapter VI, The Long Road Home* (page 170).

Personal Experience, Personal Examples

So I'm not your normal business executive. I write from personal experience and explain with personal examples. By training and in alphabetical order, I'm an anthropologist, a linguist, a mathematician, a neuroscientist, a physicist, ... One of my bios (***About the Author***, page 280) states that I've been everything from a butcher to truckdriver to Senior Knowledge Architect to Chief Research Scientist. What's my specialty? My specialty is understanding why people don't capitalize *butcher* and *truckdriver* but do capitalize *Senior Knowledge Architect* and *Chief Research Scientist*, and why most people don't pay any attention to that fact until someone references it. I don't have the training and education most business executives have. What I do have is a completely different set of filters that I apply to business situations.

And in that last sentence is something else I study and specialize in, and it points to the reason it's important for you to read this book, and I don't mean the fact that I have a completely different set of filters than you do. What I mean is that you probably understood what I meant by "filters" and "business situations" without my having to explain it to you. Those are fairly common expressions. But did anyone ever sit down with you and explain what *filters* are and how they come about or why people have the ones they do? Did anyone ever stand with you by a blackboard and diagram a *business situation* so that you'd understand the psychological, social and personal — collectively, the *neural* — dynamics involved in conducting business?

My guess is no, nobody overtly taught you the meaning of "filters" and "business situations". You intuitively knew what those terms meant, just as you intuitively accepted that certain job titles are capitalized in our society and others are not. The purpose of **Reading Virtual Minds** is to help you recognize how that same intuition might be betraying you in business, denying you opportunities and increasing your risk in future markets.

And that last sentence; if you're a business reader, you're probably a little more comfortable than you were before. If you're not a business reader? Perhaps that phrasing put you off a little bit. Phrases like that are *turning points*, and there are two kinds of turning points; *tipping points* and *tripping points*. You've probably heard the terms before and I'll bet didn't know them as turning points, definite points in mental time and space in which people's decisions, thoughts, beliefs and ideas change the direction of their lives.[c]

Both this book and this series are thick and rich, and I expect you to put some time into it and them. If you think this book is above you or beyond your capabilities, do us both a favor and put it down before it so captures you that you must carry it to the checkout and purchase a copy.

Reading What?

The title of this series, *Reading Virtual Minds*, comes from 2nd Order Cybernetics[7,198,214,239,279] and AnthroSemiotics[4,13, 14,30,152,161,201,220,264,277,278] and is used at a friend's suggestion. These two little known fields come from two very well-known fields, anthropology and neuroscience.

AnthroSemiotics is the study of how people use signs and symbols to communicate. Second Order Cybernetics is the study of how observers influence what they observe. The **Further Readings** section of this book (page 236) contains pointers and references for those interested in learning more.

This series will cover things like *Predictive Intelligence* and *Persuasive Analytics* as they're applied in business. They're fairly well-understood phenomena in anthropology and neuroscience, although in those fields Predictive Intelligence and Persuasive Analytics go by the generalist term of "mindreading", and yes, I'm serious, "mindreading".

Articles on the type of mindreading referenced in anthropology and neuroscience can be found in journals as

---

[c] – Turning points are covered in more detail in the rest of the *Reading Virtual Minds* series. The important thing to note is that what's a tipping point for some is a tripping point for others and in both cases are turning points in how people perceive the information you're giving them.

diverse as *The Journal of Sociolinguistics*, *The British Journal of Developmental Psychology*, *Evolution Psychiatrique*, *Neuropsychologia*, *The International Journal of Intercultural Relations*, *Visual Cognition*, and *The European Journal of Cognitive Psychology*. In fact, the number of fields which recognize "mindreading" is pretty vast. In these fields, however, mindreading doesn't mean telepathy and there's no hocus-pocus or mumbo-jumbo about it.

Mindreading in the form of Predictive Intelligence and Persuasive Analytics is what allows us to have anywhere from a rough to a pretty good idea of how someone is thinking just by looking at them. Everybody does it; we just don't give it the same name. Most people lump these two disciplines together and simply call it *intuition*. We predict — or *intuit* — what will happen based on x, y, z and t occurring. We don't know for a fact what will happen, we just have a good idea based on what's happened before. We persuade someone to do or not do something because they like or don't like m, n, o and p. Really what we're doing is guessing — or *intuiting* — their actions based on what we've witnessed in the past.

Being able to intuit with high accuracy is rewarded in our society. Jury selectors, FBI profilers, professional negotiators, gamblers, top-class salespeople, ... these are people whose ability to predict and persuade goes well beyond the average person's ability to intuit what someone will or won't like for their birthday or will or won't do if they win the lottery. These professionals have a great deal of training but really, when you get down to it, they're not doing anything different than what you or I do. The only real difference is that their training allows them to be consciously aware that they're predicting and persuading, why they're predicting and persuading, to extract vital information from others while they're doing it, and most importantly to know when what they're doing results in a negative outcome and how to prevent it.

These people — and you and I, don't forget — "get under the skin" of someone or "think the way they do" because it's how we function in society. Without the ability to mindread we wouldn't know when people like us or how much they like us, or that they don't like us and how much they don't like us. Psychologists and psychotherapists even have a term for people who can't mindread as well as they should. It's called "socially retarded" and it means they don't have the necessary social skills to function as well as they should. Why don't they have the necessary social skills? Because somewhere along the way they weren't exposed to enough other people for a long enough period of time to learn how to mindread; to predict how people would respond to something or how to persuade people to a certain point of view.

And strangely enough, everyone has had this kind of experience. Have you ever been in a situation where you wanted to share a very funny but somewhat off-color joke and weren't sure how the people around you would take it?

Congratulations! You couldn't mindread! Another way of phrasing that is to say that you hadn't been in enough similar situations to be able to predict how those around you would respond or persuade them to think of the joke as more funny than off-color. The person who tells such jokes when they shouldn't is described as lacking "social skills". One of the great functions of communities is to help individuals develop social skills, and the study of communities has a long and rich history.

My research for the past twenty-plus years or so has explored how virtual-space communities are causing new social skills to manifest, and how much cross-pollination there is between current, real-space social skills (such as meeting a friend at the grocery store and chatting) and recently developed or acquired virtual-space social skills (such as agreeing to chat with someone online or meet someone in a virtual environment).

What's the Difference?

Let me give you an example of the difference between everyday intuition and predictive intelligence and persuasive analytics...

Have you ever given someone a gift and seen the "Oh, God. Not another one" look on their face? Before they can say a "Thank you" or a "How sweet" or even "Oh, God. I've already got five of these" you're making apologies and offering to return it for something else they'd like.

Here's the question that starts people down the road of Profiling or Selling or whatever: How did you know the individual wasn't satisfied with the gift?

Smart money says "By the look on their face" and lets it stop at that.

Wise money says "The look on their face is the kind of look I have on my face when I'm disappointed."

And the people who earn a living at profiling or selling know that it's not just the look on the face, it's the sudden suspension of breath, the slight flushing of the cheeks, the momentary and hardly noticeable sagging of the arms, the defocusing of the eyes, the tightening of the eyelids, the shifting of the eyes right or left but not up or down, the momentary flaring of the nostrils, the tightening of the shoulders, the tensing of the stomach and abdomen, the flexing of the thigh muscles, the flexion of the neck muscles, the slight lifting of the Adam's apple, ...

Because — and here's why some people make money at this — all of those things together and a whole bunch of things I left out are what indicate that some (but not all, and here's why you have to be careful when you practice this stuff for a living) people are less than happy with the gift and just how unhappy they are, as opposed to reacting to a sudden cramp, or burping up something that doesn't taste as good as it did going down, or so many other things.

Because sometimes you'll say you're sorry and offer to exchange the gift for something else and the individual will pull the gift closer, vigorously shake their head, no, and their eyes will go wide with protest and they say, "Oh, no. I love this. I'm sorry, I was just listening to my son talking on the phone. He forgot he has to go do some errands for me before he can meet his friends."

And then you're a little confused and ask, "You're sure?"

And they reply, "Oh, please. I just *LOVE* this!"

What most people wouldn't have noticed in the above scenario is that the individual canted their head slightly and their eyes shifted to the right and held for a moment before they slightly shook their head, no. Those few movements amassed with all the others are the tip off that their attention, their focus, wasn't on what was in front of them (the gift). Instead, their focus, specifically their sense of hearing (or "audition") was somewhere else.

Where else?

In the direction their eyes shifted and held momentarily.

And how displeased were they by what they heard?

That's determined by how long they visually defocused before they started to shake their head and how vigorously they shook their head.

And how far away was this auditory cue upon which they focused their auditory attention?

That's determined by how much they canted their head (lifted and aimed their ear, so to speak) in order to hear the conversation in conjunction with how much they closed down (squinted) their eyes during the visual defocusing.

Why did intuition fail us in the above? Because our attention wasn't focused where the other person's attention was focused. We see something and think it applies to what we're focused on, and we know what a certain expression means when it's on our face, so it must mean the same thing when it's on their face, hence their expression applies to whatever we're focused on.

What we've essentially done is attempted to read their mind by interpreting their expression through what's going on in our own head. And you'll be shocked (shocked, I tell you!) to know the sciences we're talking about have their own term for what's going on in your head and why it's different from what's going on in my head. Most people are aware of what's going on around them and what situation (visiting friends, the office, a classroom setting, etc.) they're in, and they know what kind of social filters apply. Hence, these sciences and a few others use the terms "Situational Awareness"[47,131] and "Social Filtering"[153,208] to describe and often approximate what's going on inside someone's head based on what's going on around them.

All those little head twitches and eye movements and arm movements and shoulder shrugs that we don't realize we're paying attention to are called "psychomotor behavioral cues" which is a scientific jargonish way of saying "people respond physically to what's going on in their head because of what's going on around them". The basic concept was identified in 1852 and was known as *ideomotor phenomenon*. Whatever you call it, it works like this: We hear a gross story and our face twists up and we go "Ee-yuck!" or we hear a funny story and we sit back and laugh, sometimes covering our mouth or placing our hand on our chest or — if the story's really funny — wiping the laughter tears from our eyes.

Now just take a second and recognize how much everything anybody does is based on how much they're interacting with what's around them (which we call their "environment"):

    1) People are applying social filters to make sure they're behaving appropriately.

    2) They're determining what is appropriate behavior — which social filters to apply — due to their situational awareness of their environment.

    3) They're using situational awareness to monitor the psychomotor behavioral cues of the people around them to gauge how appropriate their own behavior is in a kind of feedback loop.

    4) They're using predictive intelligence and persuasive analytics (based on those same psychomotor behavioral cues) to mindread the people around them

        4.a) to determine how to interact with the people around them

        4.b) and how the people around them

            4.b.i) are interacting with them and

            4.b.ii) will be interacting with them.

So you see, everything that the professionals have been trained to do is something you do every moment of every day. The only difference between you and them is that they've had lots of training to know that they're doing it, why they're doing it, what information to get out of it and most importantly to know when their intuition is going to be wrong and how to correct it.

So What Do You Do, Again?

People who know me know I love a good question. A friend once told Susan (my wife) that he and I were driving on the highway once and "I suddenly realized I was alone in the car. I looked over and Joseph was there, but not really. A few miles later he started explaining something he'd observed about the angle of the sunlight falling on the highway. I told him, 'You're so not right in so many ways.'" An old girlfriend complained, "Every time you see a hole you have to stop and look and see what's inside. I just walk around it and get where I'm going." She couldn't understand that I could always get where I was going and unless I stopped to investigate, I'd never discover what hidden treasures were buried where others would never find them.

I have a curious nature, have yet to meet a subject that truly bores me and constantly ask myself and others questions about things to increase my understanding. Much of what this section describes came from my desire to increase both my and others' understandings.

What NextStage and I do is study, research and report on things such as you see in the charts on this and following pages. For example, figure AF1 (page 34) is a chart of how two different people responded consciously and non-consciously to the same information. This should be obvious, yes, that different people will have different responses to the same information? Think about it. People may have different tastes in food (I love spicy foods, Susan can't stand them), they may like different types of movies (westerns versus *film-noir*), intelligent, well-adjusted, interesting people like Bach and others prefer lesser composers (can you guess which way I lean?). Each of these *behavioral* differences are based on the fact that they have different beliefs, different experiences, different cultural backgrounds and so on. These differences demonstrate themselves through different responses to information.

Movies are information. If the movie is a western, the person who likes westerns will respond to it differently than the person who likes *film-noir*. Food is information. If the food is spicy then the person who likes spicy food will respond differently to it than the person who dislikes spicy food (Susan, ever-patient, always says "There'll be something I'll like on the menu" when we go out for Mexican, Chinese, Thai, Indian...well, just about anything). Music is information and the list goes on.

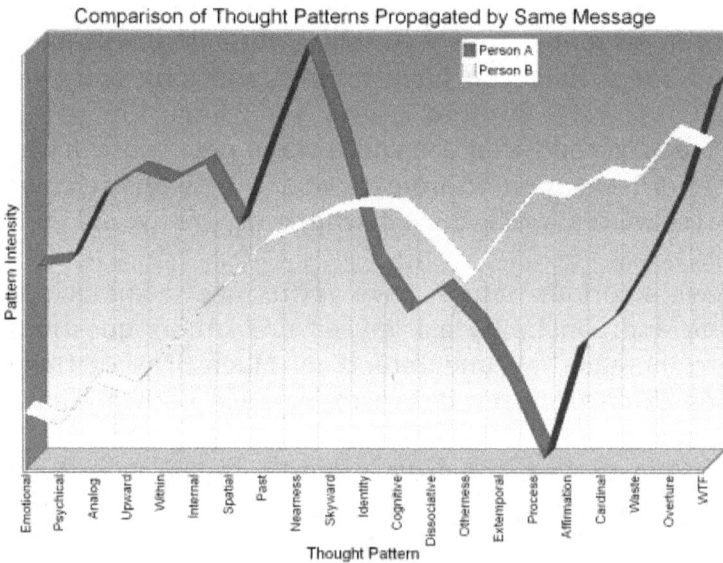

AF1 - A group of people will react differently to the same material, but in what ways and how?

And if it's so obvious that different people respond differently to the same information, how come we call our highly-expensive, broad-based marketing efforts successful when they max out at a

10% ROI when as a collection of less expensive, targeted marketing efforts could each be returning a minimum 25-30% ROI while collectively messaging a larger audience?

Simply knowing that people are shopping based on price versus product, such as shown in figure AF2 on page 35, multiplies your marketing success several times over. Figure AF2's higher right bar indicates that visitors considered price or value more important than product variety or options (lower left bar) by better than 200%. The fact that the top of the right bar is below the dark and light triangles indicates that most visitors were prepared to give or spend more for what was offered. Those same triangles just above and below the top of the left bar indicate visitors thought there were sufficient options or variety of the site offerings.

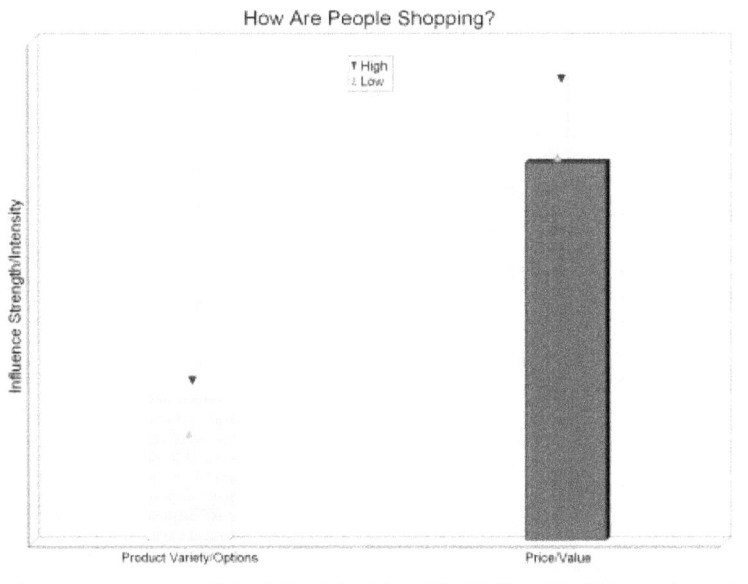

AF2 - Are people shopping by price or by product, and what can you change to make more purchases occur?

Increasing sales and upselling requires different pitches for price shoppers versus product shoppers and knowing which ones dominate your traffic becomes profits quickly and easily.

Figure AF3 (page 36) indicates how many individuals are active on a single computer during a given session. This report originated early in the days of NextStage, back when it was quite common for there to be a single workstation that was used by several different people. A client wanted to know how many different people were browsing their site because such information was a demonstration of how many dollars would result from contacting the group browsing. The circles indicate URLs that have significantly more real people visiting a site than are demonstrated by cookie counts. ET determines that different people are using the same browsing session by detecting differences in their thought patterns.

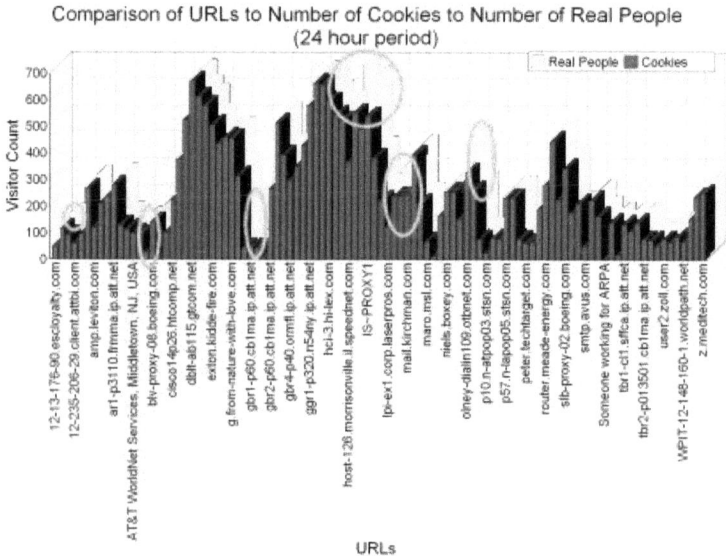

AF3 - How many people actually sit at a single computer during a single browsing session?

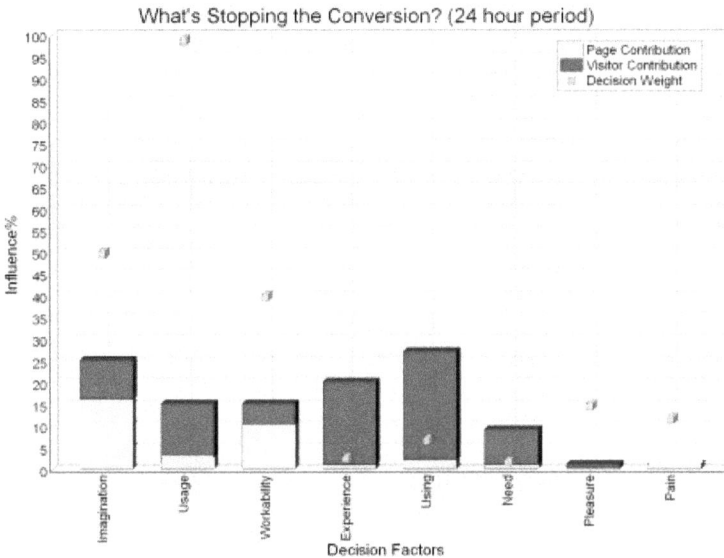

AF4 - How come there are more abandoned shopping carts online than in malls, and how do you change that?

And lastly, what can marketers and designers do so that people complete transactions on a given site? That is shown in figure AF4 on page 37. Figure AF4 is a collection of eight critical psychological factors that are in play when visitors are making conversion decisions. The light, bottom half of the bars indicate how much information the page is contributing to the decision process, the dark, top half of the bar indicates how much information the visitor is contributing from their own experience and the height of the dots indicate how critical each factor is to the individual visitor's decision process. The height of the Usage dot (second from left) indicates that product usefulness and usability are the most important factors in this individual's conversion decision. The web pages aren't providing them with that information very well (the height of the light, bottom part of the Usage bar) so the visitor is "filling in the gaps" with information (the height of the dark part of the bar) from their own experiences. The more external, personal experiential information visitors use in their conversion decision process the less control you have over the conversion process.

And that, by the way, is the end of the Author's Foreword. Thanks for taking the time to read it. Hopefully it gave you food for thought and, more importantly, a chuckle or two.

Put on your seatbelts, folks. We're going for a ride.

Enjoy.

*Vraiment etudies des vie aux sauvage:
I told a potential client about the
benefits of our technology. He asked,
"Are there any negative benefits?"
Without missing a beat, I answered,
"We haven't experienced any to date,
but we have encountered several
negative detriments." His eyes opened
wide. "Then you better tell me what
they are." I proceeded to repeat the
benefits of our technology. He nodded
as I spoke. "I've heard about things
like that before," he said.*

I – What This Book Is About

Reading Virtual Minds Volume I: Science and History is about behaviors (the whole series is, but that's another story). Specifically, ***Volume I*** is about online behaviors and the transition of behaviors from offline to online and back.

I should probably pause right here to make sure we're all talking the same thing.

I.1 – Behaviors? What are "Behaviors"?

There are lots of people in the online world who hear or see the word "behavior" and... and... and I'm not sure what they think of. I'm pretty sure it's not what I mean when I use the word.

This book considers behaviors as the external demonstration of internal states. Every thing that people do starts somewhere inside them. Allow me to use some examples from my blogs[a]:

> Attention is a behavior that demonstrates specific neural activity is taking place.[21,62,76,81,83,87,104,162,182,183,188,203,223,224,237,252,259,262,274,288-290,294,315,322,324,351]

> Engagement is the demonstration of Attention via psychomotor activity that serves to focus an individual's Attention.[74,101,102,119,121,128]

I'll agree that the ultimate outcome of a visitor's *attention* may be that they click through to the next page. Then again, the ultimate outcome of a visitor's frustration might be that they click through to the next page. It could be benign curiosity that causes the clickthrough.

And I'll agree that the ultimate outcome of a visitor's *engagement* may be a return visit. A return visit might also be to purchase one item and never come back again. A return visit

----

[a] – http://nlb.pub/7, http://nlb.pub/8, http://nlb.pub/9, http://nlb.pub/a, http://nlb.pub/b, http://nlb.pub/c, http://nlb.pub/d

might be to get one piece of information that is used to transact elsewhere repeatedly. And are they *engaged* if they spend a recognizable portion of their online time to find an alternative online experience?

One of the questions I asked myself was "If the goal is 1-to-1 interactions, why are you relying on large statistical models that record inaccurate proxies[b] and result in changes within the error margin?"

The point is that visitor "behaviors" recorded at the server and given hypothetical meaning during analysis are not one-to-one matches to *behaviors* originating in the mind. Behaviors originating in the mind are demonstrated externally through subtle, non-obvious interactions with the visitor's immediate environment and reveal more than can be imagined.[270]

So we're going to spend lots of time learning what those external demonstrations are telling us about people's internal states. How people respond to and interact with information presented via non-human mediums; emails, software interfaces, websites, online brochures and documentation, PDAs, smartphones, GPS systems, broadcasts such as TV and radio, things like that. People tell us what's going on in their minds when they're interacting and responding and nothing gets wasted. Everything people do provides information about what they're thinking and that includes things they don't know they're thinking.

Online behaviors are extremely interesting to the US Dept of Commerce. In their 15 May 09 brief they wrote:

> The Census Bureau of the Department of Commerce announced today that the estimate of U.S. retail e-commerce sales for the first quarter of 2009, adjusted for seasonal variation, but not for price changes, was $31.7 billion, an increase of 0.7 percent (±1.1%)* from the fourth quarter of 2008. Total retail sales for the first quarter of 2009 were estimated at $909.6 billion, a decrease of 1.8 percent (±0.4%) from the fourth quarter of 2008. The first quarter 2009 ecommerce estimate decreased 5.4 percent

[b] – Per Dan Linton's *Forward* (page 22)

(±2.5%) from the first quarter of 2008 while total retail sales decreased 10.2 percent (±0.4%) in the same period. E-commerce sales in the first quarter of 2009 accounted for 3.5 percent of total sales.

On a not adjusted basis, the estimate of U.S. retail e-commerce sales for the first quarter of 2009 totaled $30.2 billion, a decrease of 17.7 percent (±1.1%) from the fourth quarter of 2008. The first quarter 2009 e-commerce estimate decreased 5.7 percent (±2.5%) from the first quarter of 2008 while total retail sales decreased 11.6 (±0.5%) in the same period. E-commerce sales in the first quarter of 2009 accounted for 3.6 percent of total sales.

Let's compare that with the equivalent 19 Nov 04 stats:

The Census Bureau of the Department of Commerce announced today that the estimate of U.S. retail e-commerce sales for the third quarter of 2004, adjusted for seasonal variation and holiday and trading-day differences, but not for price changes, was $17.6 billion, an increase of 4.7 percent (±1.7%) from the second quarter of 2004. Total retail sales for the third quarter of 2004 were estimated at $916.5 billion, an increase of 1.4 percent (±0.3%) from the second quarter of 2004. The third quarter 2004 e-commerce estimate increased 21.5 percent (±3.0%) from the third quarter of 2003 while total retail sales increased 6.2 percent (±0.5%) in the same period. E-commerce sales in the third quarter accounted for 1.9 percent of total sales.

On a not adjusted basis, the estimate of U.S. retail e-commerce sales for the third quarter of 2004 totaled $16.5 billion, an increase of 5.4 percent (±1.7%) from the second quarter of 2004. The third quarter 2004 e-commerce estimate increased 21.2 percent (±3.0%) from the third quarter of 2003 while total retail sales increased 6.5 percent (±0.5%) in the same period. E-commerce sales in the third quarter of 2004 accounted for 1.8 percent of total sales.[c]

---

[c] – http://nlb.pub/e

You can see this in the 1Q'09 and 3Q'04 graphs (figures I.1 and I.2 respectively, page 43. The growth curve is solid with seasonal adjustments dashed).

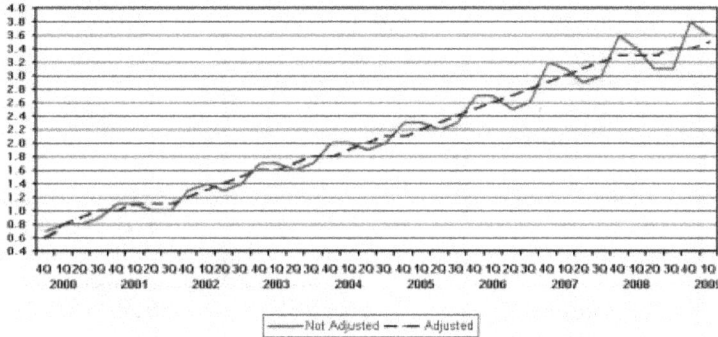

I.1 - Estimated Quarterly U.S. Retail E-commerce Sales as a Percent of Total Quarterly Retail Sales: 4th Quarter 1999 – 1st Quarter 2009

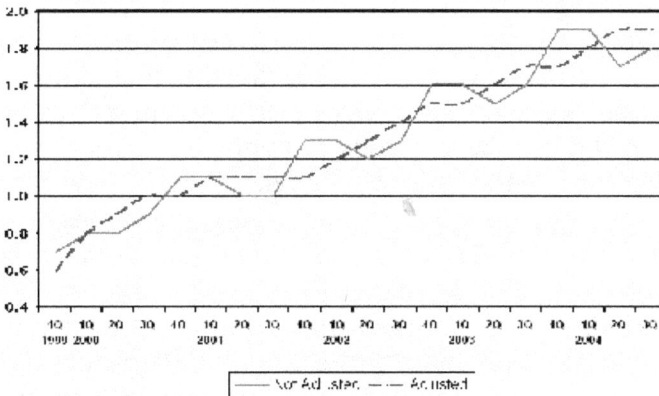

I.2 - Estimated Quarterly U.S. Retail E-commerce Sales as a Percent of Total Quarterly Retail Sales: 4th Quarter 1999 – 3rd Quarter 2004

Let's sum these up so they'll be easier (for me, anyway) to read:

	3Q'04	1Q'09
eSales (US$B)	16.5	30.2
1Q eSales Change (%)	5.4 (±1.7)	-17.7 (±1.1)
all Sales (non-adjusted US$B)	916.5	909.6
1Q all Sales Change (%)	1.4 (±0.3)	-1.8 (±0.4)
4Q eSales Change (%)	21.2 (±3.0)	-5.7 (±2.5)
4Q all Sales Change (%)	6.5 (±0.5)	-11.6 (±0.5)
e-to-all %	1.8	3.6

The US was in a recognized recession in 1Q'09. Unemployment rates were at 8.1% during this time. I had to wonder at the 8.1% unemployment rate because I couldn't find its impact in the numbers above. It might be appearing in things like the drop in eSales and all Sales. What I knew from other research was that people are becoming increasingly unhappy online. They were happy not too long ago, not so much so at this time, though.

Still, US$30.2B in online transactions and all governed by online behaviors. Just over three and a half percent of all US commerce was done online in 1Q'09. The conventional wisdom in 2004 was that the e-to-all percent would grow by better than 20% every year.

Let's see...

2004	1.8
2006	2.16
2007	2.59
2008	3.11
2009	3.73

This is impressive. The anticipated growth bears out even though 8.1% of the population has no money to spend. Things went negative in all the other numbers but the 20% growth bears out.

What's impressive about this (to me) isn't that the prediction bore fruit, it's that the prediction's accuracy is probably due to something very different than that implied. People who've studied language evolution, linguistics, sociology and ethology know there are very set rules for how new language ("jargon") moves through culture. That 20%/year increase even though everything else is going negative? That's the spread of a reluctant *meme*,[9,251] the meme of "eShopping" moving through society and becoming accepted. Ecologists know this as a traveling population wave, a special case of population dynamics synchronized in space and time across a large geographic area.

Here the population wave is the number of individuals carrying the "eShopping is okay" meme. Why "reluctant"? Two conflicting forces are coming into play; people want to spend money and people know how vulnerable eShopping is due to news articles about their personal data getting hijacked. They probably don't think about the hijacking at the point of eSale and it is in their consciousness in social settings (watercooler talk and such).

Those other numbers, though...they don't carry through with an 8.1% unemployment rate. People are still eShopping and I won't say the economic situation in late '08-'09 isn't playing a role. What I will offer is that the economic situation is only exacerbating the real problem, allowing it to demonstrate itself more obviously than it might otherwise; eShopping and various other online activities aren't living up to their promise of ushering in a better, more connected, more personally vital world. Being part of a huge online community is a good thing and it still doesn't satisfy the psycho-neural need for community, for (quite literally) that human touch. Anybody who remembers Rick Springfield's "Human Touch" music video[d] knows what I mean.

The numbers in the charts and graphs starting on page 43 reflect only US-based B2C and B2B transactions. Totally unappreciated in these numbers were B2E, C2C, PEP and other transaction areas. NextStage groups all of these areas collectively as all are governed by identical online behaviors.

The next point of clarity is *commerce*. Whatever form commerce takes — online, offline, involving goods and services in exchange for cash, currency or credit — it always involves an *information-exchange*. Information-exchange is the oldest form of commerce and all forms of commerce are exchanges of information. The information can be goods and services, the information can be email addresses and contact info, the information can be recipes and Great Aunt Hildy's directions for making chamomile soap. Commerce and information-exchange occur when I have something you value and you have something I value and we agree to trade them with each other. Commerce as we recognize it today is a subset of information-exchange. We agree on an abstraction, that some coin of some realm equals some amount of effort. That abstraction and our agreement comes from information we've exchanged overtly or covertly. The use of credit is an abstraction of an abstraction. A sad fallout of these shared abstractions is that the more we abstract the more easily we're deceived; it's easier to commit credit card fraud and steal an identity than it is to counterfeit some coin of any realm.

---

[d] – http://nlb.pub/f. And no, this isn't the Bruce Springsteen Human Touch video (http://nlb.pub/g). It's borderline sad just how different the two are and you should definitely watch the Rick Springfield one. It's quite prophetic considering they awake in 2016 and

I.2 — Electronic Behaviors

Online behaviors aren't offline behaviors done online. You knew how to behave towards someone when they were standing in front of you because you could read their behaviors — the mindreading mentioned in the **Author's Foreword** (page 27) — to get a clue as to how you were coming across. For example, you're standing next to someone in a theater line. You exchange small talk; the weather, the movie, the play or performance. Maybe you start talking about the traffic getting to the theater, maybe that goes into laughing about arguing with your kids because you needed the car tonight and they wanted to drive their friends to a game. You start paying more attention to your casual conversation partner. They have just about the same number of gray hairs you do, the same number of wrinkles in their face. They dress in pretty much the same style you do. At some point they bring their significant other into the conversation and you do the same. Then you actually introduce yourself, your partner, and you extend your right hand in a handshake. Names are exchanged. You start to talk about the joys and sorrows of married life and now all four of you are kidding and laughing. Somebody tests the waters with a slightly off-color joke. Everybody laughs hard. Someone else says, "Care to join us for a drink before the show?" and maybe that goes into getting a bite after the show. You exchange phone numbers and you've made friends.

Any one of those signs go missing and the exchange stops cold, and there are lots of signs being exchanged that I didn't bother to put in. Regardless of the missing signs, that's a pretty complex little dance.

This dance existed as a little two-person community and only to exchange goods and services — in this case handshakes, names and polite conversation — for that brief moment in time, and the only reason you knew how to create, maintain, and function in that community is because you knew the signs. You

=====
humans touching humans is lacking in the online social world.

had to know the signs because they were the ones which allowed you the right to engage in the exchange in the first place.

These same little dances go on all the time and are crucial to information-exchanges in the form of commerce. Have you ever been part of a negotiation which had every "t" crossed and every "i" dotted and was 99.999% there only to have things go sour because somebody "didn't feel right about it"?

If somebody didn't feel right it was because that person wasn't receiving the signs they needed in order to feel right. When we're starting out in the world of commerce, mom and dad go with us to teach us the signs. That way they can be sure we're not getting cheated.

Two high premium "rights of passage" in Anglo-based, western society are commerce-based; purchasing our first car and buying our first suit. In both cases, usually mom or dad and sometimes both escort us to make sure we come out ahead. Be ye male or female, the first independently purchased suit is a sign of independence from mom, the first car is a sign of independence from dad. No wonder mom wants to be there when we pick out our first suit! You think she wants people to see her child dressed as if they didn't have any mirrors in the house and were fighting with their closet? And the car? Well, if we got swindled, then chances are poppa wasn't too bright, neither, and poppa ain't gonna let that pass.

Back to online behaviors.

How do you read someone's behaviors in order to exchange information when that person isn't standing in front of you and is sitting in front of a computer or TXTing on a smartphone 2,000 miles away? How does your electronic representation — your website, your software interface, your online brochure or documentation — modify its behaviors so that an information-exchange as commerce will occur?

Online behaviors aren't offline behaviors done online. Behaviors evolve.

What used to be done by two or more people facing each other moved to being done on the phone, on the 'net, ... Face-to-face interactions obviously were between two people in close physical proximity to each other, which meant they could "read" each other and engage in a kind of silent communication. This silent communication allowed the two people to establish a rapport which led to increased comfort (or sometimes discomfort) and (in either case) an increased information exchange.

This increased information exchange was and is important because so much of communication — hence the creation of community — is not done by words alone. Take as example how often emails are misread and feelings are hurt. How can emails be misread and feelings be hurt when (supposedly) everybody's learned how to communicate through the written word? Writing ain't easy. It's amazing how many people are learning the truth of Mark Twain's "I didn't have time to write a short letter, so I wrote a long one instead" on Twitter and various TXTing platforms. Explaining the modifications to written communications due to Twitter's 140-character maxim alone are funding many an anthropologist's and linguist's research.

Still, being able to express ourselves clearly and concisely via the written word hasn't resulted in people learning to enhance their email communication skills, it's resulted in people becoming immune to all but the most emotional email exchanges. Our online behavior isn't an offline behavior done online, it's the emergence of a specific behavior to online communication.

I.3 – Digital and Analog Communications

Communication is actually done on two levels, what are called digital and analog (and not to be confused with digital and analog thinking). The digital signal is comprised of the words themselves and their meanings as distinct lexical units. The analog signal is comprised of all the minute body movements and gestures and facial expressions and inflections and so on and so forth that happen while we're exchanging words. In this context, "digital" is to "analog" as "form" is to "substance". Without that analog signal the digital signal is often unclear and misunderstood, it is form without substance. Like all good digital signals, words by themselves have a one-zero, yes-no, up-down, on-off directionality to them, and that directionality isn't governed by the person saying the word, it's governed by the person hearing the word.

It's the analog signal which lets the receiver know which direction those ones and zeros, yeses and noes, ups and downs, ons and offs are facing and how to interpret the digital signal. These analog cues are so important that people who communicate via sign-languages (Ameslan, Singlish, Freslan, Norslan, Brislan, etc.) actually make exaggerated movements and expressions, including stomping and popping sounds, in order to provide analog content to the digital content of the sign itself. The exaggerated movements and expressions are more readily seen and the stomping and popping sounds are felt as vibrations, all of which add analog meaning to the digital sign.

Here's an example of how important analog content is to communication.

Anthony is a pretty boy

The above is a pretty innocuous statement, isn't it?

Well, yes and no. It depends what I mean when I *say* it, doesn't it? And the above line doesn't provide you with my facial expressions, my body language, so on and so forth, when I type it in. If you're very clever, highly trained and monitoring me as I type, you could make a good guess whether I meant the above to be innocuous or not by how I typed that phrase (along with several other factors). But without that kind of analog information and just by reading the above phrase you don't know if "Anthony is a pretty boy" is a taunt, a definitive statement or that Anthony is a cockatiel and the sentence is how he asks for a peanut.[e]

But humans live in community and when there's no other person to provide that analog information people will

---

[e] – The amount of both semantic and shannonistic information lost in most online communications is truly amazing. NextStage did a great deal of research into how people interpret emails and the best statement was :"It's like listening to someone talking in a monotone. You really don't know what they mean just by looking at what they've written." NextStage's research has since been augmented by other researchers' findings.(1,32,35,75,113,179,200,206,219,227,232,233,280,302,306)

(instantaneously and without realizing what they're doing) create a community with themselves and get the analog information from within, from their own experience.

What does that mean? However you responded to the sentence "Anthony is a pretty boy", it was all you and none of me. Don't like what you read in an email? Make sure you're responding to what's written and not what you think is written.

Now let's add some analog information — some substance to the form, if you will — to that phrase.

Anthony is a pretty boy

Anthony is a pretty boy

Anthony is a pretty boy

ANTHONY IS A PRETTY BOY

Anthony is a Pretty Boy

Different people will have different responses to each rewrite of that phrase because we have preconceptions about what each font communicates.[23-27,54,308-310] Without my being directly in front of you and providing you with the analog information in toto with the digital information, I'm not communicating with you.

But this (e)book is.

I.4 – How Pretty is Anthony?

Most people would read each rewrite of "Anthony is a pretty boy" with a slightly different voice (louder, quieter, masculanized, feminized, ...). Without someone providing the complexities of meaning that are part of communication beyond mere words, people respond to and communicate with meanings pulled from within themselves. However you responded to each rewrite of the above phrase, you were behaving in a way which was unique to you and unselfishly you.

Behaviors. Yours and yours alone.

Right now your behaviors are governed by your own personal interactions with what's on the page or on the screen (if you're reading this electronically).

That last part, *behaviors governed by your own personal interactions with what's on the screen*, is your unique, personal, totally unselfish online behavior.

Remember the estimates for online transactions mentioned earlier? The great majority of all transactions are dropped before they're completed and the number of all site visitors returning to a given site for traditional commerce is in the low single digits. It would be nice if things changed with more and more people coming online and that's not the case. The more populated virtual reality becomes the more and more undesirable behaviors emerge.

Behaviors. Specifically, online behaviors.

We are designed to communicate and create communities by the exchange of digital (form) and analog (substance) information. Chat room and message board flame wars happened more often than not until emoticons allowed people to add some analog information to the purely digital information of their words alone, and even those have evolved from the typographical :-), :-D, |-), |-D, :->, ;-), :'-), etc,[f] which required you to be an FBI cypherologist to understand, to the recently introduced images such as those shown in figure I.3 on page 53.

More and more people are exchanging information online and are unable to communicate fully because they're only exchanging digital information (and here I mean "words", not bits and bytes). The analog information — the facial expressions, the gestures and whole lots more — is missing. As traditional person-to-person interactions such as customer support, help-desk, sales, etc., are done totally online, human-to-human interaction is done less and less and the problems of not understanding online behaviors are

---

[f] – In order of appearance " smiling; agreeing", "laughing", "hee hee", "ho ho", "hey hey", "so happy, I'm crying" and "crying with joy". You can find a description of emoticons and their kin at http://nlb.pub/h.

on the rise. When was the last time someone had a totally joyous time looking for help online or via an automated phone system?

I.3 - The latest in Emoticons

I.5 – Social Networking...
Whether You Want It or Not

People want to create communities while businesses are making it harder and harder for communities to be created. Customers and clients who want person-to-person contact find user forums and chat rooms with the latter usually being a venue for consumer angst. Automated help and support systems often fail "...because there's no human involved." The phrase "...no human involved" translates to "no community is created". Several US companies discovered this when they outsourced their help and support departments to overseas facilities.

The problem is one any company outsourcing these types of jobs to foreign countries will experience. First, people requiring help and support are willingly placing themselves in a vulnerable position by admitting they need help and support. Second, people needing help and support want to quickly create community (and probably more so than most others) because such people really,

really, **really!** want to know that they're okay, that whatever is going wrong isn't their fault.[g]

Outsourced help and support desks are losing their appeal because a community is being created but the *signs* aren't the right signs (remember discussing *our* signs versus *their* signs?). US-based companies spent quite a bit of money teaching the employees of overseas help and support desks the latest US fads, customs, jargon, and the like, teaching signs of Americana to those who don't have them. Americana signs are important for help-desk, Customer Relationship Management (CRM) and similar groups servicing Americans because if I send you a sign and you respond with an equivalent sign then you must be just like me which means you can help me. Likewise, Australiana must be taught to those servicing Australians, Franconia to those servicing the French, and so on. If I send a sign and you don't respond with an equivalent sign? Oh oh. Watch out. One of us doesn't know what the other is communicating and even though the help and support might be 100% on target, it won't be considered useful or valid and the support or help will have failed. "How can you help me unless you're just like me?" is the central metaphor of the most successful therapeutic paradigms. By engaging in small talk about recent fads and customs and by using jargon to do so, signs are given that prove the help-desk or CRM personnel are just like the caller and hence able to help them. The question might never get answered and the concern might never be addressed but the call will be 100% successful because the person calling was heard and listened to and, by golly, that help-desk or CRM person understood!

A two-person dance. Two humans engaged in the single most important function in human history, creating community. What's involved in the dance? Sharing shared ideas and beliefs. It's as simple as that.

Let me give you an example...

I called my long distance carrier's customer support one day due to a question on a bill. There was the usual period of waiting

---

[g] – This is rapidly changing in the age of Digital Divisivity(142,144,146) covered in detail in **Reading Virtual Minds Volume II: Experience and Expectation**

while my call worked its way up the queue and eventually I got a human on the line, a woman who introduced herself and offered support. The wait was longer than I cared for and I was going to share that with her. But there was something familiar in her speech that stopped the words in my mouth.

I was quiet.

"Hello?" she queried.

"Excuse me," I said. "You're from Nova Scotia, aren't you?"

"Yes, I am, sir. How can I help you today?"

"I don't mean to embarrass you. You're from Cape Breton. Sydney, North Sydney or thereabouts?"

Now it was her turn to be quiet. Then, "Yes, I am."

I laughed and said, "Ciamar tha sibh an duigh, mo charaid?"

All of a sudden the woman called out, "He has his Gaelic! He has his Gaelic!" and a wonderful conversation ensued not only between the woman and myself but between several of her co-workers who got on the line with me to talk about places we had in common, people we knew and to catch-up on gossip. Some in Gaelic, nach an Beurla (some in English).

My long distance carrier's call center is based in North Sydney, Nova Scotia, an area I'm familiar with, have called home more often than not and where Gaelic is spoken as much as English. I heard that familiar tone and speech pattern in her voice and all of a sudden I was back home, working on the farms and pulling that day's dinner from the sea.

I had a completely satisfying customer service experience even though I honestly don't remember the part of the conversation about correcting the error on my bill.

What's involved in the dance? Sharing shared ideas and beliefs. It's as simple as that.

I.6 – Attempting Community, Brands, Tribes and Ego-Identification

People will attempt community with whatever they believe is responding to them. It can be another person, a pet or some form of electronica.

That may seem strange, that last part, "...or some form of electronica." Smartphones, MP3 players, computers, information kiosks, ... Remember, though, that a function of community is to help humans create and solidify their identities and identities are important because they tell us who we are. Anybody remember the scene in *Fiddler on the Roof* where the rabbi is asked to bless the sewing machine? I've been places where the village shaman was asked to comfort the Internet Spirit when connections were slow or outright failed. And I'm probably the only one around who's ever talked to my computer when unexpected things happen. Our ancestors created community with animals, mountains, rivers, lakes, storms, plants, trees and each other in order to solidify a tribal identity.

These tribal identities still exist, most people just don't recognize it. Gang colors, body piercings, tattoos, ... these are all fairly obvious affectations of a tribal identity. Less obvious are such things as class rings, fraternity and sorority pins, power ties, club memberships, secret handshakes, buzzwords and jargon, elite credit and entertainment cards and even certain brands of cars. All of these things and many, many more are used to quickly identify you to others who are able to recognize the signs.

Consider some of the tribal markers above; the club memberships, the certain brands of cars, the elite cards for travel and business. These are tribal markers which are also corporate brands.

But if someone identifies with something, whether it's another person, a pet, a mountain or a soft drink, they do so because there's something about that other thing which reinforces their beliefs about themselves; in short, their identity. In the case of a tribal marker being a corporate brand, the corporation wants the customer to perform an act of identification with the product. This act is called *ego-identification,* meaning the person accepts the product and the brand that goes with it as part of their own existence, something they require in order to be recognized and whole within a branded (*né* tribal) community. The function of a brand is to create community, to institute a two-person dance where there is no second person involved. A brand, in essence, is a sign, and companies spend lots of money to make sure you associate the right message with that sign. There is no real difference between our ancestors saying "I'm of the Hill people" and somebody today saying "I'm a Jeep® person." Both statements are statements of tribal community.[h]

But what if there's no other person, no pet, no mountain, no jeep? What if all there is only some kind of electronica with a given software interface or website or email or this text on the screen?

However slowly, however minutely, however subtly, community will be attempted. The degree to which that community will be successful is determined by how well those involved can dance the right dance. We learn how to dance (read "socialize") from the company we keep, and there are many societies where knowing how to dance (literally) is a sign of social maturity and sophistication.[141]

Let's translate the concept of this dance to the web. The company that has a website as an afterthought, or because "everyone else has one", or has a website and doesn't really know what to do with it, or doesn't want to do anything with it because they've already spent too much money and the damn thing never lived up to its promise anyway, well, that company has sent their child to the prom not knowing how to dance, wearing hand-me-downs that don't fit and driving the manure-spreader to pick up their date.

Interfaces are like children sent out into the world. Like a child, these interfaces go out in the world and represent the parents' best efforts to turn the child out right.

Psychologists and family therapists know that families often bring in little Johnny or little Sally and say, "Our child needs help," when more times than not the entire family dynamic needs help. Little Johnny or little Sally is the family's "designated client". Make little Johnny or little Sally well and the family will be well, too. Interfaces, like troubled children, are the designated

---

[h] – See *Brand is the Art of Making the Customer Want to Know You* in the *Reading Virtual Minds* series

client in the business communication, marketing and messaging world.

Don't think much of your interface, don't put a lot of time or effort into it, don't make it a priority? Then don't have one. Save yourself the time, trouble and money, and definitely the embarrassment. Unless you're willing to put your interface out there and have it succeed, nothing you do is going to make it succeed. Then when it fails, don't start asking yourself, "Where did I go wrong with that child?" The interface, like a child, will only do what it's been taught to do. If the interface isn't a priority item then don't be surprised when it doesn't produce, because a well-designed interface that does what's intended is well worth the cost of admission.

And of course, you know I'm going to emphasize that a well-designed website, software interface, brochure, whatever, is one that sends the right signs. Signs are going to be sent whether you intend them or not, and whether you're aware of them or not. Make sure the correct signs are being sent and your website, brochure, help-desk, TV spot, blog post, video, newspaper column[i], whatever, will definitely result in predictable, persuasive action.

Know how to dance and everybody wants to dance with you.

I.7 – Online Behaviors?

Behaviors. Specifically, online behaviors.

Two people start "reading" each other and, by doing so, start communicating. Anthropologists, sociologists and people in similar fields call this mindreading. If business is to be successful, the sign "You're successful. You know what you're doing. This isn't a fluke, you're in charge and in control" must be communicated to all those hundreds of thousands if not millions

---

[i] – I may be in the minority and I still believe printed, non-web based content is viable. The key to survivability is simple; it must be a consistent and dependable single source of both trusted content and reliable information to a real-time community. The real-time community part requires online participation as the transfer mechanism between real and virtual worlds. This creates community and provides stimulus to read a print edition, essentially driving (ahem) the audience from online to off instead of offline to on.

of people coming to our websites, using our software, reading our emails, our brochures, watching our TV spots, and so on.

Each and every one of those people is doing business, exchanging information, and each and every one of them is relying on the interface to give them the proper sign that right now, right at this moment in time, they're successful, they're doing it right.

The key, therefore, to being successful in an information economy is being able to read customer and client minds through interfaces or, in short, businesses need to start reading virtual minds if they hope to create the community consumers seek.

The first communication must be instructions on how to build a receiver.
– First Rule of Semiotics

II – History

The *Reading Virtual Minds* series grew from seminars I gave throughout the US and Canada in 2003-2004. The seminars were based on research into how people interact with websites (at the time. Now we deal with all media). The seminars were entitled "What We're Learning About Visitors From Websites"[a] although we discussed print campaigns, email campaigns, software interfaces, radio and TV spots — just about everything that had a digital representation, marketing or otherwise. We studied how to get people to adopt new and transitional technologies, how to adapt a given technology to a given culture, ..., lots of stuff. The specific research this is all based on began in 1991, is ongoing, and includes studies of all information exchange technologies (if it helps people communicate, we're on it).

II.1 – Missing Links

What set me down this track? I was sitting at a cafeteria patio on a warm summer's day at Michigan State University in 1987 and overheard a conversation among people in the Educational Psychology department. A table away, a woman and some of her classmates were discussing how people learned and the different stages involved in the learning process. Their discussion focused on a "missing link" in the understanding of how people learned. These were very educated people and their discussion was very intelligent and articulate. I knew nothing of their subject or what research had been done.

I also had no social skills to speak of, so I butted in. "Excuse me for listening to your conversation. Do I understand correctly that there is no current model for how people go from what you're calling Stage 1 Learning to Stage 2 Learning and so on?"

---

[a] – It's all still relevant, despite the title. NextStage Members can access the paper as part of their membership benefits. Memberships are available at http://nlb.pub/4

The professor, an attractive, native Michiganian in her mid-30s, looked at me pretty much as if I were a tick she'd just noticed crawling on her skin.

"Yes. That's correct. And you are?"

I introduced myself. I was taking a graduate course in writing. Fiction writing. Not hard science. Not even soft science. Worse than a tick.

Ahh, but then she smiled. Her face opened, her eyes wide with possibility. "Are you writing for one of the college journals?"

Well, I was. And this was one of those wonderful moments when people will use the same word and attribute totally different meanings to it, a semanticist's wet-dream.

This accomplished woman was asking if I was writing for one of the alumni journals, research-focused journals or some such. I meant I was writing for our class' end-of-term fiction journal.

She started chatting me up and invited me to their table, asking me if I'd like to discuss her research and findings, ... oh, it was wonderful.

I listened, asked some questions then said. "The reason you're not solving this problem is because you're applying the rules of definition as if they were the rules of solution. The problem is unsolvable within a single disciplinary paradigm."

She pulled back from me slightly. Once again, and like the hero of Kafka's *Metamorphosis* (I was studying fiction writing, remember?), I was turning into a bug. "You think you can figure it out?" she asked.

"I don't know... I'll take a stab at it."

I spent the rest of that summer in her department's classes and library when I wasn't in my own. From there I contacted people in a wide variety of disciplines and traveled either to meet or study with them (back then, remember, Vice President Gore had yet to invent the Internet[b], there was no email to speak of, cellphones looked like WWII field radiophones and only worked if you climbed the tower, "Smeagol" wasn't a household word,

---

[b] – http://nlb.pub/i

NBDY CD RD THS and New Zealand wasn't the destination of wannabe Hobbits).

Understanding what happened when people learned – when someone was incorporating new information – could provide me with an answer to something I'd wondered about since I was in grade school; Why were there certain subjects I blasted through and others which completely baffled me?

I published the answer in 1991 in the form of my thesis; *How We Learn to Learn*, 600 pages covering research in some 120 branches in four major disciplines; Anthropology, Linguistics, Mathematics and NeuroScience (remember my telling the EdPsych prof that the answer wasn't going to be found in a single discipline?).

Here's why I and others can excel in certain fields and be totally hopeless in others, why some people are talented in several subjects but will never shine in a single one, why some people will never do well in traditional educational settings regardless of how much they try and what all this has to do with understanding online behaviors and *Reading Virtual Minds*...

II.2 – The Three Stages of Learning

Basically there are three stages of learning. The first stage can be summed up by "The only 'intuitive' interface is the nipple. After that, it's all learned." The next stage of learning occurs when we start to lingualize our environment and there's lots of conjecture as to when this really happens. What is "lingualize our environment"? Most people will tell you it's when we learn to talk and that's where some conjecture comes in.

Humans lingualize their environment in many ways and they all start with proto-communications. I write "communications" because lingualization doesn't have to be speech. People who use Ameslan or Singlish or Freslan or any other sign language are all lingualizing their environment, they're just not using sounds. They are using words in the way that a linguist understands words, and they're definitely communicating in a way a neuroscientist understands communication. What's the difference between a linguist and a neuroscientist? In today's market about US$25-30k/year.

So the second stage of learning occurs when people begin to share their concepts of their environment with others. True, most often this is done with words or gestures. Pre-lingual children may point at a cookie and make the sound "Uk". For that matter, the sound might just as well be "Fleebnotz!".

What's important is that the child points at the cookie and makes a sound or gesture and the parent knows that the child is really communicating "Say there, I notice that tasty little morsel over there on the counter, and you may be aware that I'm stature-challenged at the moment. Be a good egg, why don't you, and pass that sweet bit of stuff this way. What say, eh?"

It's amazing that the child gets the cookie, don't you think? Probably not. The parent is quite aware of what the child's communications mean. Not so the adult visitor who has to continually ask, "What does he want again?"[42,45,161,164,171,201,210,235,260,272,280,296,301,323,337,343]

The second stage of learning, then, is when we start to learn the rules of our immediate family or group. We learn the words or signs that are used by our family or group because it makes things so much easier. We say "UK" and our parent corrects us by gently saying "Do you want a *cookie*?" At a certain point this behavior stops and we've entered the third stage of learning. If this behavior doesn't stop, we stare at our parents and say, "'*Do I want a* cookie'? What, do you still think I'm a child? I'm talking about the UK. United Kingdom. Good grief, mother. And by the way, do you have any *mook*?"

The third stage of learning occurs when we leave the nest on a regular basis. In western culture this is called "Going to school". In truth, it is *societalization*. It's when we learn the rules of our society, our culture, our tribe.

Consider these three stages for a second and you'll notice what's really happening is an expansion of the individual's psyche. The newborn comes equipped with a neurology (barring organic difficulties there are only so many ways the human brain can function) upon which an identity either develops or is impressed, and at some later stage society lays its rules and regulations on this developed identity. What results is the individual's personality.

Our concern here is how individuals lingualize their environment. What you have is neurolinguistic, psycholinguistic and sociolinguistic rules for how people at any age interact with their environment.

The great thing about all this psychobabble is that it doesn't matter if people are using spoken words, written text, pictures, gestures, music, etc., because all of these things are simply *signs* for the concepts we carry about in our heads. What is beautiful to one person may not be beautiful to another, and the sign someone uses to convey the concept of "beauty" tells you more about that person than most people can imagine.

Take a moment and answer this before you read any further; What is beautiful to you?

Most people raised in an Anglo-based, western cultural paradigm will respond with an image; "My wife", "My daughter", "My mother's smile", "The sun peeking up from the horizon", "The mountains at sunset", "A clear night sky", "The harbor at Walker's Cay on a clear day," ... In all these cases, the response is a visual one. This is not the case in other cultures nor is it the case with all people.[35,170,209,246,281,284, 328,329,332,351,352]

For example, if you were to ask me "What is beautiful to you?" I would respond with "Bach's Toccata and Fugue in D-minor".

Right there you've learned that my basis for beauty is auditory, not visual. If you were to follow up that first question with "What makes it beautiful to you?" I would respond with "Because every time I play it I learn something new. There's always a surprise in it for me." Now you've learned that not only is my basis for beauty auditory ("a"), but also kinesthetic ("k"), cognitive ("c"), internal ("i"), and based in the present ("p", what's going on around me right now).

Based on those two questions and those two questions alone you could persuade me to do something by using a phrase like "Listen, I think once you get a feel for this it'll surprise you." This phrase (for the purposes of our discussion) sends the following messages, "Auditory internal cognitive present internal kinesthetic cognitive internal" or "aicpikci". You can think of this as a fingerprint or signature. Like fingerprints, these messages are increasingly unique as you increase the precision of the measurement (all fingerprints are made up of arches, loops and whorls. It's the combination of these elements that make individual fingerprints unique). Like signatures, they tell us a great deal about the person once you know how to read them. And because we're taking a fingerprint or signature of how people think, we use the term *memetic signatures* or "signatures of thought". At the highest levels memetic signatures are completely unique to a given individual.

The understanding of how people use signs to convey meaning is *Semiotics* and we've come a long way from eating lunch on a warm day during a summer session at Michigan State University in 1987, haven't we?

Yes and no. Back in 1987 people knew that individuals went through the three stages of learning but nobody knew how or what caused one stage to stop and another to start or if there was a smooth transition or what was going on.

What's really interesting is that these three stages of learning aren't limited to children growing up. Take any adult and put them in a decidedly new situation and they'll go right back to wanting to suck on a nipple. Humans are wired to create communities and the first community we make is with mom. Drop any one of us in a new situation and the first thing we do is look for a nipple to suck. Because we're adults we don't literally do that. Instead we drop back a little in our learning stages and test to see which learned behaviors are still acceptable.

People in modern societies have many of the problems they do because they don't have the necessary tools or training to go back far enough in their learning stages to find acceptable behaviors for new situations. They're kind of stuck in stage three because they've developed some core beliefs about themselves, their society and their role in it which they need to protect. Going back in learning stages requires the ability and definitely the desire to rearrange those core beliefs.

II.3 – Core, Identity and Personality

Rearranging core beliefs isn't easy. Core beliefs are the most deep-down, ingrained beliefs we have about ourselves. They are the hardest to shake, benefit us the most and cause us the most problems. They also form early in the life of an individual, taking shape during the transition from Stage 1 to Stage 2 learning.

This nascent self-concept, taking root and forming while we ourselves are still at a vulnerable age, requires protection in order to thrive just as we, being at a vulnerable age, require protection. In the case of core beliefs, the mind creates an identity-matrix, or "identity" for short, to protect the core. It's our identity — who we believe we are — that protects our core beliefs about ourselves and our world. This protection is necessary because Stage 2 learning occurs when we develop sufficient language skills to know that other people use words differently than how we use words. This is normally when we start interacting with society, which is when we discover that there are people out there who will intentionally lie to us and hurt us (assuming healthy child-rearing had occurred and the individual didn't come from a dysfunctional or "crazy-making" family).

We create our identity based on our core beliefs and a large part of our identity's job is to protect those core beliefs. After all, without the core the identity wouldn't exist. If we came from a crazy-making family, those core beliefs will cause us problems until we change them, especially when one appreciates that the identity will work to protect those damaging core beliefs from change. Examples of such situations occur when someone repeatedly returns to a harmful environment or willingly subjects themselves to abusive situations. These situations are not considered healthy.

Another example of the identity and core either in conflict or not in contact with each other is called "Impostor Syndrome". We often use phrases like "He doesn't know who he is" or "She has no sense of herself" when dealing with these people. More extreme cases are known as "process schizophrenia".

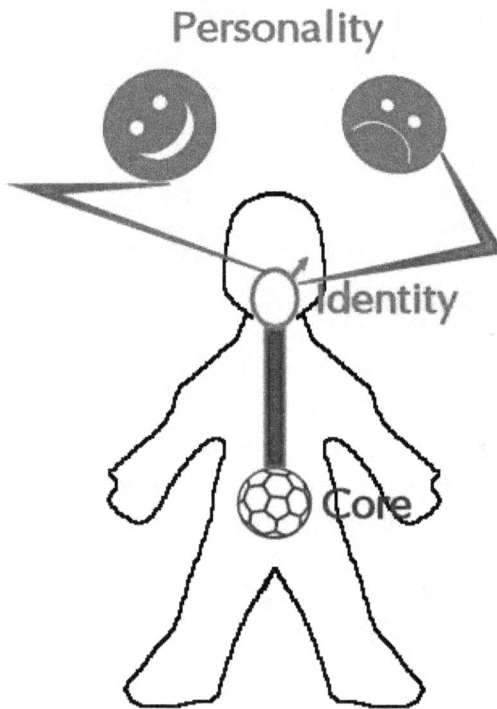

II.1 - The Personality Protects the Identity and the
Identity Protects the Core

Impostor Syndrome occurs when people either doubt or simply don't believe they have the skills to function in their daily lives and hence are impostors. The individual who claims to be a business expert and inwardly believes their success was more due to luck than anything else often lives in fear of being "discovered as an impostor". Process schizophrenia occurs when an individual has no substantial core upon which to base their identity and begins "borrowing" identities from those around them. The movie *Catch Me If You Can®* is an example of someone with process schizophrenia (not to mention incredibly good sales skills). Multiple Personality Syndrome, or MPS, is an example of the mind creating several identities in order to protect the core[c].

The need to protect the core and form the identity occurs when we transition from Stage 2 to Stage 3 learning. The identity, or sense-of-self, also needs protection and finds its protector in the personality-matrix, or "personality" for short. Our personality is our identity projected into the world. Like our identities, which are formed from the core and must also protect the core, our personalities are projected out from our identities and here's where something wonderful begins. The Core-Identity conduit is created and maintained within the self and is firmly anchored at both ends deep within our emotional-cognitive structures. It's where psychologists, psychotherapists and psychiatrists work and live.

But the Identity-Personality conduit, while having one end — the Identity — anchored firmly in the self, leaves its other end — the Personality — free to whip about untethered in the world like a sail torn from its mast. Children act like children because all they have is a Core (and usually a developing one at that). At some point children start acting like young adults because the Identity is starting to establish itself. Finally, we are adults and give up childish things because, like the Apostle Paul, our personality tells us we can't act like children anymore. At one end of this conduit are people whose Personality is their Identity is their Core. These are the "old souls" we sometimes hear about, people who are extremely comfortable with themselves regardless of the situation they're in. These people have a strong sense-of-

---

[c] – Research over the past 10+ years has offered a redefinition from MPS to *Dissociative Identity Disorder* or DID. DID sufferers don't have multiple personalities, they often have less than one whole personality such that different personality states (rather than identities) each strongly manifest themselves.(298)

self which manifests itself as self-confidence and self-awareness. When the Core is the Identity is the Personality (the opposite of old souls) we have brats and bullies and children who never grew up, people who throw temper tantrums when the slightest thing goes awry. These people have no sense-of-self, no confidence and tend to be hyper-aware of others. They feel constantly threatened and challenged by what's going on around them.

Unlike the Core and Identity, Personalities can't exist in isolation. People need to have at least one other person reinforcing their personality — echoing or mirroring it back to them, as it were — in order for that first person's personality to remain stable. So long as at least one person interacts with an individual's personality (and the interaction can be positive or negative) the personality tightens and guides the person for good or ill like a taut sail tacking into the wind. All that matters is that the interaction exists because it is the interaction, not the quality or quantity of the interaction, which reinforces the personality.

The need for interaction with people to help shape personalities goes back to people wanting to live in communities. We spend a great deal of our lives looking for people who'll accept us as we are — basically letting us know that they accept our personality...or at least tolerate it — because our personality is our self-concept (or identity) projected into the world and if our personality isn't reinforced then our identity is wrong and we're not who we think we are.

But if we're not who we think we are, then our core beliefs about ourselves and the world we live in must be wrong... perhaps you begin to appreciate how important it is that those three stages of learning and what happens between them transition smoothly.

II.4 – Echoes and Mirrors

We seek echoes and mirrors – literally reflections of ourselves in everyone we meet, every place we go and everything we do – that confirm our personalities as valid and correct in wonderful little ways. It's not apropos for us to go up to someone and ask,

"What do you think of me?" unless that person is an intimate, so we look for these echoes and mirrors in non-verbal ways.

Interestingly enough I once asked a somewhat similar question to a complete stranger and got a laugh first and then a shake of the head second; two non-verbal echoes and mirrors that, for a brief moment in time, defined who I was for that brief moment in time.

I was trying on a pair of pants at L.L.Bean™ and came out of the dressing room looking for Susan. Not seeing her nearby, I noticed a middle-aged woman appraising me from the spousal waiting area. She blushed when I caught her eye so I said, "Do these make me look fat?" The woman laughed, the tension of the moment broken. She then motioned for me to turn around so she could finish her appraisal, then shook her head, no, the pants didn't make me look fat.

I bought three pair.

I wonder how much time L.L.Bean™ spent training her?

Our society tends to frown on a middle-aged male inviting an equally-aged, unknown woman to evaluate his appearance for him. Personal appearance and such are considered taboo topics between unknowns in our society. We might think someone has never heard of a mirror but we don't usually go up to someone and say, "My God, who dressed you today? Did you have a fight with your closet or something?"

But this is where signs — non-verbal communications — come in and are so important. I'd already noticed the woman appraising me. When she realized I was aware she was staring she became uncomfortable. I made a joke and invited her to continue her appraisal. Essentially I communicated my willingness to let her look, even asking her to do so which gave her permission and thwarted any further discomfort either of us might have felt. I allowed her limited power over me (she motioned me to turn and I did) so she could feel in control of the situation and demonstrated that I valued her input, giving her a sense of importance (both to herself and to me).

Persuasive Analytics. Persuasion made simple. It's everywhere, isn't it?

But who was persuading whom? Both the woman and I entered into a little dance, something recognized and documented by many sociologists and anthropologists. This dance contained a variety of signs — some verbal and others not — and so long as each of us were willing to take part in the dance — and signal our willingness to take part by the exchange of appropriate signs — society was maintained and a happy, healthy, and rewarding interaction took place for all involved. I was flattered by a stranger's attention, she was flattered that I accepted and encouraged her attention, L.L.Bean™ sold three pairs of pants.

Everybody made out on that one, don't you think?

All because the parties involved knew and accepted the signs which allowed us to reinforce our "in-the-instant" personalities via a momentary creation of a two-person community, and nothing which happened in the momentary community caused us to question our identities or caused conflict with our greater environment or our cores within.

The *Five Man Electrical Band* sung it well back in 1970, "Sign, Sign, Everywhere a sign. Blocking up the scenery, breaking my mind. Do this, don't do that. Can't you read the sign?"

But what happens when we don't give the right signs, either because we don't know them or don't wish to communicate them? Let me give you an example...

Whatever your faith, imagine being invited by a close friend of a totally different faith to take part in their worship service. Such invitations are extremely rare historically in western cultures although, as the world becomes a smaller and smaller place, a Muslim attending a Congregationalist or whatever service is less and less rare. Cross-cultural marriages are becoming more the norm than they were in the past.

So whatever your faith, celebrate it with a differently faithed friend! Be a Baptist and go to a Catholic Mass. Or even more exciting, be Jewish and attend a friend's Shinto wedding! Now there's cultural confusion ("Why are we backing up again?" "Because the Kwan lit only two candles instead of three." "Oh, yes. I see.")!

II.5 – The Safety of the Nipple[d]

In these types of situations and especially in those less obvious as our religious service examples, we become uncomfortable, then concerned, then we start to seek a nipple (or the safety thereof) in any of several ways.

We may have the person who doesn't know the proper signs removed. In these cases our identity determines that the person who doesn't know the proper signs is "foreign" or "alien" and should be removed in order for the identity-core conduit to be maintained. Or we may remove ourselves from the situation until we learn the proper signs so that we can continue to project our personality into the world correctly in the new situation.

Alternately, we may remove ourselves from the situation until we believe the "foreigner" or "alien" has learned the proper signs. Or we could make sure our friend is there to let everyone know "He's okay, he's just doesn't know the right signs."

What are the right and proper signs? That depends on the situation you're in. We remove the person who doesn't know the proper signs and what we really mean is that the person doesn't know *our* signs, the signs we're familiar with. We remove ourselves until we know the proper signs and what we really mean is that we don't know *their* signs. The late Sammy Davis, Jr., told a story about attending synagogue with Joey Bishop to learn about Judaism before his conversion. Concerned that his friend wouldn't be able to find him in the crowd, Davis offered to wear a hat so he'd be easier to recognize. Joey Bishop rolled his eyes when Sammy Davis told the story, but everybody laughed when Sammy Davis finished the story with "How was I suppose to know all the men have to wear the same kind of hat? I was lucky he found me at all!"

----

[d] – The content is this section can be summed up best in NextStage Principles 27 and 28:
27 - Everybody knows there are classes in society, any society. Wise people don't speak of it. The wisest people don't show it.
28 - Respect people who know the name of their waiter or waitress. It shows they value people.
See http://nlb.pub/J for the complete list.

The above story is an amusing retelling of an uncomfortable situation. Now consider a situation where the individual or group needing the echo and mirror suffers from the Impostor Syndrome or something worse. Their personalities are seeking the echo and mirror that they are, for example, competent business people who know what they're doing and that they are good at what they do. Their identities, however, know that their success had more to do with blind luck than anything else. They may be or have been successful but that success hasn't been repeatable to a degree which takes it out of the realm of chance and gives it firm footing in the realm of intentional action.

The echo and mirror that such people need and seek is that they are competent and successful due to their own machinations. As long as that echo and mirror is maintained, their personalities — which require cognitive effort and control — can fool their identities — which is where the emotions and intellect battle — into acquiescence.

Imagine a situation where the necessary echo and mirror are denied for a totally mundane reason; community is attempted with someone who doesn't know or recognize the necessary signs. Remember the dance I engaged in at L.L.Bean™? A similar non-verbal dance might ensue but with very different results. Consider the following exchange between a hypothetical Tim (who is basically insecure) and Jack (who doesn't know the signs):

> *Tim*: "Hello. I'm transmitting non-verbal signs that I'm a successful business person. Please transmit recognition signs so I'll know you believe and accept me as such."

> *Jack*: "Well, I know your transmitting some kind of signs, but I've never seen them before and have no idea what they mean, so I can acknowledge that you're transmitting but have no idea if the signs are valid or not."

> *Tim*: "I just told you what the signs mean. Recognize them."

> *Jack*: "I'm sorry. I don't know what the signs you're transmitting mean. I'll start sending some signs of my own to figure out where community exists between us."

At this point Tim's identity and core are being unintentionally threatened. Even though the threat doesn't exist it must be defended against once it is believed to exist and because Tim doesn't really own his success he now transmits the *I'm a business person* signs more aggressively.

> *Tim*: "Look at the size of my briefcase! Look at the car I'm driving! Look at my house! These are all valid signs I'm a successful business person! Recognize them!"

Jack first defends because he reads Tim's more aggressive signage as a threat, although he's not sure why Tim is becoming more aggressive.

> *Jack*: "Hey, quit your shoving! Your briefcase drags like an anchor, your car is overpriced and the mortgage you're carrying makes you house rich but cash poor."

Now Jack, who still wants to create community, starts transmitting interrogative signs such as "Are you a sailor? You don't seem like a sailor to me. Are you a policeman? You don't seem like a policeman to me. Are you a tinker-tailor-soldier-spy? You don't seem like a ..."

The end result of such exchanges is that both parties leave confused at best and frustrated if not insulted at worst, and nobody is to blame. People whose Core, Identity and Personality are in alignment rarely broadcast[e] Identity signs because, being comfortable "in their own skins", there's no need to transmit identity signals for mirroring and echoing purposes. Instead, aligned people transmit comfort with themselves and comfortable

---

[e] – *Broadcasting* occurs when people send a specific signal with the intent that that signal and that signal alone be recognized as valid.

with others signals from their Core because they get along with everybody.[f] Does this seem farfetched to you?

Have you ever been in a foreign land where you were surrounded by people who didn't speak your language and you didn't speak theirs and you needed to get somewhere or do something quickly? You transmit signs taught you by your culture with which they are unfamiliar and vice versa. In the end frustration, insecurity and fear come to dominate the exchange, especially if there's only one of you and fifty of them. This is why immigrants to any country tend to seek their own people (and settle in neighborhoods such as "Chinatown", "Little Italy", "Germantown", "Frenchville", etc.) rather than others and why most people prefer guided tours rather than being dropped in the middle of a place foreign to them; they want to be around people who are able to provide the correct identification signs, the correct echo and mirror, until they learn the new environment's signs. The example of our business-person above ends with the individual or group seeking out those able to provide the necessary echoes and mirrors in order to lull the identity back into acquiescence. Tim, for example, might stop off at his club to seek the comfort of his fellow impostors and talk about Jack's arrogance in not acknowledging Tim's signs. The same error in sign transmission could occur between a person lost in the inner city and a gangmember with potentially disastrous results.

And this same exact sign confusion occurs (I'm guessing) much closer to your home. If you have birdfeeders, you can probably witness it every day.

Grackles (a black bird about the size of a bluejay) travel in flocks and any creature that exists in community (a flock is a community of birds) will develop communication — signs — simply to keep the peace. Bluejays, on the other hand, don't flock. They exist in a community but they don't flock, hence bluejay social order and structure is very different than the grackle's.

-----

[f] – The exception is people with very poorly defined Identities. They almost always recognized old souls as a threat.

The grackle dominance sign is to point the beak straight up. Two grackles get into a dominance game and the grackle who can point its beak the straightest into the sky wins. Simple, clean, neat and nobody gets hurt. The less pointing bird takes flight[g].

But that sign means nothing to bluejays. A bluejay and a grackle land on the same feeder, the grackle points mightily to the sky and the bluejay basically responds, "Hiya, how you doin'?" and merrily goes back to its seeds.

The grackle points straighter. The bluejay says, "Yeah, great, how you doin'?" and again returns to its seeds.

The third time out with no response, the grackle leaves. Jack and Tim or bluejay and grackle. When there are different social mores, strategies and beliefs, it takes intention and work to win.

II.6 – Signs Transmitted and Received

In semiotics, however, there is no reason to believe the unfamiliar response — the "Are you a sailor? A police person? A...?" signs — is invalid, only that the first person (Tim) wasn't receiving the desired confirmation sign. Human beings desire to live in communities, so some response sign was being given as described above. People who are secure in their identity will often recognize that a sign is being sent even if it's not the desired confirmation sign. Wonderful learning opportunities are the result.

Signs transmitted and signs received. One of those wonderful moments when people will use the same word and attribute totally different meanings to it. When is a "culture" not a "culture"? When a microbiologist in street clothes is having lunch with an anthropologist, checks her watch and says, "You'll have to excuse me. I have to go destroy a culture." The microbiologist isn't wearing a lab coat so an important sign isn't being communicated and the anthropologist has heart failure.

---

[g] – Don't laugh at our avian friends. Ever been to a crowded bar and watched the completely non-conscious dominance games being played there? Bluejays and grackles perch on the bar windows, look in and laugh, I'm sure.

Why do I (or you or your children or your neighbors or your neighbors' children) excel in some fields and fail wonderfully in others? Signs.

Remember our definition of "beauty"? Most people answer with images because most people are highly visual.[209] Their world is one of colors, images, sights, ... loads of visual information. That's how evolution designed human beings to be most aware. That 600-page thesis I wrote offered an interesting postulate about the deeper meaning of differences in responses to "What is beautiful?"; How people *think* is not how they're most *aware*.

Most people don't think in images — they hear their thoughts, they don't see them. Ask most people to tell you the color of their house and they can say "brown" or "white" or "red" very quickly. But ask them to remember what their house looks like and tell you the color and it takes a little longer because evolution has designed us to use our eyes to check for threats and treats (what we now call "pleasure and pain" or "profits and losses") in our environment. When we remember visual information we defocus externally because we need to focus "inside" and that requires the visual centers of our brain to ignore what's coming in through our eyes for a moment or two. From an evolutionary standpoint, thinking visually put our ancestors at the risk of being eaten by a lion or a competitor. Most people are wired to receive information visually. They internalize information audially.

Remember the auditory concept of beauty? People who are auditory are *aware* of sounds as opposed to sights. Literally, they *internalize* information differently than most people. This means that their signs for "I'm willing to learn" and "I'm ready to learn" were incompatible with traditional education's signs for "Learn this" and "Understand this", which meant most education models won't work for them. Amusingly, most people who live in auditory landscapes think visually even though their lingualization of their reality may not involve visual information.

And that, believe it or not, brings us to the meat of this book.

The semioticist's signs (be they for a student, a business-person, someone browsing the web, reading an email, using your software or attending your next meeting or presentation) are demonstrated by behaviors. We sign a greeting (we wave hello) and anticipate a sign of acknowledgement in return (a wave or nod, perhaps a verbal "Hello" or "How you doing today?"). When we receive a different kind of sign (a fit of laughter, a rude gesture or something we're unprepared for) we become confused and, if the different kind of sign continues, concerned.

But these signs — the wave, the nod, the verbalization, the laughter, the gesture — are all behaviors we learned growing up. They become part of our intuitive understanding of the world around us. If you know how to isolate and read these behaviors, and you know what information is being presented (such as a web page, a software interface, a brochure, a leave-behind, a PPT slide, ...), then you know how to predict what people are going to do and how to persuade them to do what you want, online and off, whether they're sitting in front of you, sitting in front of a computer half a world away or responding to emails on their iPhone sitting in a Starbucks™ while entering their novel into their MacBook.

III – Behaviors, Offline to On

Behaviors.

What are behaviors, exactly? The previous chapters discussed behaviors

- as the signs we give and take to and from ourselves
- as the signs we give and take to and from each other
- as what we use in order to function better in society
- and that we learn them as we learn who we are[a]

An interesting thing about behaviors is that people engage in thousands of behaviors without realizing they are doing so. These thousands of behaviors are little things that mean nothing by themselves but added up give us a pretty detailed picture of who we are.

Have you ever noticed somebody walking down the street, their back turned toward you, walking away from you, maybe even a few blocks away, and immediately known who it was? Realistically, how could you know who they were? They had their back to you, they were walking away from you, they were blocks away. Yet still you knew who they were and most times you were correct.

Have you ever heard a voice in a crowd and known immediately who it was? There were lots of other people talking, maybe music or other background noise, and the person wasn't anywhere near you. Still, you heard their voice and it rang a bell and bingo, you knew who they were and you were correct.

Have you ever wondered how you could know who someone was with so little information as a voice across the proverbial crowded room or a back glimpsed briefly in a crowd? It's not all that hard to do and the mechanism behind it is really quite simple. For example, it's much more likely you'll accurately pick someone out in these situations if you have a history with them.

---

[a] – Mark Twain's *The Prince and the Pauper* is an excellent example of different behaviors learned based upon different beliefs in who we are.

This history can be anything from a long acquaintance to a lasting but accurate impression gathered, like a snapshot, at a moment in time and known as *imprinting*.[245]

You can pick these people out because, in reality, you're not hearing just a voice or seeing just a back. Your mind and your memory are like a piece of highly sensitive film. Like that highly sensitive film, you've gathered millions and millions of points of information about that person over time or in that one powerful moment. None of these individual points tells you much about the picture as a whole but when you put all those points together in just the right order, *voila*, the shutter of memory clicks and the familiar picture develops. You've connected the person as they are today with your memory of them, run a quick analysis, determined how many points of the picture match what's in front of you now and either say, "Hey, I know you!" or "Sorry, thought you were somebody else."

Those shutter snaps don't occur because you see someone walking. If walking were all that was involved, we'd think we remembered everyone walking down a city street.

What causes those shutter snaps of memory is the *way* someone walks; the movement of the arms, the leading of the shoulders, the swing of their legs, the canting of the head as their eyes move from one item to the next, maybe even the sashaying of their hips depending on where your eye tracks them as they move. All these subtleties of movement within a larger movement are like fingerprints; they're unique to the person doing them. We're flattered when a special someone tells us nobody kisses like we do and perhaps annoyed when someone else says they could pick our gangly stride out of a crowd. But the truth is it's not the one motion, it's everything we do to make that motion. Even in something as simple as a walk or a kiss, people are giving off hundreds of clues as to who they are just by puckering up or taking a step. It's not the walk, it's *the way* they walk, it's the behavior unique to them that tells us who they are.

This is true for picking a voice out of a crowd. You don't recognize the voice. You recognize the way certain words are pronounced, the way sentences or phrases are strung together, the use of unique words in unique ways, the timbre, the tone, the pausing and inflection. When you hear a familiar voice you're not just hearing that voice, you're hearing all the experiences and beliefs of the person impressed into a string of sound. When you see a person walk you're not just seeing a walk, you're seeing all the experiences and beliefs of the person impressed into movement.

Let me offer you an example of memory's shutter in action: Remember the game show *Name That Tune*™? Contestants had to guess the name of a song based on a few clues and a certain number of notes as played by an orchestra. It became increasingly difficult to *Name That Tune*™ when contestants started bidding on fewer and fewer notes; "I can name that tune in five notes," "I can name that tune in three notes," "Name that tune!"

How good are you at recognizing someone just by their hands? How about just by their ears? Their eyes?

If you're very good you can name a tune in three notes[b] or recognize someone just by their eyes or hands, but it usually takes more. That's because we recognize people, places, sounds and everything else as a "sum of the parts". We gather information about the different parts and use them to create an image of the whole.

Recognizing people by the sum of their parts is true even through a machine interface. Recognizing individuals through a machine interface has been known since human-machine interfaces were first used for human-to-human communications. In the example given here, through the Morse-code telegraph:

> From the very beginning of telegraphy, as soon as the art began to spread, the individuality of operators became apparent. Little peculiarities in sending stood out to identify each one, just as voice quality and style do in speaking.[c]

---

[b] – The notes carry an amazing amount of information; pitch, tempo, duration, relation, time, attack, vibrato, strength, ... and this is just the music without the libretto!
[c] – From William Pierpont's *The Art and Skill of Radio-Telegraphy.*

The ability to recognize an individual as a specific person through a machine interface was so familiar that it was used as a plot element in 1934's *Brand of the Werewolf* by Kenneth Robson:

> The freckled, frizzle-haired young man stared at Doc in open-mouthed amazement. He had been listening to the wire talk. He had just heard some of the fastest and most perfect hand-sent Morse to which he had ever listened. It had been as rapid as if sent with a fast automatic key, a "bug." The freckled young man had not believed such a thing possible.

The "bug" being described was any of several mechanical devices which helped telegraph operators speed up their transmission rates (they got paid by the word, so someone able to transmit 20 words per minute got paid twice as much as someone who could only transmit 10 words per minute).

Similarly, the concept of psychomotor behavioral cuing (described in the **Author's Foreword** on page 32) is basically a fifty dollar way of saying "people respond to what's going on in their head about what's going on in their environment"[d]) can be found in scientific literature dating back to 1852, although then it went by the names of *Gedankenlese*, *Lecture de la Pensée* and *Lettura del Pensiero*, all of which translate into English as "Thought Reading" (aka *mindreading* as described beginning on page 27) and which went under the more formal name of "Muscle Reading".

> The basis of muscle reading rests upon the tendency — a marked one in some individuals, and less so in others — of involuntary movements and impulses to motor expression to accompany mental operations. Such movements find most ready expression in the contraction of delicate and specialized muscle groups, of which the hand is a familiar example. ...

----

[d] — People don't respond to their environment, they respond to their perception of their environment. Where is that perception based? In their heads, of course. Perception may be reality but reality certainly isn't based on an individual or even a group's perceptions (despite what politicians would have you believe).

> In this way it has been proved that the thought of a
> particular corner of the room is likely involuntarily to direct
> the hand towards that corner, the direction of the attention
> towards a sound is apt to start a movement towards the
> locality of the sound, and so on. In brief, the local direction
> of the attention is more or less readily reflected in the
> accompanying involuntary movement.[e]

In the 1870's professional "muscle readers" would put on performances and "mind read" members of the audience. Likewise, the concept was so familiar that it appeared in the pulps as well, this time in E.E. Smith's 1950 novel *Second Stage Lensmen*:

> ...and Samms' daughter Virgilia — who had inherited her
> father's hair and eyes and who was the most accomplished
> muscle-reader of her time — went first.[f]

What's most important to remember, be it telegraphy, muscle reading, psychomotor behavioral cuing or recognizing individual behaviors via a machine interface, is that the individuals in question aren't recognized by any one thing they do but by all the things they do. People are the sum of their parts, and once you appreciate that the way you use a mouse is different from the way I use a mouse, and that the way you type in your name is different from the way I would type in your name and vice versa, then it's no great leap at all to understand that recognizing individual behaviors, offline to on, is merely a mathematical exercise in recognizing the sum of the online parts. What people do either non-consciously or through extensive training can be done by a computer with sufficiently developed mathematical models of the dance that occurs between the person using an interface (PDA, computer, smartphone, kiosk, ...) and the interface itself. As noted before, people will strive to create community with whatever they feel is responding to them at that

---

[e] – http://nlb.pub/j
[f] – Today "muscle readers" are mostly known as "cold readers". You can find them practicing their craft everywhere from real-life detectives to detective novels to stage performers to police and beyond, as mentioned on page 28.

moment in time. If all that's in front of them is a computer, then it's just the computer and the person in the dance.

The interfaces learn the right dance just as a child does,

- by first mimicking what is around it (Stage 1 Learning),
- then by testing past experience in new situations (Stage 2 Learning),
- and finally by adapting their behaviors to new environments (Stage 3 Learning).

In other words, the interfaces, like a child,

- first learns by interacting with its user. It can then take what its learned from its user and determine how well what its learned works with people similar to its user
- then take what it learns while doing that see how well it works when interacting with people completely different from its user.
- Lastly, the interfaces determine how what they've learned from people similar to its user should be applied to people it might encounter once and never again and learns from that.

Mother, family, society.

Workstation, workgroup, office network.

Intranet, extranet, internet.

My web session, my family's web sessions, the web sessions of others browsing the same website.

Anthony may be a pretty boy, and the computer's part of the dance is to determine *how* the person currently sitting at a computer will and is responding to that phrase. The *how* is communicated to the computer by psychomotor behaviors; thousands of little, non-conscious behaviors everyone does but nobody knows they do. In this case the psychomotor behaviors are those we've transferred from our offline world to our online experiences. People coming of age in an information-rich, digital culture are creating online behaviors which are a jargon of offline behaviors just as their language is a jargon of the words and phrases used by their parents and others around them.

Why create and use jargon behaviors? To establish community by sharing shared ideas and beliefs. I wd nvr txt msg. Wd u? Chances are the generation which text-messages as part of their identity knows that and would respond accordingly when they saw the errors in my messaging.

III.1 – Creating Community

People communicate and create community, and the ways people communicate tend to be both common to a specific community (sociolingual and psycholingual) and unique to an individual (psycholingual and neurolingual). A wonderful and necessary by-product to communication and community is that people recognize each other by the sum of those common and unique communications. Those common and unique communications — the individual's psychomotor behavioral cues — are the behavioral parts that summed together allow recognition to occur. People don't look at one thing, people look at many things and build an inference based on the total of those many things. More correctly, people don't watch what someone does to figure out who they are, people watch *how someone does what they're doing.* Everybody walks, it's the *way* someone walks that lets you know it's them and not someone else. Everybody talks, it's the *way* someone talks that lets you know it's them and not someone else.

These psychomotor behavioral cues — the parts we sum — are so unique people can recognize each other through a machine interface (as in the earlier telegraphy example). Being able to recognize people by their behaviors through a machine interface must mean the interface is collecting and transmitting those behavioral cues to and from the people on either end of that interface.

And if the interface is collecting and transmitting those behavioral cues, it can also monitor and interpret those behavioral cues in order to establish community between the user and the interface itself because people will seek to establish community with whatever they feel is responding to them. They'll transmit recognition and attention signs until they are recognized and paid attention to.

Imagine an interface that could recognize and respond to your signs, that could create community with you based on you being you and not you being the 803rd person who typed in "Reading Virtual Minds" in the past ten minutes. Google™ would be a whole lot better if it knew what you really meant when you typed something in, wouldn't it? And if it only responded with the links you were really interested in? Imagine Amazon™ suggesting books based on a recognition that you were buying a book for your nephew and not for yourself, or that what you're shopping for today isn't what you were shopping for yesterday and might not be what you're interested in tomorrow.

III.2 – Summing the Parts

Creating community is therefore also an exercise in the summation of the parts and, once recognized as such, becomes a simple mathematical exercise. The maturing mind of a child learns to create community over time and the inference engine they build during that time is truly wondrous due to the number of datapoints children collect and integrate over time. Software interfaces and websites don't have the luxury of time. What they do have, however, is thousands upon thousands of users or — in the jargon of the day — user populations.

A child learns over time and starts with one person, then a family, then an extended family, than a peer group, a tribe, and eventually a society. Computers get to do it the other way around; get a society (the user community as a whole), start calving the user community as a whole into smaller and smaller groups. Are all of these users responding to the presentation the same way (or "Are all their online behaviors similar")? Then there must be similarities among their offline behaviors as well because online behaviors are based on offline behaviors (at least until we start jacking in a la *The Matrix*). Perhaps these users are all from the same demographic, maybe all males. Within that smaller group, are there further differentiations? There are, so now our first calving (males and females) is also calved (men over 35 from men under 35). And so on until, at last, the interface is able to recognize one-for-one who is using it and how to best respond to that particular user at that moment in time, much the same as when first meeting someone your interaction is based on your experience of society and, as you get more comfortable, your interaction is based on the individual him or herself.

And the interface does all this by recognizing the user population's signs, then the signs of a group within that population, then the signs of the group within that group, until finally it differentiates an individual from all other individuals by doing exactly what you and I do when we see someone walking down the street or hear someone speaking in a crowd. Mathematically and information mechanics-wise[g], this is known as *identity-relational modeling*[54] and is based on the same memetic signatures mentioned on page 66.

Interfaces can learn to create community over time, essentially going through the three stages of learning, then use what they've learned to start calving and recognizing individuals. Stage 1 learning is based on a common neurology — the human brain is designed a specific way and is bound by the rules of that wiring. Anything which can't be attributed to the direct cause and effect of that design must be unique to the individual using the computer (Stage 2 learning, and psychological). Similar responses to similar stimuli across a broad spectrum of users must be sociocultural and there we have Stage 3 learning.

Online behaviors, the little and largely non-conscious psychomotor behavioral dance between an interface and the person using that interface, and involving such things as how someone uses the keyboard and the mouse, taps the screen, rolls the cursor button, the size of the screen, the number of windows they have open, and so much more.

---

[g] — *Semantic* information mechanics, not *Shannonistic* information mechanics

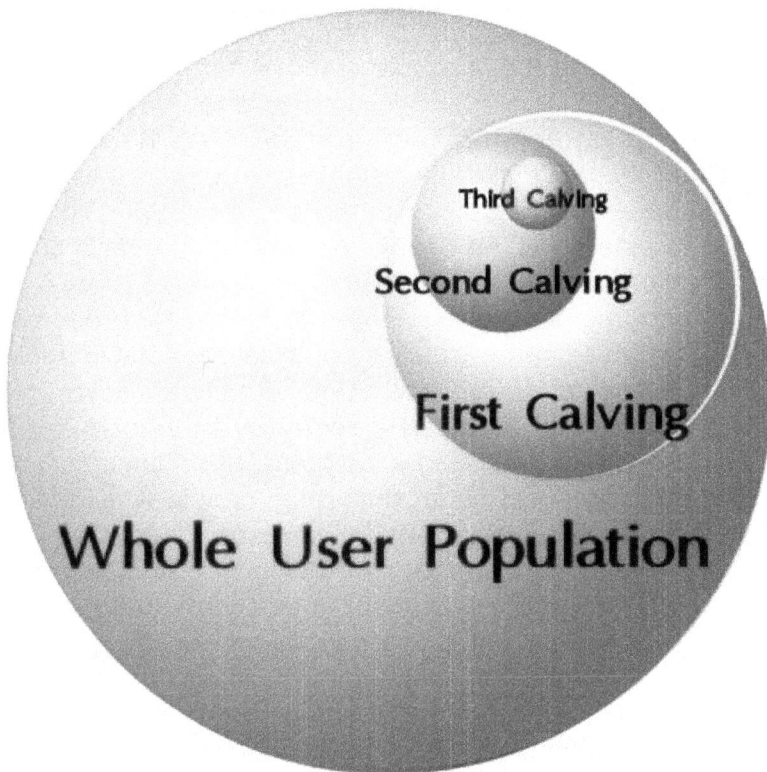

III.1 - The computer can cull you from the herd by recognizing your signs

Each of these separate items — how someone uses a mouse, how they type, their language style and rhythm, the color depth of their screen, ... — summed together form a pattern. The complexity of the pattern is determined by how many data points are contained therein. "Lives in the northeast USA" is a pattern which is contained in the pattern "Joseph Carrabis". "Maleness" is another pattern that is part of the pattern of "Joseph Carrabis". However, "Lives in the northeast USA" is not part of the pattern of "maleness" or vice versa. If you know what patterns to look for, you know a great deal about who someone is (their buying habits, decision making rules, etc).

Oh, if only these interfaces could talk!

Well, they can! Not at first, of course. First they must say *"mook!"* and be sure they're understood. After *mook* their lexicon grows and grows.

The next chapter in *Reading Virtual Minds* deals with how that lexicon grows and demonstrates that growth through a number of anecdotes. Before doing so, however, I'll share a personal example of offline behaviors forming the basis of a new, online behavior.

My rules for business telephone etiquette have been pretty well-fixed for quite some time; I don't call anyone before 9am their time and not after 7pm their time. I believe I learned these rules by watching my father. He regularly brought work home from his office and completed it at home after dinner. Dad had some hard and fast rules about disturbing people when they were "at home and in the privacy of their own house."

Recently NextStage has started using internet telephony as an inexpensive way of staying in touch with our distributed workforce. For the longest time I held by my business telephone etiquette rules for internet telephony until one morning I noticed that my internet telephony client indicates whether or not someone is available to take calls (a little box appears beside their name indicating their status). Just looking at that box made me feel odd, as if I were violating some rule (which I was! The rule was my own rule about business telephone etiquette). I looked at the clock on my desk. It was 8:30am. Too early to call. But their status box indicated they were available to take a call. And obviously they were at the computer because the internet telephony system indicated so, which meant they were working.

There are several assumptions about my co-workers in the above and all are based on my own behaviors. I only use my computers for work (okay, I play solitaire once in a while) therefore all others must do the same. I don't surf the net just to surf the net (a growing population does just that in the same way that people of my generation use to go for a ride in the country, just to sight-see). My internet telephony client is only on if I'm willing to take calls therefore all others must shut theirs off when they're not willing to take calls.

It was 8:30am and I didn't want to intrude on (my assumption of) their privacy. I compromised and sent an IM (instant message) to my co-workers to learn if they were available to talk.

How did I determine that an IM was less intrusive than their telephony client ringing?

I'm primarily auditory, remember?

And that, dear readers, is a very real example of offline behaviors being the basis of and morphing to form new, online behaviors.

What really blew my mind is that he had it working ten, almost fifteen years ago.
— Adam Laughlin, Senior Software Engineer at Attend.com and Creator, Inside, to Boston Quantified Self Meetup (23 Jan 2014)

IV – Anecdotes of Learning

These anecdotes — all documented and used with permission where individuals are named (**Appendix A – Anecdotal Correspondence**, page 178) — are shared chronologically as happened and give an example of an interface learning both the rules of society and that society's lexicon as it goes. Technically, such an interface would be called a *Symbiotic CyberSemiotic System*, and who in their right mind wants to read that more than once in a book? Let's compromise and call the interface *ET*. In many ways, the interface is an alien, silicon-based lifeform visiting planet Earth and attempting to learn how we carbon-based lifeforms get along.

Perhaps most important is that ET learns as it goes from its interactions with people. It doesn't use surveys, polls, other internet databases, logins, or anything like that. It compares this person to that person but it's self-contained (something worth remembering as you read through these anecdotes).

What's could be most important is that these anecdotes are from 2002-2008. ET has been fully functional since about 1999. Keep in mind the following quote from Doug Brown[a], currently Consulting Sales at Oracle:

> I first encountered NextStage back in 2003-4. Joseph was demonstrating how Evolution Technology could determine things like site visitors' ages and gender, how they made purchasing decisions, what they liked and didn't like about a website and the only inputs were a mouse, keyboard and browser, and this was with the site's entire visitor population, not a focus group or marketing panel or people answering a popup questionnaire.
>
> Then he showed us how Evolution Technology could read a website and figure out how different audiences would react before the site was published. All the calculations were being done on a laptop.

---

[a] – http://nlb.pub/k

Interesting enough, neuromarketing and sentiment analysis companies seem like they are just now executing the kind of functionality that NextStage showed me back in 2003-4. Joseph was and I imagine now continues to be ahead of the curve when it comes to this complicated technology.

IV.1 – Dave Nelson Was Hungry (2002)

ET had only been in existence as an interface for about a month. It had learned all it could from me and had some experience with others in the tribe (students, friends, family and peers). Could ET take what it had learned and synthesize new information, essentially

1) learn and interpret the signs of someone it had never met (i.e., *acquire them*),
2) make an accurate analysis of that person's behaviors in order to understand how they think (i.e., *read their mind*), and
3) predict that person's needs and future plans based on what it had discovered in 1 and 2 above (i.e., *synthesize outcomes*).

I went to see Dave Nelson, then Director of New Hampshire's Small Business Development Center office at Rivier College in Nashua, NH. There were two other gentlemen in the office with him, and I started to explain what ET was and what it could do. It was 10:30 in the morning.

Their eyes glazed over very rapidly.

Dave Nelson started working on his computer. I figured he was bored and checking his emails or some such. Little did I know he was navigating the NextStage Evolution website. The site is very different now from what it was then. Back then it would display little charts about you based on what it was learning about you while you navigated.

Dave stopped and, as I continued to explain how ET worked, he said, "I'm on your site."

He said it very dryly, very deadpan. I figured someone had hacked into our site and replaced it with porn or something.

"Oh? What do you think?"

"Your site says I'm highly visual and that I'm thinking about something in the near future."

"Oh? That's nice."

Dave paused, then looked at me. "My wife always complains about how visual I am and I was just wondering what I'd have for lunch."

Like I said, it was about 10:30 in the morning. Near future. Highly visual.

Acquire, read, synthesize.

Dave has been one of NextStage's strongest advocates ever since.

IV.2 – The Investors Heard the Music (2002)

One of the early incarnations of the NextStage Evolution website self-modified in real time based on how individual visitors were interacting with it[b]. Two people could be sitting in the same room but using different computers to browse the site and ET would deliver content customized to each visitor's unique cognitive, memorization, and comprehension styles. These styles are collectively called the "{C,B/e,M} matrix", meaning "cognitive, behavioral/effective, motivational matrix".

The {C,B/e,M} Matrix[51,52,90,116-118,120-122,126,134,137,138,140, 236,269] is quite literally a shorthand notation for how people interact with their world. What is covered is very rich and detailed and can be summed up into three basic categories:

- Cognitive - "How do they think? What do they think about?"

---

[b] – *Self-modifying* sites are what now might be called "morphing" sites. I have a challenge with the term "morph" due to the concept of Turing machines. A site, like you, should modify its behavior based on who it's communicating with. People (and true Turing machines) routinely modify their behaviors based on who they're communicating with, but only true psychotics "morph", i.e., become a completely different being.

- Behavioral/effective - "What do they do that
  demonstrates how they think?"[c] and
- Motivational - "Why do they think the way they do? Why
  do they demonstrate it the way they do?"

Differing {C,B/e,M} matrices were demonstrated when two investors called up from their office in San Francisco. I was sitting in my office in Nashua, NH, and they had asked for a demonstration of ET.

"Have you been on our site?" I asked.

Yes, they had, of course. So?

"Are you near a computer hooked to the internet right now?"

Yes, they were. So?

"Log onto the site. Pick any page off the menu you'd like to visit and tell me which one it is, okay?"

Okay.

I navigated to the same page they were on. "I'm going to describe to you what I'm looking at. While I describe it to you pay close attention to what's actually on your screen. You'll notice some differences." I started reading some of the text.

Yes, the text on their browser was slightly different.

I started describing the size and placement of images, as well as image content.

Yes, in some cases they didn't even have an image I was describing, often they had one I didn't have, etc., etc.

Then, while I was talking to them, their browser started playing music.

"You didn't tell us your site had music," one of them said.

My response didn't make sense to them at first. "ET determined that you weren't paying attention to the website and were focusing on an auditory stimuli, so it started playing music in the hopes of bringing your attention back to the website. It's attempting to substitute its own auditory stimulus for the one you're focusing on."

----

[c] – The way I use the word "Behavioral" has next to nothing to do with how the term is used in the industry today, me thinks. See *Section I.1 Behaviors? What are "Behaviors"?*, page 40)

"Why would it do that? There aren't any *auditory* stimulus in the room."

I remember both the emphasis and the lack of grammatical expertise on the investors' parts. My explanation stopped them cold. "Yes, the auditory stimulus is that you're talking to me. ET doesn't know that you're talking on the phone, but it can determine that some sound event — in this case our conversation — is where your attention is focused. It wants you focused on the website, so it's playing some music in order to draw your attention away from this phone call and back to the screen. Like a child, ET wants to be the center of attention."

I heard them click onto another page and the music stopped.

"How come the music stopped?"

"Because your attention was focused back on the website. It didn't need to play the music anymore in order to get your attention."

A brief discussion ensued in which they expressed a great concern about my ability to access and distribute fertilizer.

And the music started playing again.

IV.3 – The Toddness Factor (2002)

Todd Sullivan is NextStage's IP attorney and often serves as general counsel when he has the time. He was given a password to access the back end of our site during development of the patent application.

It so happened that one day I had just completed work on the "sum of the parts" formula so ET could recognize individuals based on their individual signs — their psychomotor behavioral cues — as they interact with it rather than some login criteria. That's a fancy way of saying you don't have to worry about ever remembering your password again. From now on, the computer will recognize you just by how you interact with it.

A problem with implementing such a formula is that there's no literature on how many parts people look for in order to recognize someone.

You and I don't recognize a person's face only when we have 100% of their face to look at. Many times we can recognize people just by their eyes or their nose or their lips or even their hairdo. Earlier we mentioned being able to recognize someone just by their walk or by hearing a few words across a room. We also mentioned telegraphers being able to recognize each other by the way they tapped out a message on the telegraph key. And of course there's *Name that Tune*™. As I described in **Chapter III, Behaviors Offline to On** (page 82), it's rare indeed that we wait until we have 100% of something or someone before we can recognize what or who it is.

So how to instruct ET? Wait for 100%? ET works by recognizing general and specific neurologic, psychologic and sociologic behavioral patterns. None of us acts the exact same way two days in a row. None of us acts the same way two minutes in a row because we're thinking, learning and changing every second of our lives. What was completely unacceptable a few pages ago is totally believable now and what is totally unbelievable now will be completely accepted when we turn the page.

Our ability to think and learn is both unique enough and general enough that ET can select, for example, which learning style best suits someone or which sales pitch best suits someone based on what it's learned by showing the same information to others who behaved similarly. As of this writing (30 Mar 2015), ET has a catalog of some 3,500,000 *digital personae* (we prefer the term "synthetic users" and have referenced them in various research papers as *bioginots*). Basically ET "remembers" its interactions with some 3.5MM people at present and uses this experiential memory to decide how to interact with other individuals. This number continues to grow as ET interacts with more people.

But figuring out how someone learns or which sales pitch will work best is kind of a "general" thing and doesn't require much effort on ET's part.

ET figures things via *engines* and *channels*. An engine is a mathematical equation that adapts itself to what is being calculated, as if the equation first determines which types of variables it's been given then decides which parts of itself need to be used in order to perform the calculation. A channel is like a variable in an equation, except that a channel knows when it needs other variables in order for the equation to calculate correctly. ET can determine best learning style or sales pitch using two engines and six channels. The unique part is that ET, when running all 70 or so engines on all 90 or so channels could identify you in a crowd of 10^{153} people. Talk about stars in the sky or grains of sand on the beach![d]

However, identifying one individual from another based solely on each individual's psychomotor behavioral cues meant that ET needed to pick up aspects of an individual's Core in order to recognize an individual as the same individual from one session to the next. To understand how to best serve you, ET only needs to know something about your basic thought patterns and the society you were raised in. To know you as uniquely you, ET needs to identify elements of your Core. An individual's Core rarely changes, and when it does it's usually slowly and over time. Often the individual does "core" work, such as deep psychotherapy, in order to invoke a core change to rid themself of long-lived problems interfering with their leading a fulfilling life. Rapid core changes usually are due to a *re-missioning* of the individual. Re-missioning is exactly what it sounds like; an individual has to create a new mission for their life. Dramatic spiritual conversion, such as the Apostle Paul experienced when the lightning bolt knocked him off his donkey, is an example. Another, more modern example is when someone undergoes a complete and inexplicable remission from cancer, which is why the term is used in that context.

The question comes down to this, "How much of a person's Core is required to identify them as who they are?"

Well, this particular day I said, "Oh, let's go with 75% of a person's Core is enough to identify them."

----

[d] – Originally ET analyzed some 65 channels with some 27 mathematical tools.

And about an hour later our site notified me that someone was using Todd's password but wasn't behaving like Todd.

I called Todd up. "Hi! How you — "

"Yes, I'm on your &&#(*$)!**W site."

You have to understand that Todd is a very soft-spoken, quiet, friendly kind of guy. Sweet. Gentle. Nice.

But right now it wasn't Todd The Nice Guy saying, "Yes, I'm on your &&#(*$)!**W site."

"Something wrong, Todd?

Todd was looking for something, was in a rush, was under some pressure, needed to get some things done. Todd was being hassled and, as they say, the detritus was migrating a negative slope.

I talked with Todd a bit and helped him find what he was looking for. As we talked, ET's numbers on him rose back up to where ET was convinced it was getting 75% of the Todd it knew and was happy.

This is one of my favorite anecdotes about ET and Todd and there are several others. Sometime you'll have to ask him about them should you ever meet him.

IV.3.A – How Much of a Person is Enough?

It turns out that about 68% of a person is enough of a person for ET to recognize them as who they are on most days and still allow for the changes that occur in our psyches from day to day. More than that and ET will reject a person if they're having a bad hair day. Or are, perhaps, being threatened to compromise something. Like a pilot with a gun at his head while the plane is in flight.

ET's mathematics will support any human-machine interface. Imagine a weapon which could recognize which police person or soldier it belonged to and would refuse to fire for anyone else.

When ET is turned up full bore I need to meditate before it will let me in. At 98% ET will let me in only when I'm calm. At 95% ET will let me in unless I've eaten within the last half hour (kind of like swimming, I suppose). Below 90% ET will let me in most of the time. Under 75% ET will let me in and sometimes ask a challenge question. Below 70% ET will let me in but not Susan (my wife, business partner and one of the best natural language theorists I've ever met) if she has my login credentials. Under 15% and ET will recognize that I'm not Susan and will provide us with information customized for each of us.

By the way, The Toddness Factor is now incorporated in ET's DejaWho Tool.

IV.4 – Hans Reimar Gets Offered a Job in Sales (2002)

I mentioned in the **Author's Foreword** (page 24) presenting at an MIT Enterprise forum. One of the people attending that forum was Hans Reimar, President and CEO of Market-Vantage[e]. Hans was one of the people who came up to me enthusiastically after that presentation to talk, and we did. We also followed that conversation up with some phone calls, ending in a plan to meet for lunch at his office one day the following week.

It might help at this point to know that NextStage is self-funded, which means I needed to find creative ways to have ET learn about people, but not all people at once. I wanted ET to be exposed to specific types of people for controlled periods of time so that ET could learn what makes one group of people different from another. The way I chose to do this was to sign up for contests. Submit your site to a contest for best website and you're going to be browsed by lots of website designers. Submit your company to a business plan competition run by a bunch of venture capital firms and you're going to be browsed by venture capitalists. Submit your company to an MIT Enterprise forum and, well, you get the idea. When ET found a new set of psychomotor behavioral cues and we knew the majority of new visitors were coming to the site based on some contest we'd entered, those behavioral cues were by definition indicative of the people most involved in that contest.

---

[e] – http://www.market-vantage.com

Let me tell you, if you want to do massive amounts of socio- and psycho-linguistic research in a short amount of time, use the web and pick your targets wisely. The ROI is astronomical.[f]

So ET, by this point in time, had learned a great deal about how different people thought, made decisions, learned, remembered, so on and so forth. In fact, ET had learned enough that it could determine what kind of job a visitor would be best suited for should said visitor be searching for a job. No need to submit a resume, no need to fill out a form. ET would automatically make a decision regarding your aptitudes and abilities and, if such a position was available at NextStage, that position would be offered to you.

Hans, when we met, had this wry smile while we talked. It was a pleasant meeting and he had some of the other folks in his office come in to say hello. Hans introduced me as the fellow who'd come up with that interesting ET stuff, on that website he'd asked them to browse. I noticed that everyone looked at me a little strangely and I wondered if somehow I had once again transformed into Kafka's bug à la *Metamorphosis*.

Finally Hans told me that he'd went to our jobs page.

"Oh?"

"Your site offered me a job."

I wasn't sure what to say. "Did you take it?"

He laughed. "It offered me a job in sales."

I thought for a second. "Isn't that what you're doing here?"

Then he really laughed.

When I asked Hans if I could use this anecdote he wrote

> "...it was rather funny (and incredible) at the time. In the interest of journalistic integrity, my actual title at Marketreach was Director of Business Development, but everybody knows that means "glorified sales rep.""

Hans introduced to me to a female co-worker who had also gone to our Jobs page. She shook my hand while looking at me quite warily. It turned out she was leaving her present position to

---

[f] – Now most socio-population studies are done on the web.(135,136,336)

go to another firm. ET had offered her a position in research and development, something she'd always been interested in. What was she going to be doing at the new firm?

Research and development.

IV.5 – Mark Broth Discovers What Makes a Lawyer a Lawyer (2002)

I was invited to give a two-day seminar[g] at the law firm of Devine, Millimet and Branch (DMB). The invitation came when DMB was undergoing a rebranding to Devine Millimet (DM). Part of this rebranding involved a new, full-page print ad (figure IV.1 on page 104) in the top financial and law journals. As part of my seminar, I offered to demonstrate ET's effectiveness in determining how different people would respond to the ad.

I had not known at the time that there were various and non-quite sundry conversations among the partners about this ad, or that the firm was divided pretty much 50/50 regarding how useful the ad would be in the rebranding efforts.

The audience was filled with lawyers and some of them were litigators. Much of their interest and many of their questions focused on the ability to use the techniques I was demonstrating for jury selection and interrogations. The ability to predetermine someone's testimonial and prejudicial predilections fascinated them, and especially Mark Broth, a litigator and partner in the firm.

At the end of the seminar I shared that I had shown the ad to three people — a female graphic artist in her early 40s based in New Hampshire, a male marketing specialist in his mid 40s based in South Carolina and a male attorney in his early 30s, also based in New Hampshire — and then had ET analyze each person's responses to the ad. Each of them had a different response as shown in figures IV.2-4 on pages 106 through 107. Note that

---

[g] – The seminar was *Know How Someone's Thinking in 10 Seconds or Less*. NextStage offers that and similar trainings and seminars as time and requests dictate. You can keep up-to-date on what trainings and seminars are being offered where and when via http://nlb.pub/l or NextStage's RSS feed, http://nlb.pub/m.

channels are on the horizontal access and intensities are on the vertical access in the majority of the following charts. Internally, we call these graphs *neuroprints* for a number of reasons, their similarity to the outputs of voiceprint technology being one.

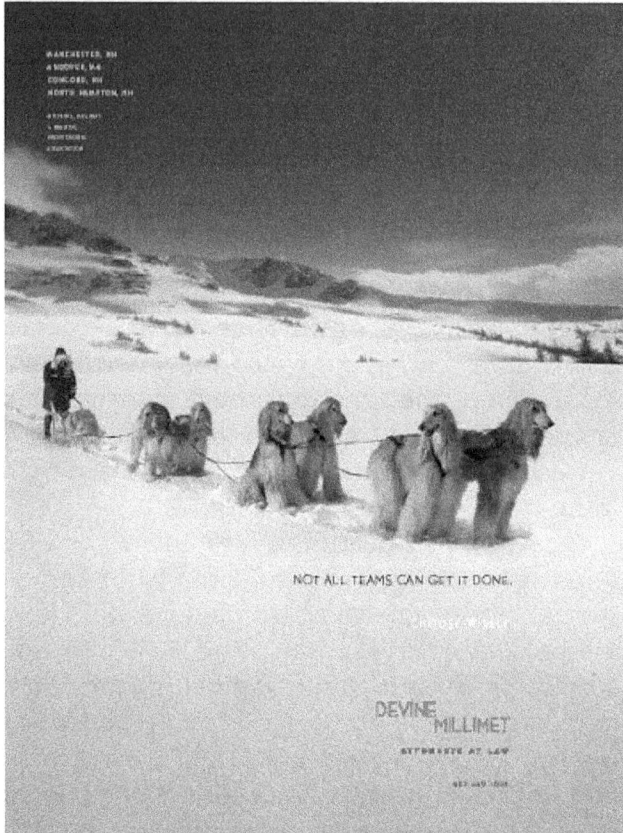

IV.1 - The DM ad

Now consider this same information grouped together into a single Intensity by Channel chart as shown in figure IV.5 on page 107. This chart shows three bars for each channel, one bar per channel for the male marketing specialist, one bar per channel for the female graphic artist and one bar per channel for the male attorney. The height of each bar indicates the intensity of the response of these individuals for that specific channel. Some channels are common to all three individuals, some channels only show up on two of the individuals while others are unique to a specific individual.

The Intensity by Channel chart shown in figure IV.5 on page 107 is interesting because those distinctions exist even though the three people themselves would say their opinions of the ad were in agreement. On the conscious level, yes, they were in agreement; none of them liked the ad.

However, on a non-conscious level, *what* they didn't like was different, in some cases slightly and in others cases greatly. Even more important, *how* they demonstrated their dislike was different. Remember that it's not that somebody's walking, it's *how* they walk, it's not that somebody's talking, it's *how* they talk.

In this case, it's not that they dislike something, it's *how* they disliked it and *what* they disliked about it. The *how* and *what* are, at a non-conscious level, like a fingerprint (another reason we use the term "neuroprints") of who they are. These neuroprints are shown in the Gender by Channel chart (figure IV.6 on page 108).

Here we discover that there are not only gender differences in response, but regional differences in response as well. I'm not saying this is definitive by any means. I'm merely pointing out that differences exist in this admittedly small sample and that these differences posed a curiosity to the researcher in me.

For example, what makes someone female? Perhaps what makes someone female is shown in the "Female Markers" chart (figure IV.7 on page 108). Should marketers include these elements when marketing to females?

What makes someone from New Hampshire? Is that shown in the "New Hampshire Markers" chart (figure IV.8 on page 109)? Are these the elements that insure successful marketing to New Hampshirites?

What makes someone from South Carolina? Do the unique spikes in the "South Carolina Markers" chart (figure IV.9 on page 109) show you that? Will successful South Carolina based campaigns include those elements in their pitches?

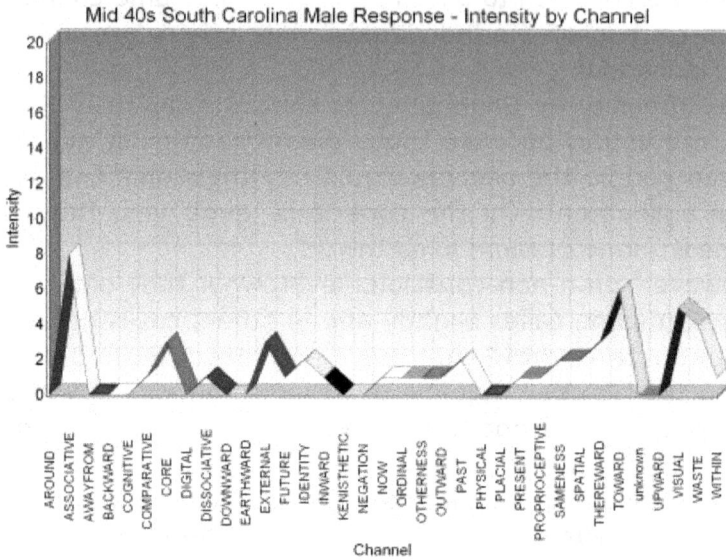

IV.2 - South Carolina mid-40s Male Response by channel

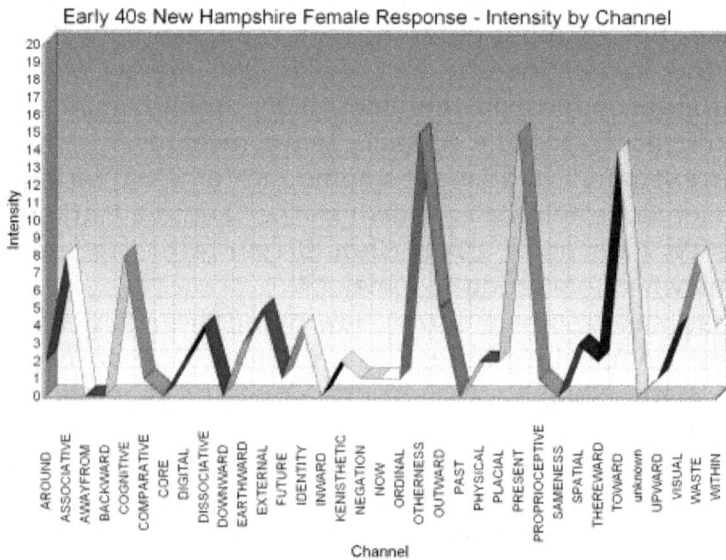

IV.3 - New Hampshire early-40s Female Response by channel

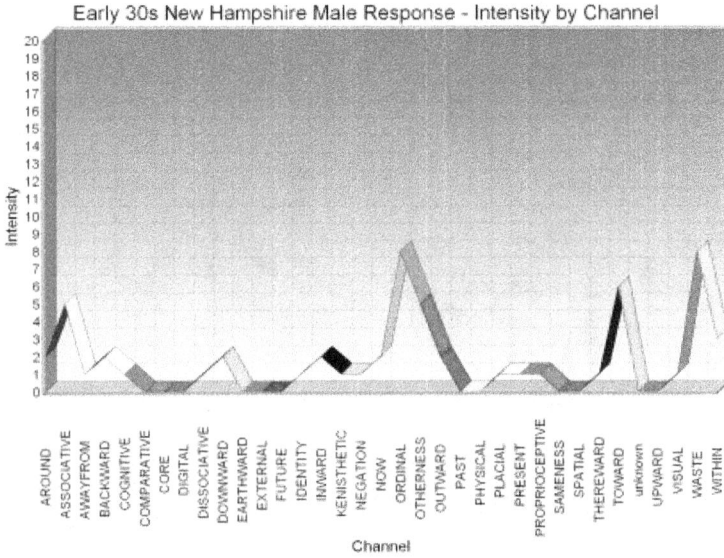

Early 30s New Hampshire Male Response - Intensity by Channel

IV.4 - New Hampshire early-30s Male Response by channel

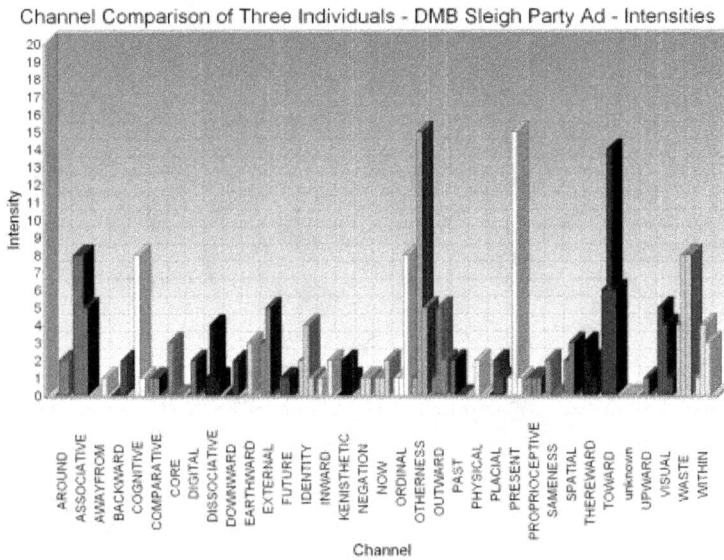

Channel Comparison of Three Individuals - DMB Sleigh Party Ad - Intensities

IV.5 - Note the similarities and differences in intensities for each channel of three different individuals responding to the DMB ad

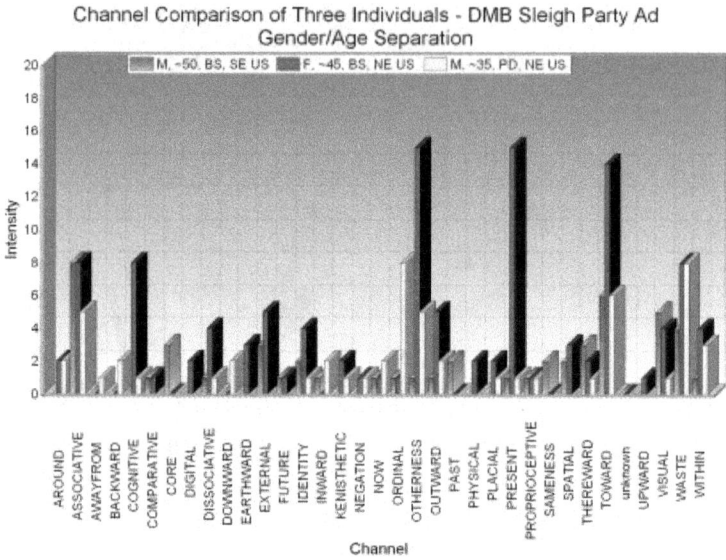

IV.6 - Separating the responses by channel along gender and age
lines highlights unique features of each individual's take on the DMB ad

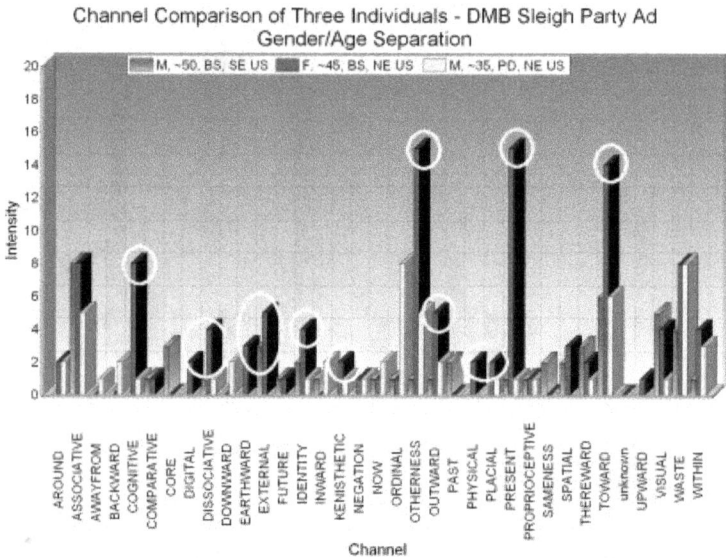

IV.7 - These highlighted differences were unique to female
responses to the DMB ad

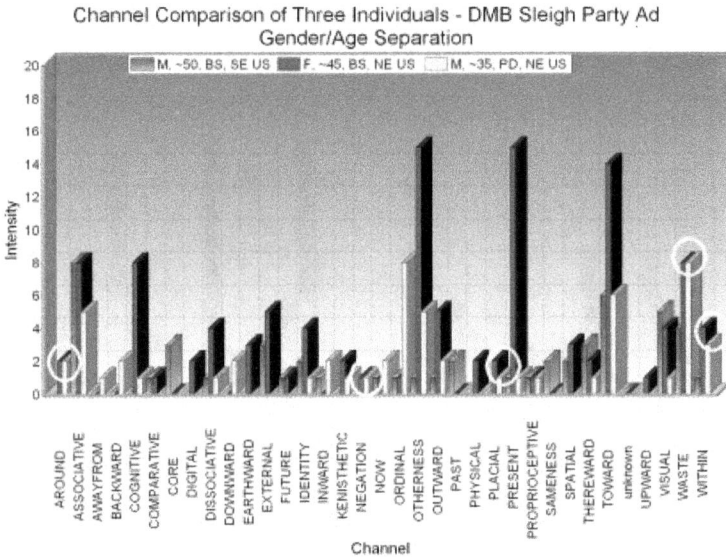

IV.8 - These highlighted differences were unique to responses from New Hampshire based people

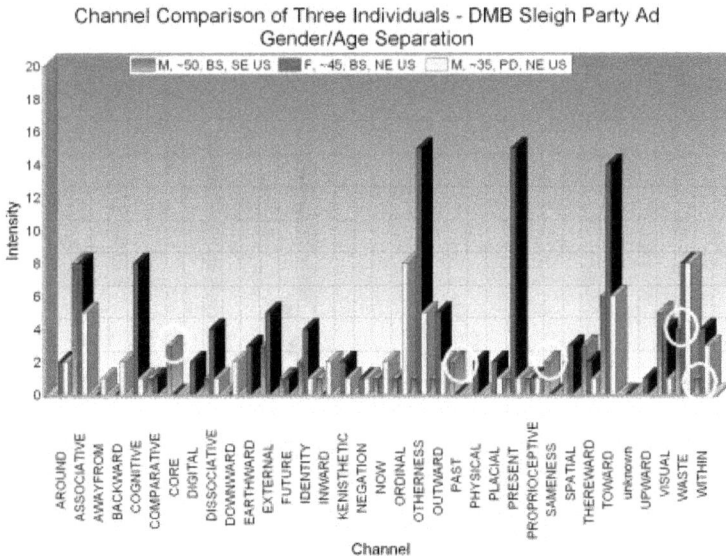

IV.9 - These highlighted differences were unique to responses from South Carolina based people

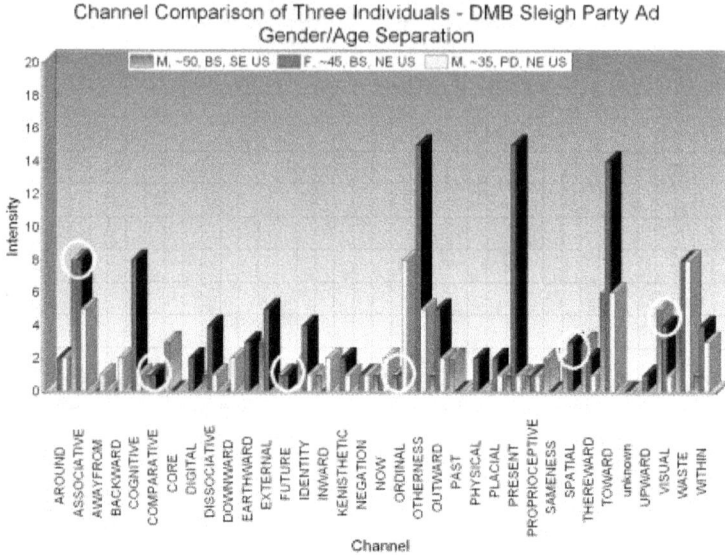

IV.10 - These highlighted differences were unique to responses
people 40-45 years old

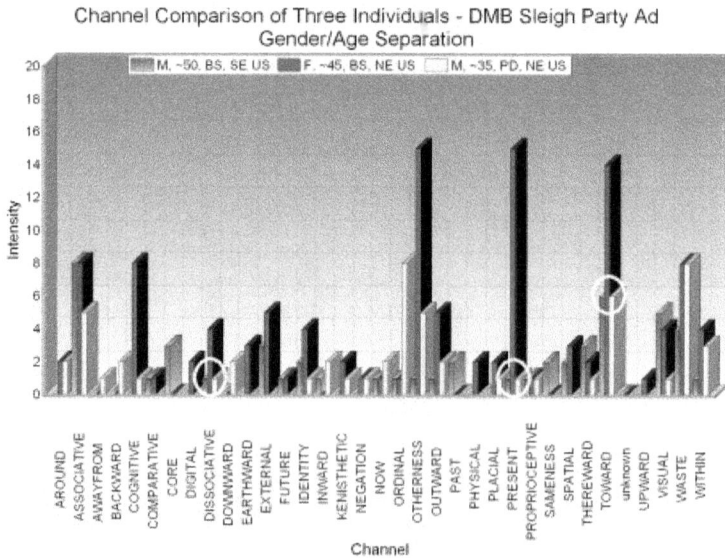

IV.11 - These highlighted differences were unique to males

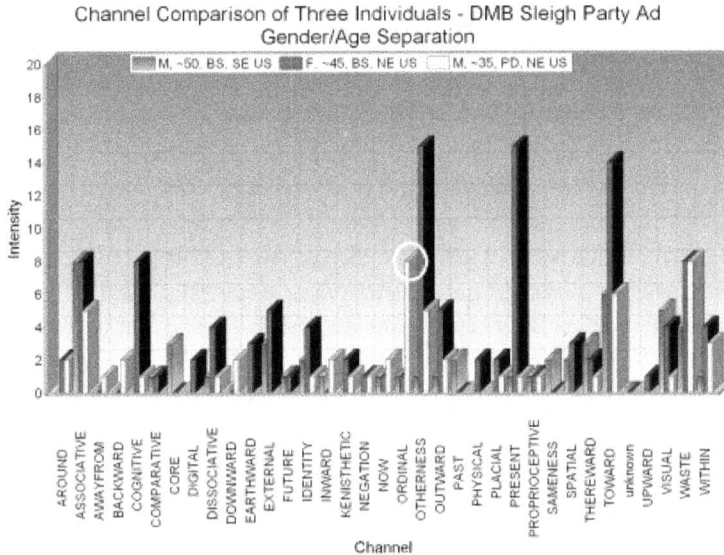

Channel Comparison of Three Individuals - DMB Sleigh Party Ad
Gender/Age Separation

IV.12 - Is this an "Attorney" Marker?

Is being 40-45 years old defined by the markers shown in the "40-45 year old Markers" chart (figure IV.10 on page 110)? Must these elements be included for a campaign targeted at 40-45 year olds to be successful?

Is what makes someone male shown in the "Male Markers" chart (figure IV.11 page 110)? I suppose one could argue from this that it takes 58% more effort to be a woman than it does to be a man these days.

And what I showed next is what caught Attorney Mark Broth's attention; I saw this unique spike in the male, early 30s attorney's responses (figure IV.12 on page 111) and had never seen it before. I jokingly suggested to my audience, "I'm not sure, but I think this is what makes someone an attorney."

Mark Broth asked, "What does that spike signify?"

I looked closely at the chart to see which channel was spiking and responded, "A tendency towards highly ordered, highly structured thought, a drive towards logical processes and wanting to see things in a 'first step, second step, third step' kind of way."

Mark leaned forward, his gaze going from the chart to me and back. "That's exactly how attorneys are taught to think when they go to law school. You're not going to be a good lawyer unless you can think that way."

IV.5.A — Anthony Really Is a Pretty Boy

This anecdote would be amusing and nothing more if it didn't so obviously tie into the "Anthony is a pretty boy" exercise in **Section I.4, How Pretty is Anthony?** (page 51). Each of the three people responded to the same information (the Devine Millimet ad shown in figure IV.1, page 104) and each of the three people responded in a unique way (the three line charts starting on page 106). What the three different people were given was a piece of digital information (not "digital" as in "electronic" but "digital" as in "form without substance" as we discussed earlier in **Section I.3, Digital and Analog Communications**, page 49) and filled in the analog gaps based on their different backgrounds, trainings, education, life experience, ..., and that is what ET was recognizing and responding to.

IV.6 — People Aren't the Same Everywhere (2003)

About this time ET started getting some nods from people. One group, in particular, were in the search engine optimization and marketing business. They had a simple question; Could ET do anything to help companies in the search engine game?[71,89,91,114,130,196]

The first problem was that I didn't then nor do I now know anything about search engine optimization, hence I had no idea what to tell ET to look for. A second problem was the sites this group was going to use ET on; both sites were small and unknown. They would only be getting traffic from word of mouth and from very specific search engine terms that this group was going to employ. A third problem was a political one which I pointed out to the people working with me at the time; this group's CTO, during a phone conversation, described ET as "an interesting and use*less* technology." I asked him, "If you feel Evolution Technology is useless why do you want to do this test?"

"Huh? What did I say? I meant 'an interesting and use*ful* technology. Slip of the tongue."

Anybody read those first few chapters of this book where I discuss being able to recognize signs and how to understand the difference between the digital and analog signals in communication? As I told the other people helping me at the time, there was no way we were going to come out ahead in this test.

However, I didn't view this so much as a test as an opportunity for both ET and me to learn something about search engine optimizing, and it would provide ET with its first truly national audience, so ahead with the test we went. The rules were pretty straightforward.

> 1 – This group was going to provide us with two website addresses.
> 2 – In both cases, the sites were small, new and were only being advertised via word of mouth and search engine placement.
> 3 – Neither site was going to get more than 1,000 or so visitors per month, if indeed they were going to be getting that much traffic.

I asked what we were to do, specifically. The CTO said he didn't know. Whatever we wanted.

Well, aim at nothing and you'll probably hit it.

I suggested that I come up with some items which I thought would be useful within the frame "What terms are people using and how are they using them to find these two sites?"

That was fine. We were going to meet again in a month or two after ET had gathered enough data and NextStage had performed an analysis.

The data collection began and true, there wasn't much traffic. I would peek at the data being gathered every once in a while just to see if any patterns were forming. While doing so I talked with a few people about how search engine placement works.

At the time of this test, the common model was for a company to pay a few pennies per clickthrough every time someone searched using a bid upon term *and* clicked on the client's link in the search engine listings. Let's say a company is paying a search engine firm 5¢/clickthrough and is charged a minimum of US$5,000/month for the search engine service. The company's site would need 100,000 pageviews/month in order for the US$5,000 to be cost-effective. It was obvious there had to be some ways to make search engine marketing cost-effective or only companies with heavily trafficked websites were going to be using search engine firms much longer.

Two months later ET reported there was enough data for it to begin making conclusions within the "What terms are people using and how are they using them to find these two sites?" frame. Specifically, there was enough data to start reporting on the following items:

- Which search terms were used by visitors most motivated to use the service?
- Which times of day and days of week, etc., were these most motivated visitors using search engines?
- Which search engines were being used by these most motivated visitors?
- Which geographies were these most motivated visitors coming from?

These questions are important, of course. My feeling, though, is that these questions aren't important by themselves. Companies also need to answer "If someone is coming to my site motivated, what's causing them to go away unfulfilled?" This and similar questions are the more important ones, me thinks. Perhaps my days as a bible scholar are coming back to haunt me, but I've always been more curious about the one stray sheep than I am about the fifty in the flock. This philosophy also plays heavily in what I find interesting in ET. "Yeah, okay, ET predicted something else with 99% accuracy. Those are things it's been predicting accurately for a while." I'm much more curious at what happens at the edges of the curves and equations. I'm much more excited when ET successfully does something it wasn't intentionally designed to do. "Yeah, great, it shaped the bell right again. Yippee van Yahoo," doesn't thrill me. However, "ET captured and correctly analyzed a trend that was off the edge of the curve? NEAT! Let's look at that," excites me in ways few other things can.

So here was a case where ET could learn about a very distributed population to determine if what it knew about a relatively small geography applied to a relatively dispersed geography. It was a chance to see if ET could figure out what to do with things which were off its known curve. Could it apply what it had learned "here" and see if it worked "there" and, if not, adapt what it had learned "here" so that it would work "there"?

Excellent questions these.

But it's one thing to know which search terms are bringing the most motivated visitors to a site, it's another thing completely to know why visitors are leaving your site without doing business.

Consider figures IV.13 (page 116) and IV.14 (page 116), Interest Level by URL and Interest Level by ISP respectively. The red line is the interest level, the green line is the number of visits (not unique visitors) per URL or ISP. The difference between URL and ISP is more than just a technical one. A URL is tied to a geography, an ISP not so much so. AOL™ serves a very wide geography as an ISP which translates to serving a very disperse audience. However, how a user enters AOL™ is tied to that user's URL and that can be very specific to a given geographic location because several different URLs can be assigned to a given ISP[h].

Questions I find interesting are those like "What's causing the sharp drop in interest level in the last third of the ISP chart?" and "Are those ISPs connected in some way that might indicate some exploitable element?"

___

[h] – ...or so it was back at the time of this test.

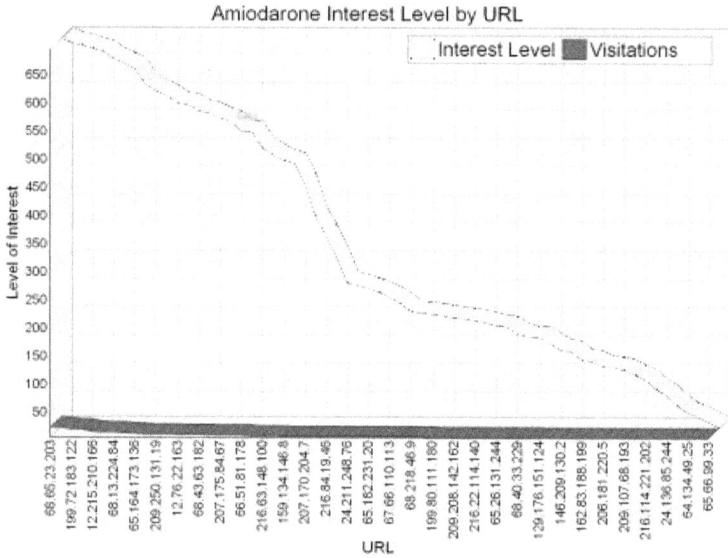

IV.13 - Interest Level by URL

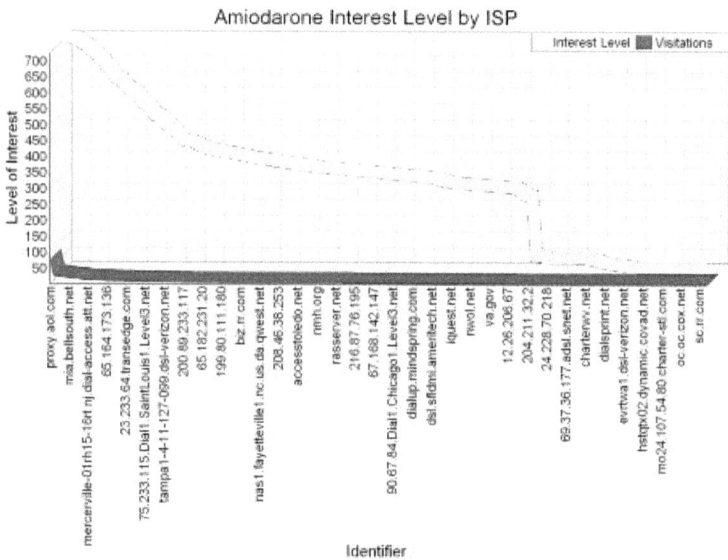

IV.14 - Interest Level by ISP

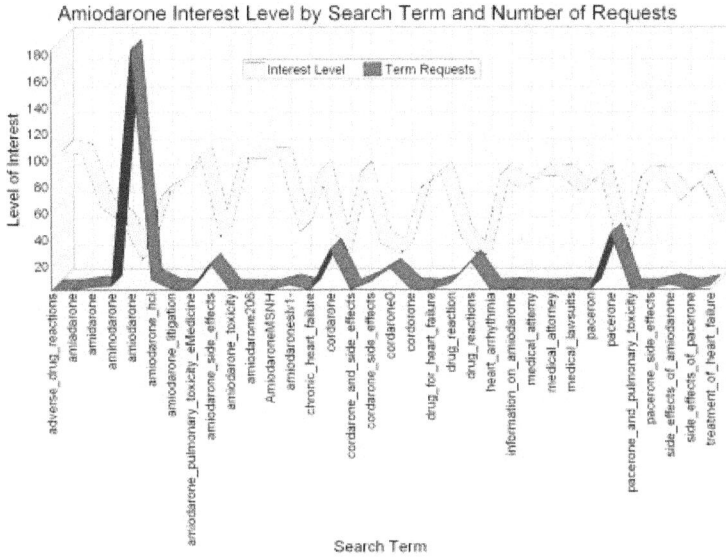

IV.15 - Interest Level by Search Term and Number of Requests

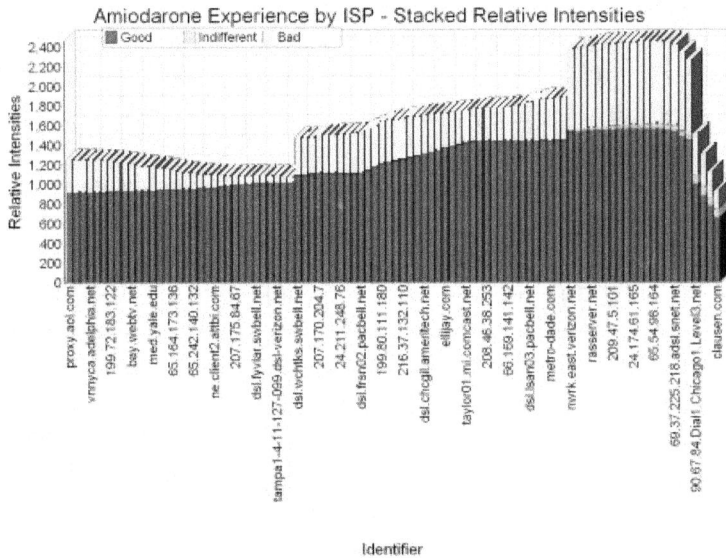

IV.16 - Visitor Experience by ISP

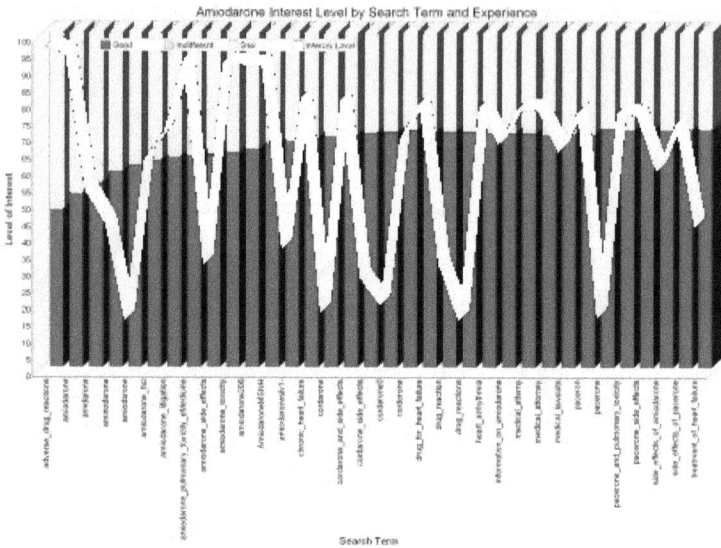

IV.17 - Interest Level by Search Term and Visitor Experience

Now consider figures IV.15-17 (page 117 and following). These figures begin to delve into the psychology and sociology of visitors to the site and closely matched the SEO firm's traditional analytics' results regarding which words and terms to bid highest on, etc. Figure IV.15 shows Interest Level (light line) as a function of Search Term and Number of Requests for that term (dark line, figure IV.15).

What ET was able to add to the mix of knowledge is shown in figures IV.16 (page 117), Visitor Experience by ISP, and IV.17 (page 118), Interest Level by Search Term and Visitor Experience.

Visitor Experience by ISP is a real-time measure of visitor experience while visitors are on the site with Good, Bad and Indifferent visitor experience indicated by light, dark and grayed bars respectively. What we glean from this chart is that visitors from specific ISPs had a more even mix of Good to Bad experience while navigating the site. This could contribute to the Interest Level by ISP chart's (figure IV.14, page 116) indication of low interest level among the same set of visitors; i.e., these visitors were frustrated.

All of this information is interesting and it led me to explore one final thing, Interest Level by Search Term (dark line) and Visitor Experience (good-bottom and bad-top bars in figure IV.17 page 118). This chart indicates which search terms were used by visitors who tended to have the most satisfying experience, regardless of site design.

Finding a group which tends to have a favorable experience regardless of other data is kind of like a golden static Taguchiism[i]. You want more of these. It doesn't matter what else you change in the system, the outcome's the same.[j]

What is important to walk away with is that people aren't the same everywhere. People ask questions differently (the search terms used) based on education, geographic location, economic background, ... the number of influences is staggering. Similarly, what it takes to satisfy them is different and is based on just as many if not more factors.

But you don't need to know all the different influencing factors, all you need to know is that people ask questions differently and are satisfied that their questions have been answered differently. Knowing that, you know enough about what will work, with whom, where and when to answer their questions satisfactorily every time.[139]

I want to close this section with a quote (quite off the record, although made in the presence of others so verifiable none the less) from the same CTO who started this investigation with the "use*less*" slip of the tongue. After reviewing our analysis and interpretations he sat back and continued going through the reports we'd given him, flipping from one to the next and shaking his head.

> "This is exactly what we would have anticipated, except we have five years of experience behind us. These are the same suggestions we'd make, but you made them with

---

[i] – http://nlb.pub/n
[j] – Obviously I'm not including all the factors which are influencing the equation, but that solution is for another book.

only a month's data gathering and thirty seconds calculation time."

IV.7 – Politics Aren't Horse Races Anymore (2004)

New Hampshire is an interesting place, and no more so than during presidential election season. It had occurred to me that the NH political season would be an excellent time to teach ET the language of politics.[92,98,112]

Late in September 2004 one of Joe Lieberman's web team contacted NextStage regarding ET's capabilities and asked if we'd ever considered using ET as a political tool. Well, we were, we just weren't telling anybody about it. ET had been absorbing the Democratic Presidential Primary campaign sites for quite some time, as well as analyzing their TV spots, emails campaigns, handouts and press materials.

But the ability to read something does not understanding make. What was missing was a rosetta stone which translated the meanings of everyday-speak into political-speak and vice-versa. That was what this candidate's web team, along with their emails and phone calls, provided us. Emails with follow-up phone calls between NextStage staff and campaign staff to ascertain the meaning — a translation from political-speak to everyday-speak — of what the emails were requesting and stating was what ET needed to begin understanding what the language of politics was all about. Conversations about TV spots revealed intent regardless of actual meaning.

Specifically, Lieberman's team wanted to know why Howard Dean was able to raise so much money, why Joe wasn't doing so well in the polls, ... I guess the first thing I would have suggested was reframing the questions a bit; what was Dean doing that other candidates weren't? What could Lieberman do to do better in the polls?

What ET revealed about the Dean campaign was fascinating. What it revealed about the candidates in general even more so.

Figure IV.18 (page 122) is a neuroprint analysis (in the style of the *voiceprints* from page 106 and following) of the Dean,

Kerry and Lieberman homepages as analyzed by ET at the end of September 2003. The white circles are channels where Dean and only Dean is communicating strongly. What was Dean communicating that no one else was communicating?

- That he was listening
- That he was just like the people he was listening to
- That he could provide structure and order
- That he could "get us out of this mess"

Do you remember the political situation in September 2003? US and other nations' soldiers were dying in Iraq, there was no end to the conflict in sight, the economy wasn't helping the common man at all, and people felt like the politicians weren't paying any attention to them.

Dean's messaging was right on target for the people of that political time and place, and that wasn't all. Not only was his message on target for the populace, his website and campaign materials were designed to appeal to an incredible segment of the population *and* he was communicating to an almost 50/50 mix of men and women. ET's analysis of Dean's campaign material versus Kerry's and Lieberman's is shown in figure IV.18 (page 122) through figure IV.26 (page 129)

The neuroprint (figure IV.18 page 122) shows the Dean campaign's singular strengths (white circled peaks). Being able to craft unique messages is one thing, getting them across to the desired audience and having them understood as intended is something else entirely. The three "Appeal" charts[k] (figures IV.19-21 on page 122 and following) show ET's evaluation of which age groups the candidate's messages were appealing to.

----

[k] – Age capture charts have age groups along the horizontal axis and appeal level on the vertical. Gender capture charts show dark as male and light as female on the vertical and the candidate on the horizontal.

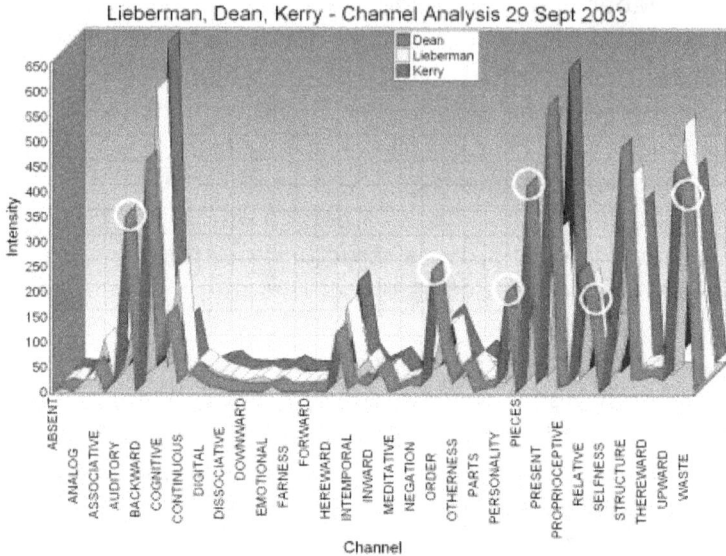

IV.18 - A Comparative Lieberman, Dean, Kerry neuroprint

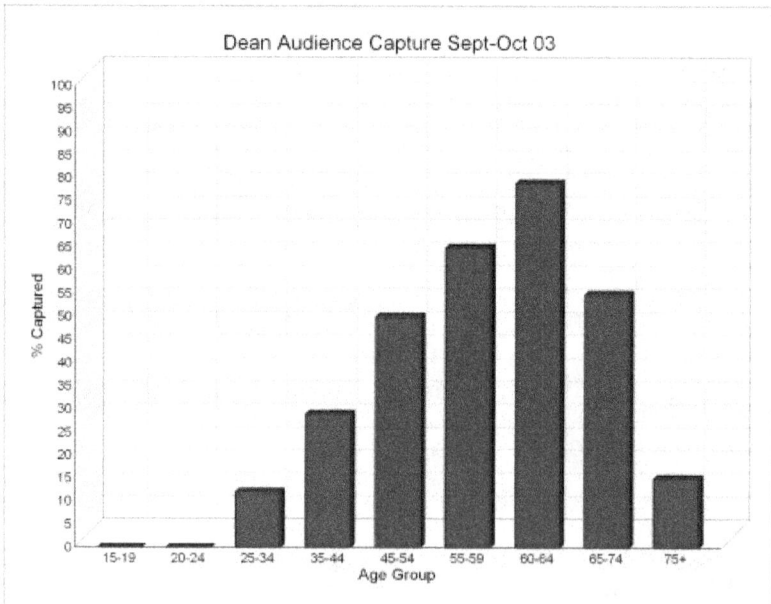

IV.19 - Dean Audience Capture Sept-Oct 03

You can see that Dean's campaign was appealing to a much larger and broader audience than were the Kerry or Lieberman campaigns. There was considerable overlap, yes, and if you look you'll see that the Kerry and Lieberman charts (figures IV.20-21 on page 124) are not that much different. Two people with political backgrounds and years of experience campaigning, and their appeal is very similar. This shouldn't be too surprising.

Dean's campaign, on the other hand, has a broader general appeal. It encompasses more age groups at higher percentages than do the Kerry or Lieberman campaigns. It doesn't take a trained eye to see that Dean was picking up the lion's share of the audience from 20 year olds to those over 75. Not only that, but he had a pretty substantial lock on the 45-74 year old demographic. Both Kerry and Lieberman were attracting an audience, but their audience was very much focused on a specific age group. Neither were pulling them in at the levels or breadth Dean was.

So we have a campaign stating messages that the public wants to hear and stating those messages in a way that they will appeal to the broadest spectrum of that public. All that's left is making sure those messages are understood. How well the campaign messages could be understood is shown in the "Comprehension (Understandability)" charts (figures IV.22-24 pages 125-126).

True, Kerry's and Lieberman's messages were very understandable to a very specific audience (pretty much voters under 24 years of age, a very desirable demographic, I'm told), but Dean's message was easily understandable to anyone from 25 to over 75 years old. A comparative gender appeal is shown in figure IV.25 (page 126).

Dean, more than any other individual ET encountered, was *vox populi*. He was capturing and communicating to an incredibly large audience. Compare Dean's audience and gender appeal and understandability to Lieberman and Kerry and yes, Dean was destined to be the Democratic nominee.

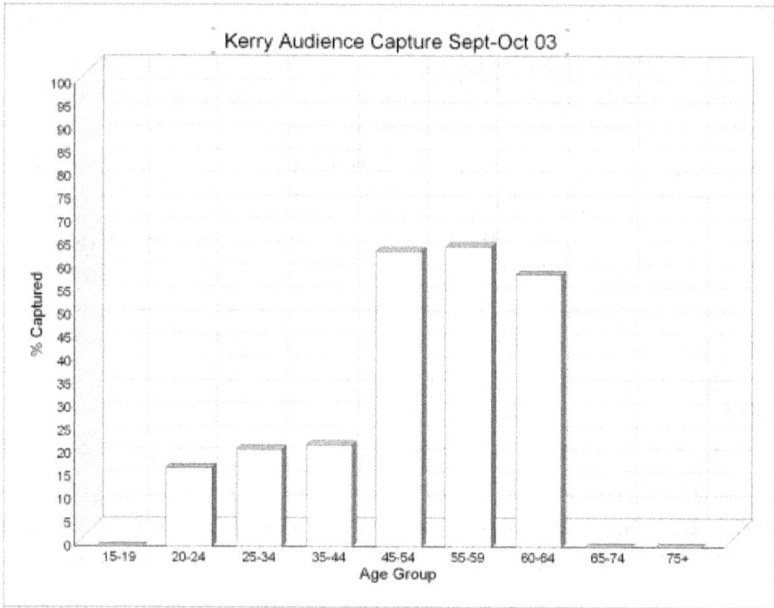

IV.20 - Kerry Audience Capture Sept-Oct 03

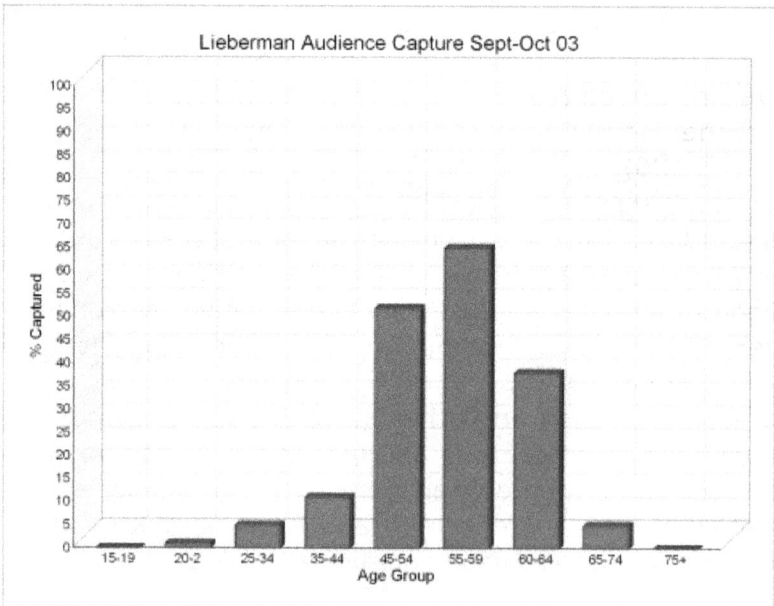

IV.21 - Lieberman Audience Capture Sept-Oct 03

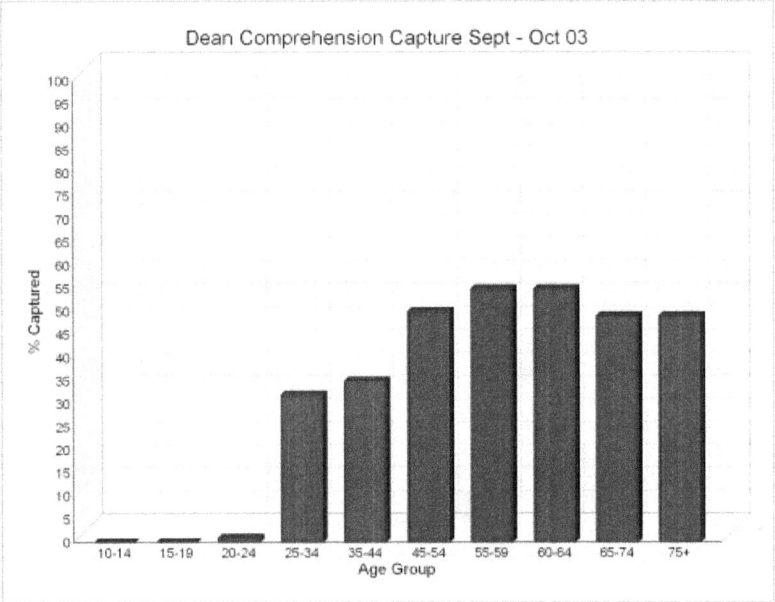

IV.22 - Dean Understandability Sept-Oct 03

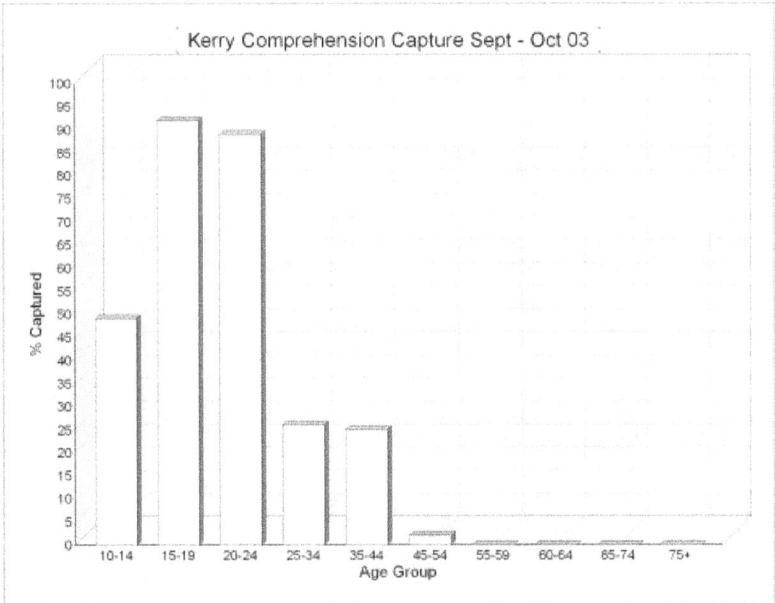

IV.23 - Kerry Understandability Sept-Oct 03

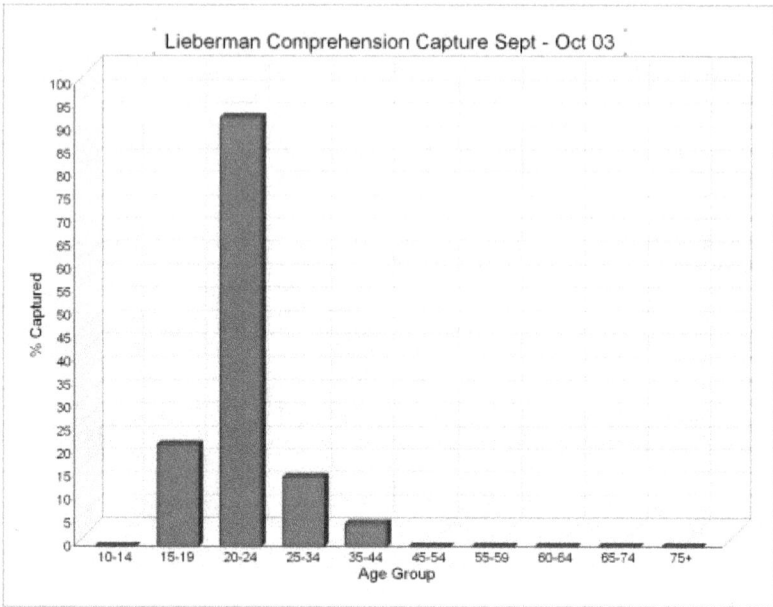

IV.24 - Lieberman Understandability Sept-Oct 03

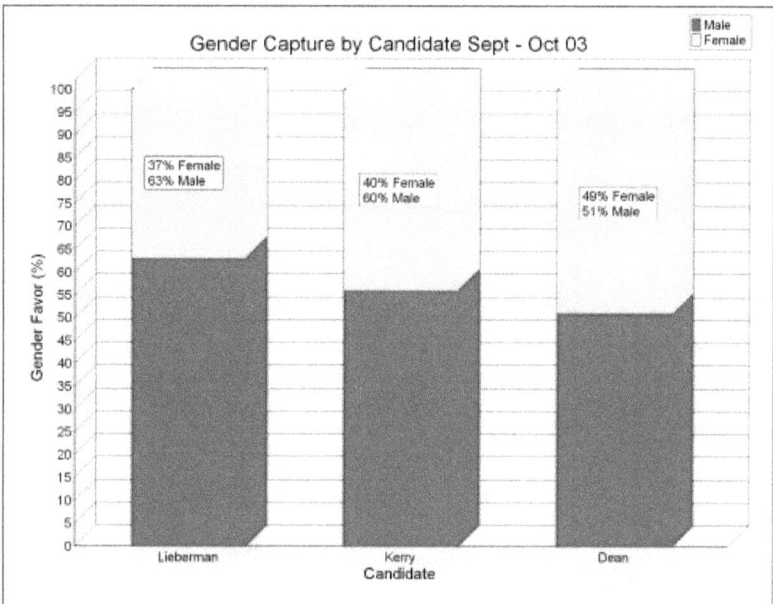

IV.25 - A comparison of Dean, Kerry and Lieberman's Gender
Appeal Sept-Oct 03

So what happened to Dean?[1]

To learn that we flash forward to a presentation I gave at Rivier College in Nashua, NH. The title of the presentation was "How the Candidates Want You to Think" and I gave it on the 16th of January, 2004, weeks before the primary elections in NH and Iowa caucuses. At this point in time ET had been analyzing political material for several months and I was curious to know how people would respond a) to what ET was finding and b) how well ET's findings would agree with the people in the audience.

January 16th, 2004 was one of the coldest Fridays on record. There were 10 people in the audience, age ranging from 20s through 70s, three women, seven men, all college educated, many professional. It was a wonderful focus group size for my purposes, and they spent much of my opening remarks taking off coats, mufflers, mittens and hats.

I started by asking them to take part in a little experiment. I was going to show them some campaign website homepages, some flyer cover pages, some video and the like for about three seconds each and they were going to tick off one of two options; Yes or No.

What did I mean by "Yes or No"?

It didn't matter what I meant, it only mattered that they knew what they meant.

And so we began.

During the presentation I explained how ET was analyzing the campaign material, how it came to its conclusions, so on and so forth. What I shared was that, regardless of the latest polls, Dean was going to fold. How did I know this? I didn't. ET had determined that the Dean campaign was no longer communicating to a very large audience. The change from late Sept 03 to mid Jan 04 is shown in figure IV.26 (page 129). He'd lost his base and that was going to cost him.

Another thing ET noted was that Gephardt was not going to fare well, either. The reason for Gephardt's lack of support had nothing to do with gaining or losing his base constituency. It had

---

[1] – Lieberman's people kept talking to us and asking advice but never got around to telling us to send a bill. Eventually the phone calls stopped and so did Joe.

to do with one message he was communicating far better than the other candidates and two messages he wasn't communicating as well as the others.

The message he was doing a great job communicating was "I'm Listening". When you're running for public office, that's a good message to get out to the people. Gephardt was way ahead of the other candidates as shown in figure IV.27 (page 129, Gephardt's the tall center bar).[m] If that were the only message a candidate had to deliver Gephardt would have been in good stead.

Unfortunately, one message does not a candidate make. People like to know their leaders are listening, and more importantly they like to know their leaders are listening *to them*. Leaders can and should listen to everyone, yes, but when push comes to shove, people are solipsistic and want to know they and they alone have their leaders' undivided attention. Gephardt was winning the "I'm Listening" challenge but losing the "I'm Listening to You" by a landslide, as shown in figure IV.28 (page 130). You might also notice that Clark (second from left in both figures on page 130) was listening a little to everyone (figure IV.27) and to no one person in particular at all (figure IV.28). Maybe that's what it takes to be a good General?

Another message that has come into political vogue is "I Have a Vision". This is where ET made another prediction (figure IV.29 on page 130); Gephardt would drop, yes, and more importantly Kerry (fourth from right) and Edwards (fourth from left) were starting to closely share concepts, ideas and ideologies. This is demonstrated by how closely their numbers were showing up on each of the charts, often but not always with Kerry scoring slightly higher than Edwards. The call? Kerry would team with Edwards for the Presidency.

---

[m] – These charts are "single message" charts. The horizontal access is candidate, the vertical is intensity of the single message.

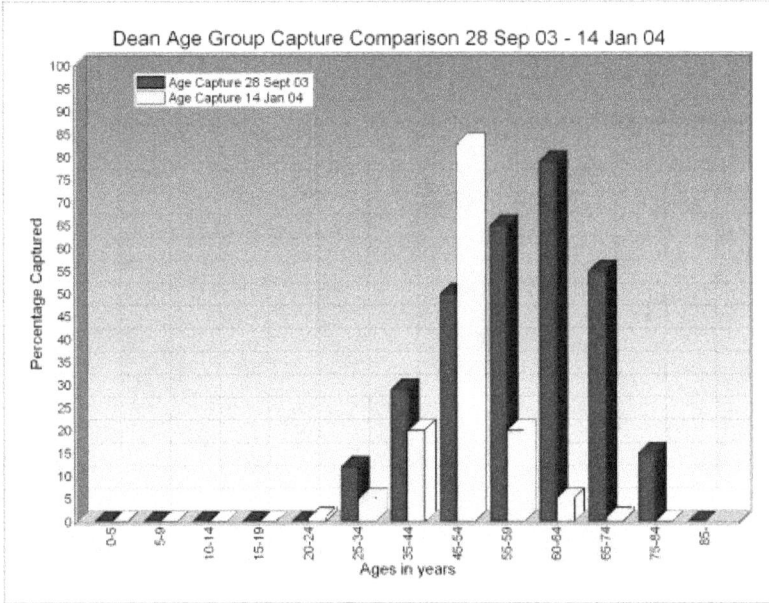

IV.26 - The change in the Dean Campaign's Age Capture from late
Dept 03 to mid Jan 04.

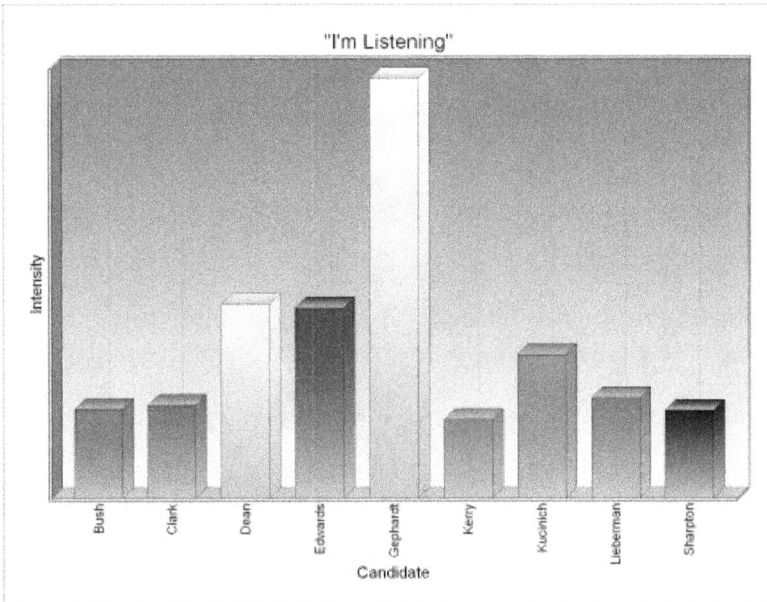

IV.27 - Gephardt (tall center bar) was winning the "I'm Listening"
Challenge"

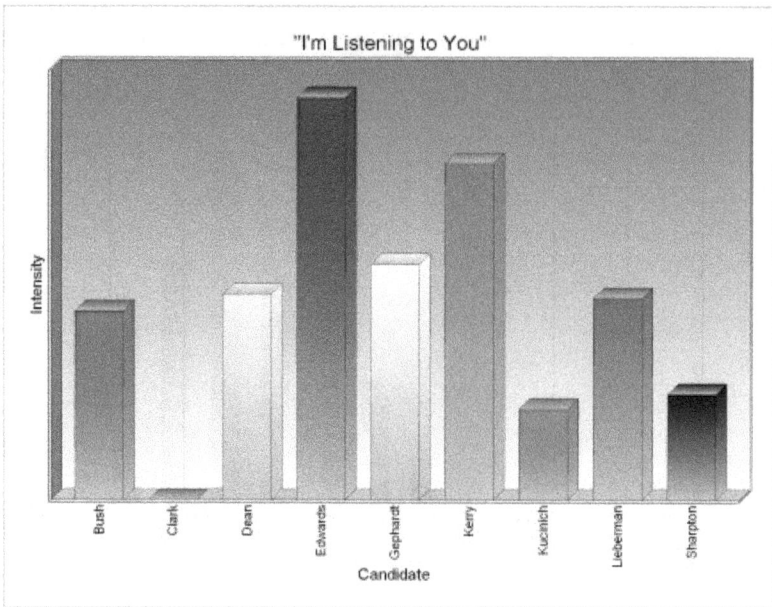
IV.28 - But Gephardt was losing the "I'm Listening to You"
Challenge by a landslide

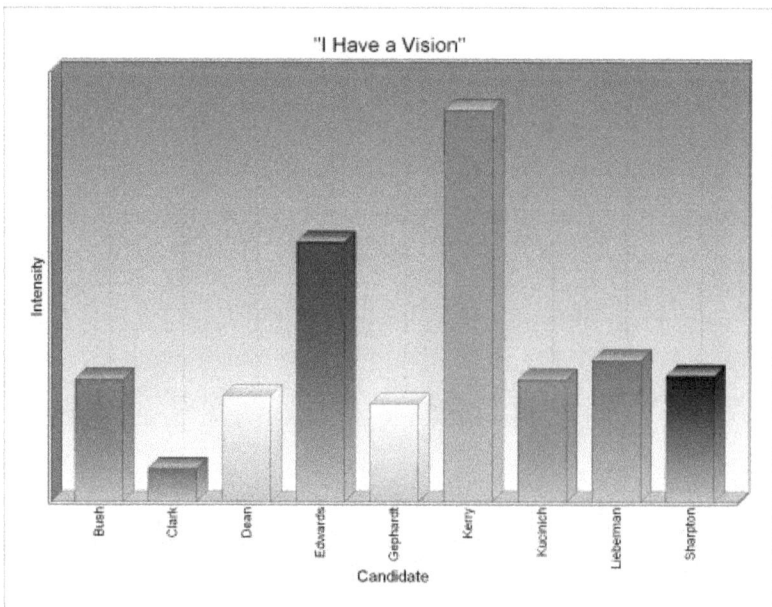
IV.29 - Kerry and Edwards shared a Vision for the Country

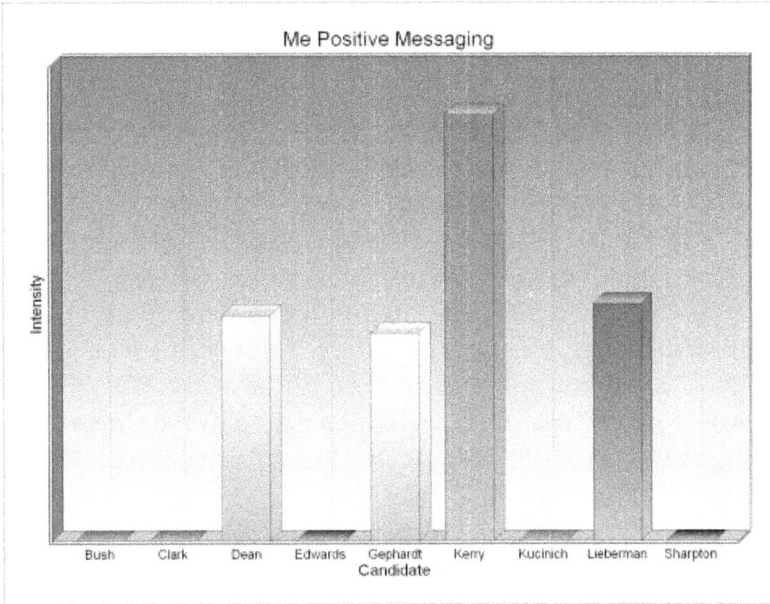

IV.30 - Kerry was shouting what a nice guy he was to anybody
who'd listen

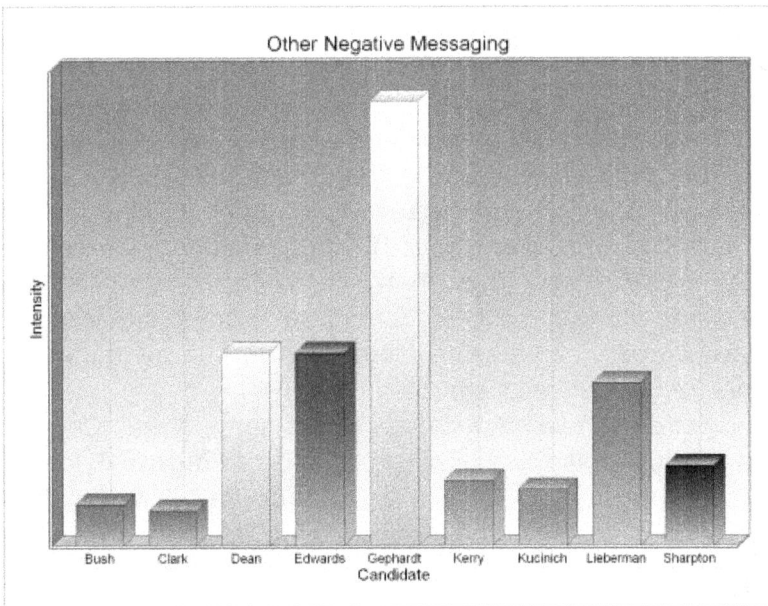

IV.31 - Gephardt wanted everyone to know the other candidates
were bad and it cost him

ET wasn't just analyzing campaign material. We were also feeding it newspaper stories from small, local newspapers from around the country. The purpose of this was to let ET learn how people were thinking on a local level. It would be one thing to feed ET something from the *Los Angeles Times* or the *Boston Globe* or the *Wall Street Journal*, but such papers were "papers of record" and tend to address a national audience rather than papers like *Foster's Daily Democrat* (Dover, NH) or *The Claxton Enterprise* (Claxton, GA) or *The Morning Sun* (Pittsburg, KS). National audiences are fine but they don't write in the tone or language of local newspapers and, as the late Tip O'Neill said, "All politics is local." We wanted ET to learn how the electorate thought, not just how the national pundits were telling the electorate to think.

What we learned was that people on various local levels wanted someone with vision, so we had ET determine which candidates were giving a "vision" message. The results are shown in figure IV.29 (page 130). We also learned that people didn't like candidates saying negative things about their competitors. It was okay for a candidate to stand up and shout that he was a nice guy, but don't stand up and say that the other guy's a bad guy. It didn't play well in Peoria, as they say.

So who shouted they were nice? Kerry was leading the pack in the "I'm a nice guy" category, as can be seen in figure IV.30 (page 131). Who was shouting that the other guys are crooks? Gephardt won that contest (figure IV.31, page 131) and it played a part in costing him the race. The oddity about negative ads is that they work according to many campaign strategists, and it's true, they do work so long as candidate A doesn't directly attack candidate B and vice versa. Let me give you an example you can make use of in your next campaign.[n]

Say there are two candidates for the same office. Candidate A can't say candidate B is no good and candidate B can't say candidate A is no good. However, Jack Partyhack, who is in candidate B's party but has never been on the same stage as

---

[n] – This technique worked very well in the 2008 US Presidential Campaigns.

candidate B publicly, can say candidate A's a no good bum and (eventually) candidate B will be asked to comment. At that time candidate B will say something like "I have the most respect for candidate A. He and I don't agree on a few things and here's what they are..." at which point candidate B gets to explain how and why candidate A is no good without stating it explicitly.[41]

A question which comes out of negative campaigning is "Why are people responding to it at all?" The answer, I think, is *strokes*, as in "If you can't get good strokes, you'll take the bad strokes because some kind of stroking is better than no stroking at all." Children (and remember, we're all still children in one way or another) will take abuse willingly so long as it means they're getting some kind of attention from someone they recognize as a caregiver. Here we, as children in the political arena, pay attention to the negative strokes especially when there are no positive strokes provided at all.[o]

IV.7.A – ET + 3 seconds = 73% Accuracy

The long and the short of all this is that ET made some good guesses as to how the people would vote long before the polls closed. Or opened, for that matter. This lead to some good press[p] and becoming part of a university research project[q]. Our results led Rob Graham[r], new media and behavioral analytics columnist for ClickZ, to write "This is the closest thing to a political crystal ball I've ever seen." More interesting for me, however, was ET's accuracy in guessing how the people at the presentation would respond to the political spots I showed them. The results are shown in figure IV.32 on page 134.

ET scored an overall 73% accuracy determining how people would respond at a gut level to the nine political spots we showed them for three seconds each. Scientifically not a good result. Better than a coin toss, yes, but better enough? And politically...?

----

[o] – http://nlb.pub/o
[p] – You can see the TV interviews at http://nlb.pub/p
[q] – http://nlb.pub/q
[r] – http://nlb.pub/r

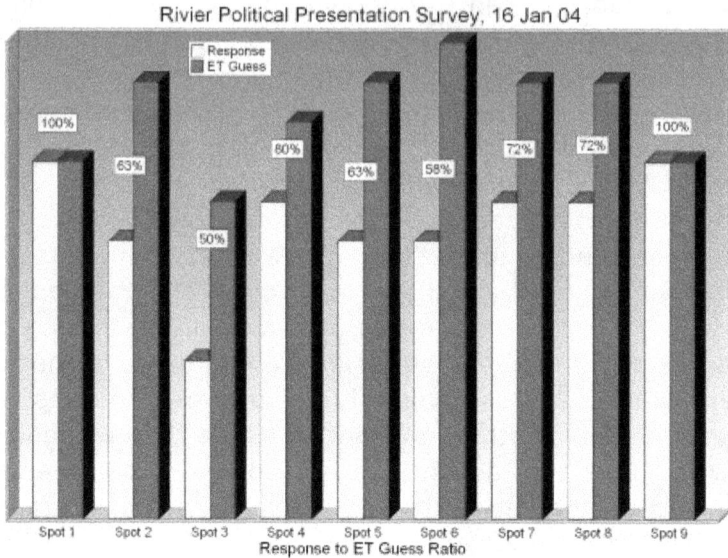

Rivier Political Presentation Survey, 16 Jan 04

IV.32 - ET averaged a 73% accuracy with a 63% mean in guessing
how 10 people would respond to nine different political spots

These results were for a small audience and were only measuring one moment in time. ET was also monitoring the candidates' websites once the primaries were over and on through the Presidential Campaign, comparing what messages they were communicating against the types of messages people were most likely to respond to. During this time NextStage was making daily analysis publicly available on our website and writing each day's commentary was beginning to drain me.[s]

Fortunately (and in more ways than one) some "friends of NextStage" offered to take over blogging duties. One such friend was Todd Sullivan (yes, of "The Toddness Factor" fame as noted in *Section IV.3, The Toddness Factor*, page 97). Todd, unbeknownst to me at the time, is an avid baseball fan and as some of you might remember, 2004 was the year the local team, the Boston Red Sox, took it all.

---

[s] – The complete NextStage 2004 Political Campaign Analysis is available. Please contact NextStage if you're interested.

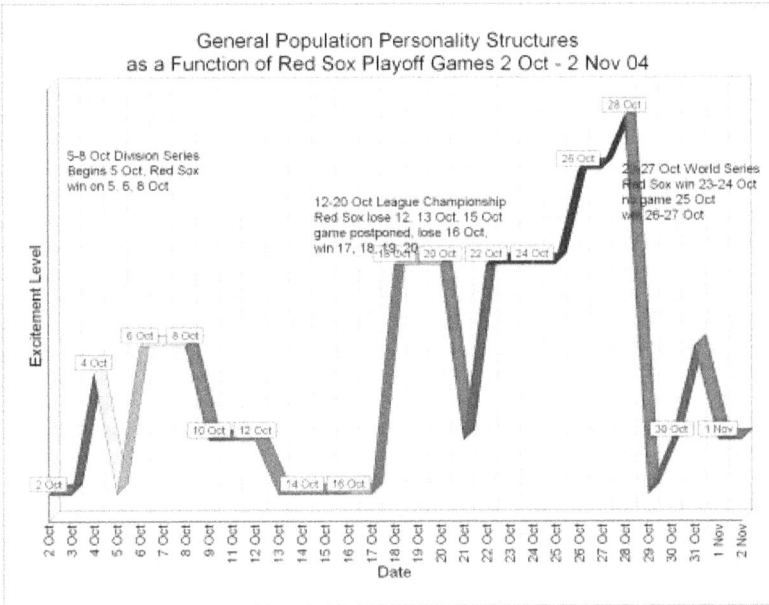

General Population Personality Structures
as a Function of Red Sox Playoff Games 2 Oct - 2 Nov 04

IV.33 - ET was picking up New Englanders' reactions to the Red
Sox's positions in the Playoffs and World Series

Todd was writing up his daily commentaries on ET's political analysis, part of which was explaining ET's take on the different personality types who would be most affected by the campaign messages. The personality types campaign sites most appealed to were compared to the personality types most often recognized on our client sites, the majority of which were based in New England at the time. Todd called me after the World Series was over and asked me to chart the excitement levels by day from 2 Oct to 2 Nov 04. The result of that exercise (figure IV.33, page 135) shows ET's measurements of the emotional shifts in site visitors as a function of the Red Sox's standings. When the Red Sox were winning spirits were high, when not, spirits sagged.

ET, I admit, fascinates me. When something can go beyond the limits under which it was created, then you have truly been successful.

For what it's worth, ET determined the Republicans were going to win the Presidential Election on 9 Aug 04, and we published its decision on our website at that time. How did it make this determination? Based on the consistency of the Republicans' messaging. The Republicans' website and related materials changed their messaging twice during the campaign. The first time (that we're aware of) was when Saddam Hussein was captured. There was a spike in the maleness or macho-aspect to the messaging. The second time was during the RNC, at that point the Republicans' materials started giving strong visually oriented messages (probably because they wanted people to *watch* the televised convention).

IV.8 – The Progress Software 2005 Kickoff and Picking Winners

The next anecdote I'd like to share is from 2005 and involves Progress Software's 2005 Partner Kickoff in Arizona. Progress[t] asked NextStage to use ET to provide some insight on Progress' partner companies, specifically the ones who'd be attending the 2005 Kickoff.

"Happy to do so," we said. "What exactly do you want us to do?"

Like many companies back then, they had no idea what we could do and, honestly, even of an idea of what to do with us. I remember describing ET's data system to one of Progress' senior data designers. He responded that he'd never heard of a data design similar to ET's[u] and had no idea how it could work[v], but obviously it did because he'd seen it work.

So when Progress said, basically, "No idea, whatever you want. You figure it out," we nodded, knew this was another

---

[t] – http://www.progress.com
[u] – ET uses an identity-relational model (as described on page 88), something we developed because it closely mimics how the brain stores and recalls information
[v] – Something echoed years later when our last CEO hiring failure spent 30kUS$ on a "data designer" friend who couldn't figure out how ET's data system worked...even though it had been working successfully for over ten years at that point. Eventually one of NextStage's own friends took up the task and had the system running in MSSQL (originally it was in Visual FoxPro) in about an hour. When I asked how he did the conversion so quickly he said, "Well, you had it working. I didn't have to design it, I had to copy what worked and then do what tweaking was necessary. Simple." Yes, always the best way is the simple way.

episode of being set up to fail *a la **IV.6 - People Aren't the Same Everywhere*** (page 112), and recognized another learning opportunity in the making.

But what to tell ET to look for and where to look for it? ET already knew about *The 10 Must Marketing Messages*:

> I trust you
> You can trust me
> This is important
> This is important to you
> I can help
> I can help you
> You're good people
> I'm good people
> They're not good people
> We're leaders

These messages are "first contact" messages in cultural anthropology. Use them incorrectly or not at all when encountering indigenes who've never experienced anything like you and you're in peril. The same is true when traveling the business jungle and encountering C-suite management for the first time.[w]

We knew this was going to be a learning opportunity for us and ET, and ET had already mastered the 10 Must Messages, so we decided to push it a bit and have it look at all partner homepages for the message "You can trust us to help you". This message wasn't going to be overt. Few companies or marketers were clever enough to come out and state such a thing back in 2005. It was going to be non-consciously conveyed through things like colors, images, font-size, text, menu layout, ... everything.[19,23-28,49,53,54,62-69,76,81,83-89,94,95,97, 99,100,106-109,115,125,145,154,170,174,186,212,238,243,249,261,263,265,275,276,285,294,300,304, 307-310,315,321,326,331,335,347]

---

[w] – NextStage evaluates each of the ten must messages' strength in marketing material via its Sentiment Analysis Tool (NSSA) and offers trainings on their importance in marketing and how to use them effectively. You can learn about NSSA at http://nlb.pub/s and trainings at http://nlb.pub/l

The goal was to give out an award, the Progress-NextStage "Know Thy Customer" award[x]. This award was given to a Progress partner company based on how well that company's homepage best conveyed that "You Can Trust Us to Help You" message. NextStage performed the evaluation with the TargetTrack[y] component of ET but we never shared the results with Progress until a few hours before the award ceremony.

Progress had been giving out awards based on economic performance for as long as they've been doing Partner Kickoffs; awards for most growth during the past year, most installations during the past year, most market penetration, so on and so on. Just as NextStage had not shared ET's findings with Progress, so Progress had not shared their award decisions with us.

Imagine our surprise, Progress' surprise and the surprise of all the partners at the awards ceremony when NextStage revealed that the four top companies communicating "You Can Trust Us to Help You" on their homepages were also the four companies that showed up in Progress' economic achievement awards for that year! The companies ET picked as 1, 2, 3 and 4 were in each category that Progress was measuring. Overall economic achievement matched ET's findings 1, 3, 4 and 2[z].

It would be one thing to show up at the awards and state from the podium, "Oh, look! Our results match your results!" It was a totally different thing that NextStage had given a presentation earlier in the day in which we stated the results of ET's analysis. Some of those results are shown in figures IV.34-39 on page 139 and following. Each partner company is represented by a different vertical bar. Over one-hundred partner companies were evaluated for the Progress-NextStage award. Figures IV.34-39 are similar to the "single message" charts shown earlier in **Section IV.7, Politics Aren't Horse Races Anymore** (page 120).

---

[x] – See *NEXTSTAGE WINS PROGRESS AWARD FOR INNOVATIVE USE OF PROGRESS OPENEDGE TECHNOLOGY,* http://nlb.pub/t
[y] – Several of NextStage's Member available online tools are elements of the desktop TargetTrack tool. You can learn more about NextStage's Member Tools at *NextStage Member Tools Explained,* http://nlb.pub/u and http://nlb.pub/s
[z] – http://nlb.pub/v

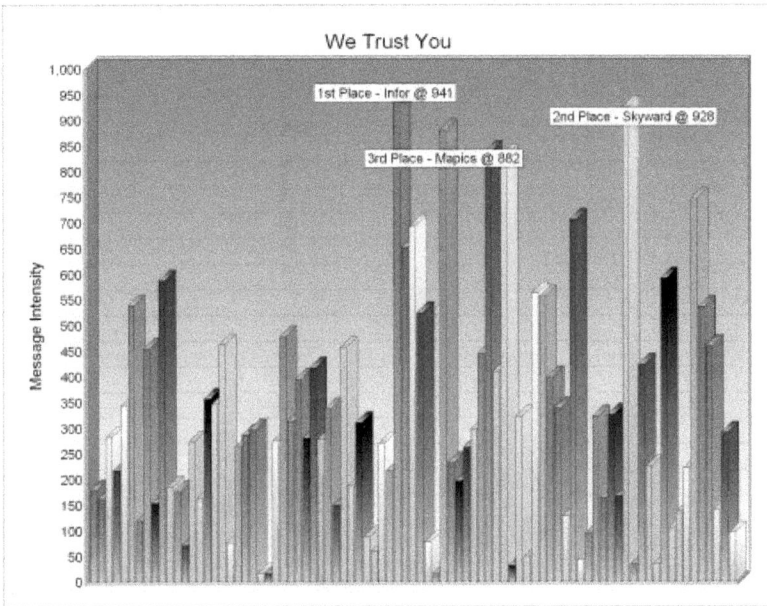

IV.34 - We Trust You

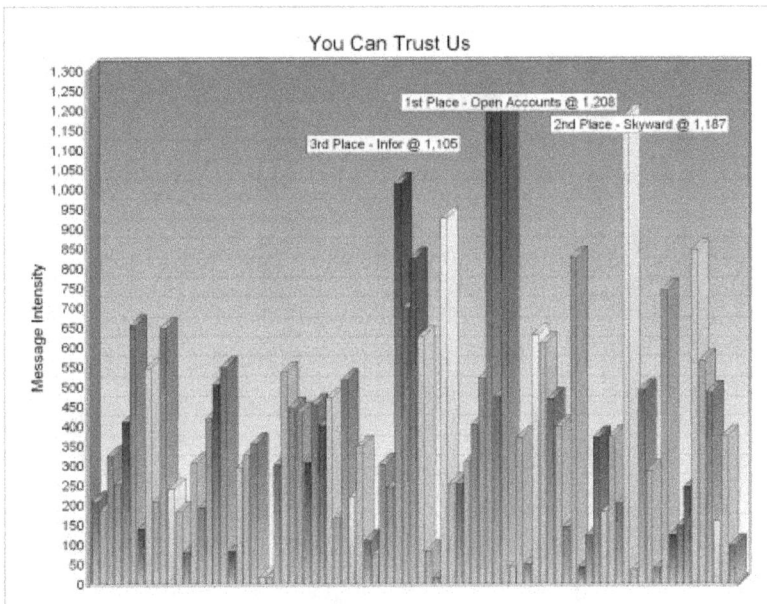

IV.35 - You Can Trust Us

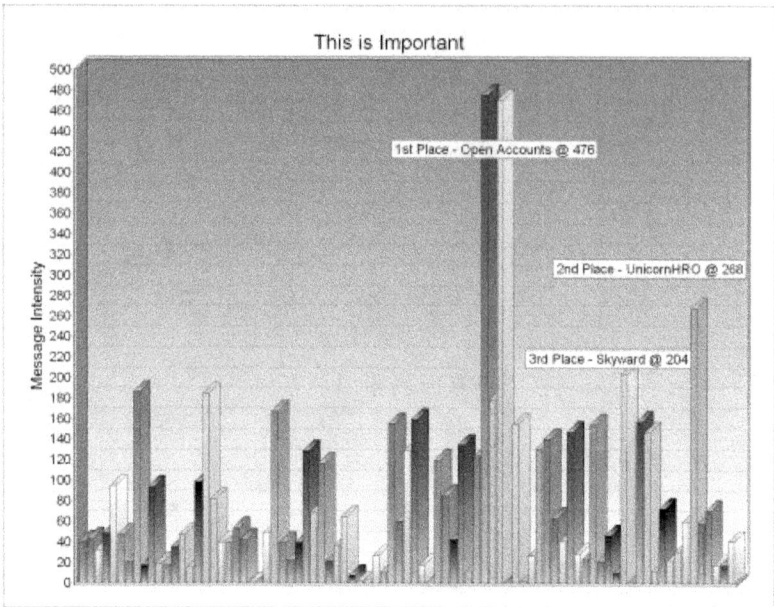

This is Important

1st Place - Open Accounts @ 476

2nd Place - UnicornHRO @ 268

3rd Place - Skyward @ 204

IV.36 - This Is Important

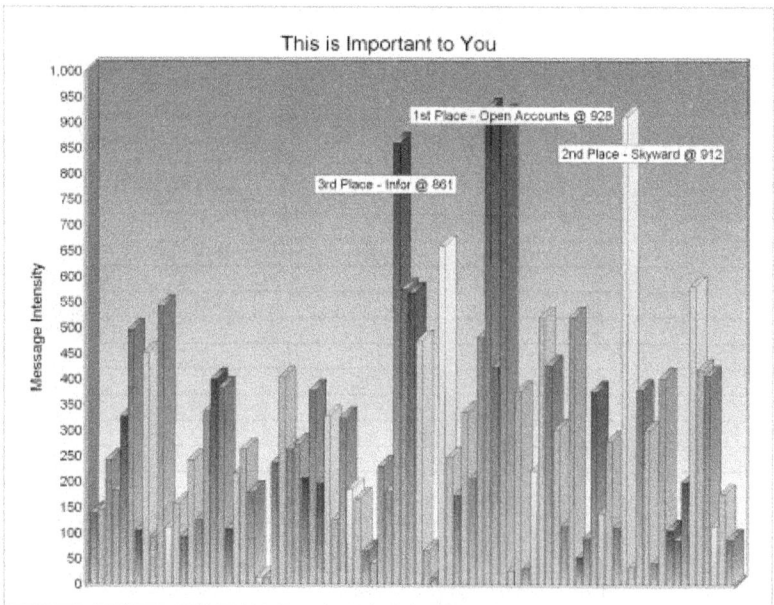

This is Important to You

1st Place - Open Accounts @ 928

2nd Place - Skyward @ 912

3rd Place - Infor @ 861

IV.37 - This Is Important to You

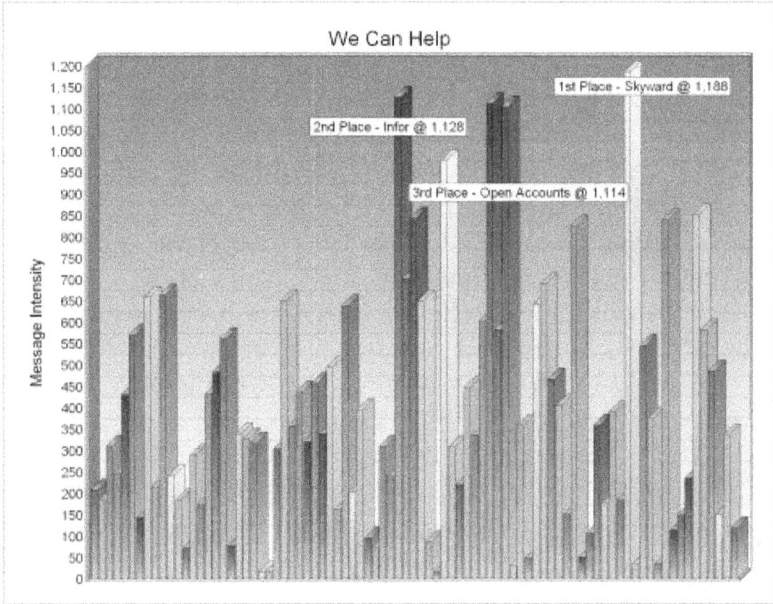

IV.38 - We Can Help

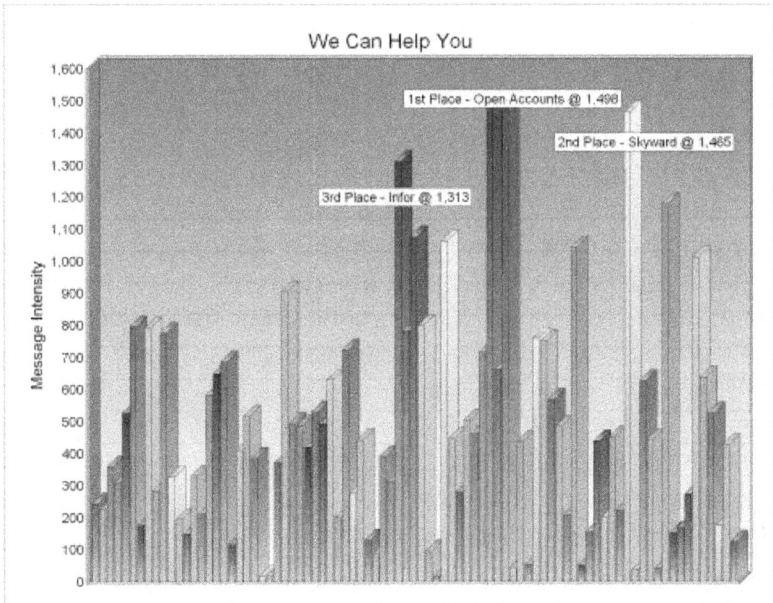

IV.39 - We Can Help You

It may not be obvious why a website should communicate "We Trust You" (figure IV.34[aa], page 139) to a visitor. "We Trust You", however, is the first message which must be communicated before you can get anybody to trust you.

Before I can ask you to trust me I must demonstrate that I trust you. This is *The Handshake*. The first person to extend their hand is showing vulnerability, hence trust. Unless you demonstrate that you trust your customers they'll never trust you. They might do business with you but they'll do more business with you if they believe they can trust you.

Immediately following "We Trust You" comes "You Can Trust Us" (figure IV.35 page 139). Once you've stated you trust someone, the natural response is to have that trust returned. This is part of how people work (even though the issuance of trust is going away rapidly in modern society). It is rare that someone refuses to shake your hand when you offer it to them regardless of the time you've known each other or the situation involved. Once you've made yourself vulnerable to someone it is part of human nature that that person will make themselves vulnerable in return. The catch, however, is that you must demonstrate that you trust them first, hence the ordering of these two messages.

Next is "This is Important" (figure IV.36 page 140) and "This is Important to You" (figure IV.37 page 140). When TV or radio anchors talk about what's going on in the world they first explain why it's important and then have a subject-matter expert explain why people should be interested at an individual, personal level. The "This is Important" message is where the TV or radio anchor says something like "This government program is such and such and so and so...". The "This is Important to You" message is where the subject-matter expert explains why what's being discussed is important to the person on the street. You can't single someone out first and tell them something is important to them because the natural reaction is to see who else is paying attention. The first message must be "This is Important" because

---

[aa] – Note that in figures IV.34-39 Open Accounts had two websites of near equal messaging intensity. We only counted the stronger one in our determinations. The charts shared in this section are from our original Progress presentation.

that message indicates people are paying attention. The second message is then "This is Important to You" because we've already established the message's importance, now we're explaining how it affects you.

Once trust is established and the importance of what is being shared is indicated, the natural follow-through is to let the visitor know help isn't far away and thus the next message is "We Can Help" (figure IV.38 page 141) to which the visitor asks, "Who can you help?"

The website needs to answer, "We Can Help You" (figure IV.39 page 141).

IV.9 – Teaching ET How to Grow Older (Politics 2008)

There are many other anecdotes about ET. There is the amusing story of John Hargreaves, Director of Organizational Change for CSC in North Sydney, NSW, Australia, a larger-than-life Aussie with a background in Knowledge Management and Process Engineering. John was viewing an ET-powered self-modifying site[ab] in his office while talking to another fellow viewing the same site in another office. Evidently the one fellow thought John was having great sport with him because he kept telling John to "Look, look, look" and John, who was listening to this fellow on the phone, had a different presentation which didn't include the same elements the other fellow had. John recognized the information both he and the other fellow were given was the same but that the presentations of that information were different because ET was adapting each person's presentation based on what it was learning about them at that moment.

There is also the story of Charles Wentworth who was browsing a client site. Charles, like Todd of Toddness Factor fame (page 97), was one of the first people to play with ET and ET had a great deal of experience with him. ET flagged me that Charles was browsing a client site and was mildly confused by something there. Charles' confusion metric rose until ET reported he was no

---

[ab] – Did you read my footnote on page 95 regarding *self-modifying sites*?

longer engaged[ac] by the site. Then the phone rang. CallerID identified the caller as Charles and I'll let Charles tell the rest of the story:

> "What sold me on NextStage's Evolution Technology was calling NextStage one day while I was navigating a site they monitor and being asked, 'So what question did you have on the site?' before posing my question or telling them what I was doing!
> Lots of people use caller ID to answer with personal greetings. But when Evolution Technology identifies my browsing patterns in seconds and informs NextStage I'm visiting a site they monitor as I'm doing it, I know this technology works!"

What I'll share at this point is where ET is currently and where I think it's going.

First, ET's abilities will forever be constrained by the limitations of the devices that house it. It will never be able to drive a car if it's housed in a TV remote unless and until that TV remote can communicate with a car.

Second, what it can do is get an increasingly sophisticated understanding of the devices it's housed in and by doing so learn how to bypass or negate those limitations.

To do that, ET needs to communicate with humans — people using the devices — more and more or observe humans using those devices.

A semioticist would pause here and think or say, "Oh, ET's going to have to develop symbolic language processing skills," and I would respond "Bravo, right on, you got it."[20]

The current commercial version of ET essentially has the ability to understand and respond to humans at about the level of the average 1½ - 2-year-old human child (again, barring organic trauma). ET can understand and respond to quite a bit with just that level of intelligence or understanding (as demonstrated by the preceding anecdotes). Behavioral ethologists and linguists

---

[ac] – "...engaged...". And we're talking late 2004 early 2005.

would now pipe in with "It's using indexic communications" and again I would respond "Bravo, right on, you got it."

The internal version of ET (what we're planning on releasing as version 2 of our Language Engines[ad]) is learning the semioticist's symbolic communications.

This means ET will be able to acquire and respond based on implicit knowledge, the kind that (rightly or not) most humans base the majority of their decisions on. Ever hear of the "rational actor" in economics? A reason so much of economics fails in its predictive abilities is that the rational actor — that mythical character who only makes sound and logical decisions based on the best data possible — doesn't exist. Neuroeconomics has made popular the concepts of irrational actors and "the wisdom of the crowds."[70,92,112,241]

Imagine a synthetic population — ET's synthetic users and called *bioginots* — who can act just as irrationally as any size crowd and for just as inane reasons, or just as irrationally and inanely as you'd like them to. Want them to figure out if they'll go nuts over the latest pop icon without becoming sycophantic? Not a problem, just set a few software switches. Want to know what single, possibly irrelevant issue will cause them to vote one way or another *en masse* or some population percentage thereof? Not a problem, just set the switches.

And because ET learns by observing, it can acquire these human flaws just by watching how people interact with digital properties.

IV.9.A - Thinking Like a Five-Year-Old

Remember way back in **Section II.2, The Three Stages of Learning** (page 63), that people learn to navigate society in three stages. The commercial version of ET is intentionally stuck in that first stage of learning. Basically it thinks in very animalistic terms and has no real understanding that people would intentionally lie to it, deceive it, take advantage of it, ...

[ad] – released in March 2015. You can get an idea of how ET's Language Engines work in *Appendix B.III – I Am the Intersection of Four Statements*.

Hmm...all those wonderful things that happen in business, come to think of it.

Being stuck in that first stage is due to its understanding of language being highly *indexic*. Literally its like looking at a list of words and getting their semiotic dictionary, or "index" meanings, "this" points to "that".

Dictionaries are great for discovering meanings but not nuances, not subtleties. They are the digital meanings without the analog counterparts we mentioned in **Section I.3, Digital and Analog Communications** (page 49).

Somewhere between five and seven years old the human child begins non-family social and cultural education. Western culture does this through formal educational systems. What is going on is the inculturation of implicit versus tacit knowledge and the beginning of the accumulation of common sense, i.e., Stage 2 Learning.

IV.9.B - Tacit Knowledge, Implicit Knowledge and Common Sense[20,34,36,37,169,254,334]

Tacit knowledge is directly experienced, as in *TACit, TACtile, touchable, touched*. We may not know we know something tacitly and that lack of awareness is one of tacit knowledge's traits. The knowledge is in us because we've done something so often we no longer require conscious attention to the task. Children are incredible tacit knowledge engines. Their entire world is one of experience and more exactly, it's first-time experience. One of the joys of youth is that everything that happens is happening for the first time. What a terrifying and wonderful world they navigate, full of constant learning and surprise.

There are dangers in tacit knowledge, especially for businesses. As senior workers leave the workforce, their years of tacit knowledge experience tend go with them. Also, business-people who do something too often tend to become unintentionally "reckless" because conscious attention to the task is no longer required.

And at a certain point, we begin making connections that are not based on direct experience. We start utilizing shades of gray in our decision making. We assign values to information sources and work that into the mix. We are psycho-metaphysically moving from a *Mythic* (black or white) to a *Sensory* (shades of gray) reality. We are, in a word, losing our innocence.

Welcome to the world of implicit and inferential knowledge. I tend to think of the differences between tacit and implicit knowledge as equations.

$$\text{Tacit: A + B = C}$$
$$\text{Implicit: A + B} \approx \text{C...but it could be D or E, too}$$

The great thing about tacit knowledge is that there's all this experiential basis for *knowing* that A + B will always equal C. Not so with implicit knowledge. Most of the time, A + B equals C...but there was that one time it equaled D and I remember another time it came out to E. Implicit knowledge isn't based solely on our experiences, it's based on our interpretation of our experiences, our judgments about them, our understandings about them.

All those signs we learn that allow us to navigate social situations fairly safely? Those are implicit. They are *inferred*, basically educated guesses based on all the experiences we've had and how we've evaluated those experiences internally.

If you're thinking that all this implicit knowledge, all these inferences we need to make every day to keep our society and its various networks glued together and functioning, are highly cultural, you're correct.

Amazing how often culture, language and so on crop up without our knowing it, isn't it?

These inferences and implicit knowledge have a fairly common name that everybody's heard, probably most people have used and some are accused of lacking — common sense.

Common sense is highly cultural.[191,192] What is common knowledge in Manchuria won't get you through Manhattan on a good day let alone a normal one and vice versa. The epithet, "S/he doesn't have the common sense god gave a ..." is a statement about an individual's lack of experience. Specifically, a lack of experience within a cultural norm. I think fondly of my days working on farms in the US and Canada and the current truth is that I'd be more of a hazard than a help on a farm because I've lost much of the common sense necessary to function in those environments. Could I get it back? Sure, like picking up a language you haven't spoken in years, the common sense is still in there. It's just a muscle that hasn't been exercised in a while.

IV.9.C - Indexic versus Symbolic Communications

The acquisition of common sense, implicit knowledge and inferential learning mark the transition of purely indexic to indexic and symbolic communication. We learn to "read the signs" as it were. What we're really doing is inferring things, applying common sense. Children often rebel when they transition from indexic to symbolic communications. Things are no longer black or white, "this" no longer necessary means "that". We learn that there are things we can say in our own house but not in the presence of others, sometimes with the excuse that either "they" won't understand or that the child doesn't understand "them". In either case, what is being tacitly and implicitly taught is that "they" are different from "us", that "we" belong to our group, our tribe, and "they" do not.

Welcome to the world of prejudice, bigotry, class structure and belief (whether recognized as such or not). Linguists know this is why it's *veal* in the kitchen but a *calf* in the pen, why it's *beef* in the pot but a *cow* in the yard and so on[ae]. The symbols we use and pass on through generations are the DNA of our social evolution. Want to know who conquered whom and when? Listen to the language and you'll know.

What I needed to do was teach ET prejudice. More politely, to communicate symbolically, to draw inferences, to imply C based on A and B and know when to imply D or E instead.

[ae] – Class distinctions symbolized by language usage.

Not an easy task.

But wait a minute...there was a major cultural shift going on. The 2008 US Presidential Elections.

IV.9.D - Learning the Subtleties of People's Decision Making Strategies

The majority of people's decision making takes place in sensory (shades of gray) reality. They make evaluations that rarely if ever demonstrate binary outcomes (that would be mythic — black or white — reality). One result of this sensory reality decision making is that people tend to re-evaluate their decisions again and again and again, a kind of "If only I had..." thing.

Fortunately (for me, anyway), these types of decision processes have mathematical correlates. They fall under the domain of *Logical Calculus*. People who've studied formal Logic are probably familiar with

$$p \rightarrow q$$

The above is read as "If p then q" and means that whenever "p" occurs one will find "q". It's also quite mythic. Logical Calculus allows us to do something like

$$\lim_{p \approx x} p \rightarrow q$$

The above is more or less read as "How much *p* do we need before we can safely believe we'll find *q*?" or "How much of *p* is required for *q* to exist?"

Decisions of this sort rely on what's called *inference* and *inductive logic* and is what people use to make the majority of their decisions because you don't need complete data to act or make a decision. You first decide (consciously or not) how much data is necessary to make a decision then you make the decision. Mythic reality is the realm of deductive logic (there's unambiguous, conclusive evidence) but people live, work and breathe in sensory reality where inductive logic (not conclusive, merely sufficient evidence) rules.

Where o' where to teach ET to think like a 5-7-year-old, to use the rules of Logical Calculus and to infer rather than deduce...

Late in Aug '08 I sent a request out via a personal email list, SoMe, LinkedIn and Facebook and received responses from 29 Aug to 11 Oct 08. The request was simple enough, please send me your thoughts on the '08 US Presidential Campaign. That was it. Extremely general and not directed to any group in particular. My hope was that the request would spread virally (it did) and that I'd get responses from a broad cross section of society (I did).

ET had been monitoring the US political process much as it did in '04 via its tacit understanding (equivalent to about a 1½ - 2-year-old's knowledge base).[98] I wanted to expose it to non-public, reflective, sometimes highly personal thoughts. Not public blog posts and newspaper columns and the possible vitriol or rhetoric they carry with them. I wanted ET to learn from people who — knowing they were responding to me — would put their common sense, their implicit knowledge and inferential understanding, into words.

Those words would be highly symbolic and minimally indexic.

I collected 961 responses. Removing responses from people who couldn't vote in the US left me with 851 from across the US and Puerto Rico. The question ET had to answer was a simple one; based on a single instance of information (a single data point, a snapshot in time when people provided their individual responses), could ET determine who would win the election regardless of what was actually written by the individuals?

Think of it this way; there can be a difference between what someone says they're going to do and what they've non-consciously already decided they're going to do but don't yet realize they're going to do. Could and can ET detect the differences? Doing so would mean it was using the equivalent of a 5-7-year-old's knowledge base.

Mathematically, I had ET create an 80-dimension covariance matrix that measured how closely people were thinking to the main political philosophies as demonstrated by the major candidates, then Senator Obama and Senator McCain. This is important. I wanted to determine which philosophy made the most sense to people regardless of candidate or candidate's rhetoric. In non-mathematical terms, I wanted to find out

1) How far off the political philosophies were from where people believed they were and
2) Whether people were leaning towards or away from their stated beliefs.

First, it is rare that people think monolithically. Except in politics. I once sent a letter (back before emails) to the NH Senate delegation (comprised of four republicans) and received four identical responses. I mean, truly identical. Word for word. I was amazed.

But common citizens? Monolithic thinking is a sign of psychologic trauma (hmm...is that a prerequisite for politics?) and is rarely seen outside of psychiatric and penal institutions. I didn't expect to see a one-to-one correspondence between what people were thinking but not stating and the major political philosophies of the day. People may claim to be single-issue voters and that tendency is demonstrated most often in times of economic extremes (see **Appendix B.II.1 - Machine Detection of Website Visitor Age and Gender via Analysis of Psychomotor Behavioral Cues**, page 193, for an example of how economic extremes can affect thought and behavior).

What I was surprised by was just how far off Republican correspondents and Republican philosophies were. Figure IV.40 (page 152) shows a neuroprint of the Republican platform's symbolic communication (dark) and the average neuroprint of pro-McCain respondents.

About the only places where they overlap is in how the symbolic communication is occurring, not in what it is. This means the message is being clearly understood but the message isn't a welcome one? How unwelcome?

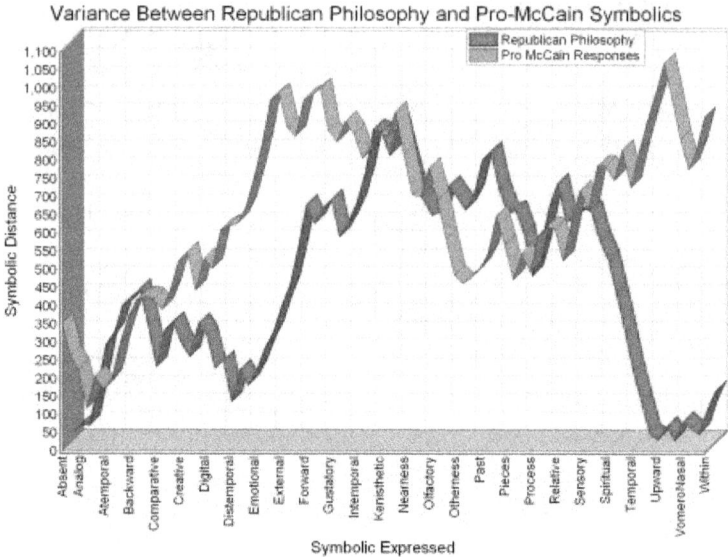

IV.40 - Recognizable differences existed between people who stated they were pro-McCain and where they thought the Republican Party was going

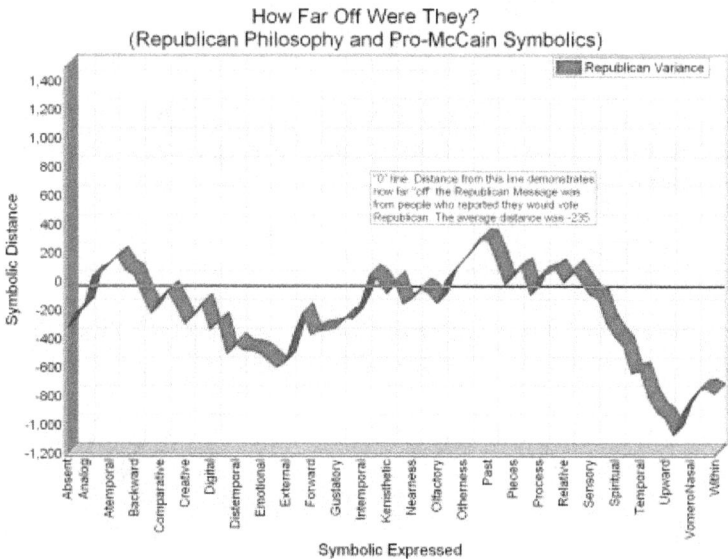

IV.41 - A psychological distance of -235 existed between the Republican Philosophy and pro-McCain respondents

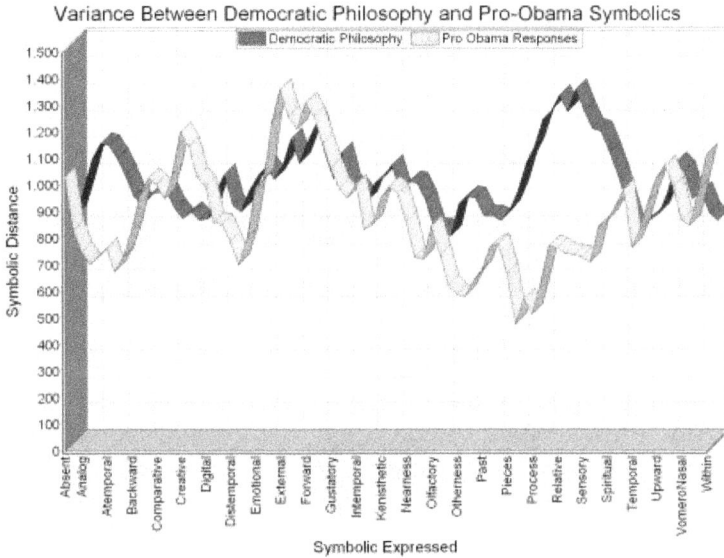

IV.42 - The Democratic philosophy and pro-Obama respondents were much more closely aligned in the symbolic communication

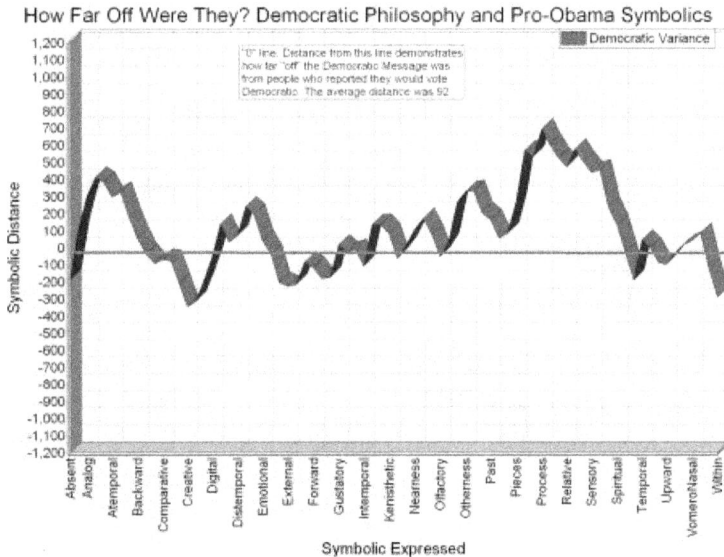

IV.43 - Pro-Obama respondents didn't have to change too much to align with the Democratic message

Figure IV.41 (page 152) shows the average distance between a "0" line — complete agreement with the Republican Philosophy — and pro-McCain respondents. Not only is the average distance recognizable at 235 units, it is a negative 235 units. The "-" is significant. Not only were pro-McCain respondents psychologically distancing themselves from the Republican party, they were symbolically demonstrating a healthy discomfort with what it meant to be "Republican". Following the Republican platform meant becoming someone these people didn't want to be. Not a good situation for the Republican party, period.

What about the Democrats?

The Democrats were demonstrating something equally interesting (figure IV.42, page 153). There was some alignment in how things were being communicated and not as much as I would have thought considering the then Senator Obama's "rock star" status in the press.

The close alignment was in what was being communicated, not necessarily how it was being communicated. That, and the consistencies of the intensities was impressive. Not quite monolithic thinking and a reasonable demonstration in the population sizes we were working with.

The Democratic message wasn't always understood but it was always welcome, a distinct difference from the Republicans. Republicans were getting the message and not liking it. How much did Democrats like their party's message?

The average psychological distance between the Democratic philosophy and pro-Obama respondents was +92. The "+" is important because it indicates that pro-Obama respondents would embrace a move towards being more Democratic. Pro-McCain respondents were moving away from their party, pro-Obama respondents were moving toward their party.[75,110,111,113,133] Good news for the Democratic Party, that. Later research demonstrated that the Democratic message was *protentious*. I wrote in a blog post[af]:

[af] – http://nlb.pub/w

> Protention is to Expectation what Hope and Emotion are to Belief and Logic. Protention is what we really, really, really want to have happen, Expectation is what we think will really happen. Obama's message -- Change -- is a protentious message. Voters (I'll offer) expect some kind of change to occur regardless of who gets into office.

About a month before the general elections there was no question that the Democrats would win the election. Their strength was that people who were admitted Republicans didn't like being Republican, were increasingly uncomfortable with what the party stood for and how it demonstrated itself. It's amusing in its way, a political party's advantage is that nobody wants to be part of the opposing party. The pro-McCain supporters weren't necessarily pro-Obama, they were simply increasingly anti-Republican in their symbolic communication, in the *implications* of what they wrote and said.

IV.9.E - Symbolic Communication and the Transmission of Meaning
or
"Whether thou goest...I don't know, maybe I'll follow...what exactly are you getting at?"

The Judeo-Christian Bible's Book of Ruth tells the story of Ruth the Moabite who, offered the opportunity to return to her native lands or remain with the Israelites, replies, "...for where you go I will go, ..."[ag]. Thus was the power of belief back then. Belief was communicated via language and as then so now with the caveat that the closer the ties in language the closer the shared beliefs.

Doubt me? Do you easily understand the jargon your teenager uses? Especially when they don't want you to know what they're talking about with their friends?

Ah...jargon again.

[ag] – Ruth 1:16 RSV

One of my goals is to have ET transcend jargon. It's one thing to have a tool that can read French, extract the meaning and produce the correct English equivalent (for example), it's an entirely different thing for a tool to take perfectly good but jargonized English and produce perfectly good, correct but differently jargonized English. Imagine taking something written by a lawyer for other lawyers and having a tool that can translate it into something understandable and actionable by a lay person (and if it's a lay person speaking another language, all the better) and you get the idea. To a certain extent we've already done that with some of our Language Engines (the RWB Language Engine comes to mind. We use it to understand investor-speak. Next time we're at a conference together ask me about it).

The most confusing jargons to translate aren't related to professions, however. They are related to age and gender.

Ah...marketing.

Imagine a 54-year-old white Eurocentric male writing a marketing piece for a service or product with a target audience of 15-24-year-old Asian-American impoverished, inner-city females. Now imagine a tool that can take what was written and quickly and correctly translate it into understandable and actionable 15-24-year-old Asian-American impoverished, inner-city female speak.

That's a challenge. Being able to take the symbolic communication of one individual and put into the symbolic communication of a completely different individual — different history, different education, different belief system, ... — and have it make sense?

This is "...for where you go I will go..." on a global scale. The Tower of Babel will sink into the Earth if this is possible and Nimrod's arrow will ascend into the heavens at last.

So I took what ET had done with the responses to my political question emails (see page 150) and asked it to translate what it had learned into the symbolic meanings of age and gender combinations not represented by the responses.

Figure IV.44 (page 157), published online on 3 Nov 08[ah], shows ET's determinations ("projections", if you will) of who would take what age groups and by what numbers. ET made these determinations using version 2 of its Language Engines[ai] by

1) taking the respondents' symbolic communication (the "what they meant" rather than "what they said"),
2) determining if that meaning could be accurately translated across age and gender boundaries and
3) determining how individuals in those non-respondent groups would act in response to that meaning.

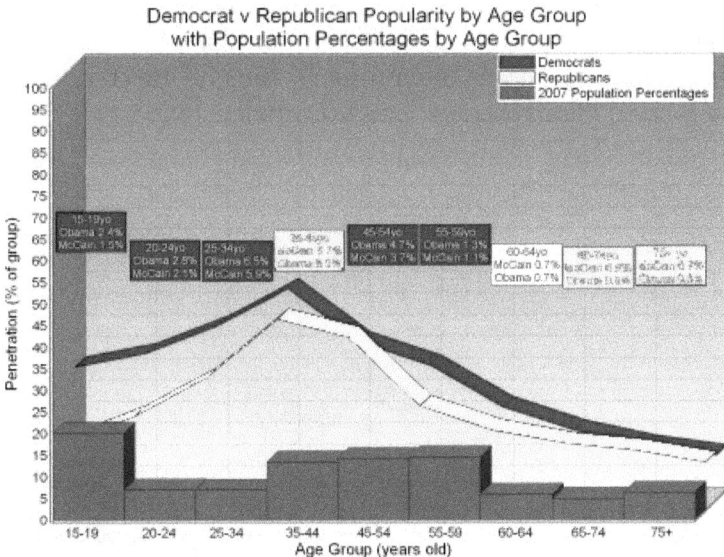

IV.44 - ET correctly translated symbolic communication among age and gender groups, although Senator McCain's ability to carry the 65-74-year-old age group was higher than ET estimated

ah – http://nlb.pub/x
ai – ET's v2 system wasn't commercially available at this time.

A reader contacted me to let me know that ET was accurate across the board albeit a bit low on its determinations for the 65-74-year-old age group. But otherwise accurate.

I tell you, I'm loving it.

IV.10 – The Learnings

ET, our extra-terrestrial, has gone from being able to recognize the most basic aspects of human behavior to understanding the behaviors of selected groups of individuals to understanding the behaviors of people at large and finally to understanding business behaviors well enough to correctly pick websites which will best satisfy a given audience's needs, hence generate revenue for their parent companies.

Implementing those learnings is for the next books in the *Reading Virtual Minds* series. See you then.

Most science consists of elaborations on well-tested themes. The discovery of something genuinely unexpected, however, kicks over the traces. Even the discoverers find it hard to accommodate the new arrival in a picture they have, perhaps inadvisedly, taken for granted.
— Henry Gee

V – The Science Behind Reading Virtual Minds

This chapter deals more directly with some of the hard science and philosophy which goes into Evolution Technology. It's not intended for the squeamish, although I hope it's a blazing good read for those with the heart to go through it.[a] Evolution Technology is based on sciences that explore the meaning of myth, specifically personal myths, those things which give meaning to every individual's life. As Arthur Young wrote,

> Science...has become so fragmented into separate disciplines that it has lost sight of the unifying principle that the word "universe" implies... Science, like a map, can furnish information, but it cannot provide a compass. Myth supplies this compass. With its help we can discover how to orient the map.[b]

V.1 – Overview

Reading Virtual Minds is based on studies and research started in 1987 (that chance conversation mentioned in **Section II.1 – Missing Links**, page 61) covering some 120 disciplines in four major fields; Anthropology, Linguistics, Mathematics and Neuroscience. These studies and research resulted in NextStage's proprietary Evolution Technology (ET). Starting in 1991, eight basic tests have been performed and repeated at regular intervals in order to insure ET's being calibrated for the current on- and off-line population. These eight tests include

- Gender Linguistic Modeling
- LexicoStatistical Modeling
- Memetic Recognition Modeling
- Presentation Format Preference

---

[a] – More detail is given in **Appendix B – Proofs** (page 187)
[b] – Arthur Young was a 20th century mathematician and an engineer, a practical man who knew how, in the Yankee tradition of know-how, and as such was the most significant single figure in the development of the Bell helicopter.

- Sensory to Δt Mapping
- Teleology
- Time Normalization Studies
- Ungoaled Persistence

From these eight basic tests, 24 further tests were developed and are used to refine ET's capabilities starting in 1995. Research continues in a variety of fields and often at the request of our research partners and clients. The types of tests we perform and what ET's able to determine is constantly growing.

NextStage Evolution's ("NSE's") research and methods apply to determining which parts of an individual's mind and brain are active when information is encountered, evaluated and acted upon. The current state of the art knows where neurologic activity occurs and can neuro -chemically and -physically quantify it. Further, the ability to correlate experience to where it occurs in the brain is well-documented.[163,248] Knowing where this activity occurs, we know what types of experience it's producing, which is culturally based.[162]

ET's function is to determine an individual's state-of-mind by observing how the individual interacts with information. How crucial is knowing people's state-of-mind? According to Bakan, it's crucial:

> Politicians concern themselves with the mental states of their constituents and others. Military commanders are particularly concerned with the mental states of those against whom they are warring, as well as the mental states of those on whom they spy. The mental events in the minds of Einstein, Fermi, Szilard, and other physicists, in connection with atomic energy, were of no small moment with respect to the physical world. Deceivers are very concerned with the mental states of those whom they deceive and vice versa. Lenders are concerned with the mental states of those who borrow. Salesmen and advertising agents are concerned with the mental states of potential and actual customers. Everybody has an interest in the mental states of motor vehicle operators."[12]

A common eCommerce use of ET is determining if online visitors are researching a purchase or are ready to purchase and either responding or directing others to respond accordingly.[c]

V.2 – Subjective versus Objective Experience and Why it Matters

There is a field of research called "NeuroCognitive PsychoLingualAnthropology". As its name implies, it's a synthesis of several disciplines some of which don't even appear in the name. What it deals with is subjective versus objective experience. Anthropologists, linguists and neuroscientists regularly utilize the concepts of subjective and objective experience. The rest of this section provides an overview of the differences between objective and subjective experience and why it matters when developing and modifying websites.

Objective experience is experience everyone can agree to. We all saw something happen, we all agree on what we saw. Objective experience is what trial law is concerned with; we all saw the car go through the red light, we all saw this person take something from that person.

In science, objective experience is what rules and something isn't considered true until the statement "we duplicated it therefore it must be true." is made.[d] But the rule of objective experience comes with a great price:

> "Copernicus gave preference to man's delight in abstract theory, at the price of rejecting the evidence of our senses . . . It becomes legitimate to regard the Copernican system as more objective than the Ptolemaic only if we accept this very shift in the nature of intellectual satisfaction as the criterion of greater objectivity. This would imply that we would rely increasingly on theoretical guidance for the

---

[c] – Papers detailing more of NextStage's research are available to NextStage Members as part of their membership benefits. See http://nlb.pub/4 for membership info.
[d] – The rule of Objective Experience is fairly recent in human history, only going back some 400 years. According to Jonathan Shear of Virginia Commonwealth University's Dept of Philosophy, "...the notion of what we today call 'science' evolved during the sixteenth century."

interpretation of our experience, and would correspondingly reduce the status of our raw impressions to that of dubious and possibly misleading appearances."[286]

As the quote above implies, the price is our ability – some might say "our right" – to accept our subjective experience as valid. There is a problem with objective experience which is hinted at in the above; Objective experience is not where we live.

We live in subjective experience.[56] We eat there, we sleep there, we think and love there, we laugh, cry, and grow old there. Subjective experience is our own, private, internal understandings of things. It doesn't rely on the beliefs and ideas of others, and is the most easily destroyed of all experiences.

Why is that?

Someone will say, "I think this about that" and someone else will respond "Oh, you don't know what you're talking about" and depending on the first person's ego-state, that first person's subjective experience is gone. Someone will say, "I feel this way" and someone else will respond "How can you possibly feel that way?" and again, depending on the first person's ego-state the subjective experience is gone. Very often the child in the back of the car will say "I have to go to the bathroom" and the parent who's driving and on a schedule will say "No you don't, not yet" and sometimes the child's subjective experience becomes the parent's objective experience before anyone can stop it.

Because we are a culture which believes the only real experience is mutually agreed to experience (objective experience), we deny and/or negate subjective experience when it doesn't fit the needs of the objective norm.[230,312,314] This belief is that subjective experience can't be real because it is not externally verifiable.

But despite the past 400 years of scientific method, subjective experience is making a comeback in what some might call the extreme sciences:

"Today the small community of experimental high-energy physicists . . . — a select few who survive a long process of formal training and research apprenticeships — [cannot rely on] independent replication of experimental results . . . Instead, influential physicists assess the skill and trustworthiness of experimenters and reach agreement as to whether a particular set of findings merits acceptance."[40]

Subjective experience, on the other hand, is a personal, private experience and deals with the intimacies of how we respond internally to what goes on around us. Finding something funny that others do not is an example of subjective experience. Knowing the comic spoke and hearing people laugh is objective experience. Our finding the comic's joke funny and laughing is due to our subjective experiences of humor and amusement. Subjective experience is where we live the most real, the most intimate, and the most truthful moments of our lives and is defined by the following attributes:

- Subjective Experience is always correct[282]
- It is always from the "I/me/my/mine" viewpoint
- Subjective Experience always places the individual having the experience in the center of what's happening around them
- It is rarely discussed or accepted due to our adversarial society
- It no longer exists as soon as it is questioned[e]

Whether we like it or not, the majority of our daily decisions are based on subjective experience (the cars we drive, the people we associate with, our tastes in food and clothing, mates and partners, etc.). Studying subjective experience also has a valid scientific basis:

---

[e] – Readers may appreciate that the first, third and fifth elements in this list can be used to describe quantum interactions. The similarity is purely intentional, as a portion of ET's mathematical basis is quantum mechanical in nature. Consider that the collapse from subjective to objective experience is much like Schrödinger's Cat; it's both alive and dead until someone looks in the box. Like a quantum state, all the possibilities of subjective experience cease to exist once a single objective "state" is looked for, such as when focus groups look for some one "thing", the subjective quantum states collapse to reveal only that one "thing".

> "There are further grounds for claiming scientific respectability that a first person approach of the kind proposed here could also be expected to meet. The fruits of such inquiry would be *describable* in ways that others with similar training would probably recognize. They might well be *generalizable*, in the same sense. In at least some cases, they might also prove *replicable*, at least at a certain level of inquiry. Finally, they might lead to *prediction* as to the kinds of experiences that other researchers pursuing this approach are likely to have."[282]

It is on this bridge between subjective and objective reality that ET lives. It makes no claims to know what an individual's subjective experience is, only that it understands that that experience has happened. ET can do this because humans respond to information subjectively and *non-consciously* before the conscious mind responds to that same information and such non-conscious behaviors can be mathematized via "a computational theory of near optimal performance".[166] As Berger and Schneck write in the *Journal of Scientific Exploration*:

> "Long before 'cognition' and 'psychology' became buzz words for analyzing and defining human experience, the organism responded first and continues to so respond, even in its most recent evolutionary version, *sub-cognitively, intuitively, and spontaneously by means of genetically inscribed, emotionally driven* instincts."[22]

Most of these responses come and go within the first three seconds of an individual encountering information.[18, 57,157,172,234,246,247,284,338,339] It is highly unlikely this information will be captured using traditional methods and using synthetic methods (strapping focus group participants to EEGs, MEGs, fMIRs, PETs, etc.) invalidates the testers' ability to gather genuine information.[2,16,44,148,177,258, 319,327,346]

What all this means to people making a living from online traffic is that you have at most three seconds to get and keep your visitor's interest and attention, and you have to figure this all out without the visitor knowing you're doing it because the second they know you're watching their experience goes from totally subjective to mostly objective and they're no longer engaged in what you want them to do (probably make a purchase or otherwise convert while they're on your property).

Let me give you an example of subjective experience immediately collapsing in the face of "objective" experience. I was at a conference and a presenter put up some slides. During the Q&A, I offered that I truly appreciated the clarity of the charts. During lunch, another fellow, someone highly respected in his field, quietly shared with me that he thought the slides were far from useful but when I spoke and he saw others nod, decided he was "wrong" and kept quiet.

I shared that his decision to keep quiet denied everyone in the room a possible learning moment and encouraged him to voice his thoughts early and often...provided he was willing to learn from others as well.

V.3 – Internet Anthropology

So now we come to the Internet.

How do we observe subjective experience when someone is browsing the web?

We use the tools of anthropology. We create a "blind", a common practice in anthropology, ethology and behavioral etiology[31,158,162,316,317] and probably something you've seen on TV or read about in magazines. We create a blind from which to observe undetected a selected population (lions, chimpanzees, walruses, people). The Chinese General Solicitation is the closest measure to a blind available in investigator-(human)subject exchanges. True blinds involve the use of cameras, tape recorders or similar agent-style recording equipment which act as surrogates for the investigator. The obvious advantage to using a surrogate is that the investigator is distanced from the observed event and is deprived of the ability to assign meaning to the event other than what is impartially recorded by the surrogate apparatus.[f] The best blinds share some common qualities:

------

[f] – "A feedback mechanism, carrying unadulterated messages, required that an observer

- They are designed so that the observer can hide from those being observed
- Observations can be made from the blind without interfering in the subject's activities
- Observations are constantly and instantaneously calibrated to the subject's behavior in order to
  a) remove observer bias and
  b) ensure that what's being evaluated is what's being monitored and not the observer's reactions to what's being monitored

In this case, the blind is the internet and NSE's Evolution Technology is the recording equipment in the blind. ET gathers the data and posts results based on a living, growing knowledge-base of some 300,000 interactions.[9] And here is an amusing (to some) aspect of what NSE, its subsidiaries and ET does; when animal ethologists perform blind based studies they work to stop themselves from anthropomorphizing their subjects (animals in the act of living their lives).[178] Anthropomorphizing was a useful tool for the old Disney™ documentaries on raccoons and fox and cheetahs, giving them enough human characteristics and qualities to keep viewers young and old interested, but it is not a useful tool when observing creatures – be they human or otherwise – and learning their motivating behaviors, decision processes, etc.[178]

======

standing outside the system report on it without in any way participating. Container and conduit metaphors leave no room for negotiated meaning."(266)
[9] – As of 06 Apr 2015, ET's knowledge-base has 3.5M human-information interactions catalogued. These interactions comprise several tens of millions of unique events. ET's knowledge-base is self-modifying and rebuilds itself whenever a new interaction-response pair occurs.
ET's "unique event" is quite different from a "unique visitor" to a digital property. Hundreds of millions of people may have the same or at least similar responses to a given event or stimulus. If they didn't, mass marketing would fail completely.
ET's unique events fall into the category of "first kiss", "first love", "first taste of chocolate", "first roller-coaster ride", essentially "something never encountered before". Because they are the first experience of something, they create exemplars against which all similar experience are measured.

ET is a useful tool for three reasons. First, ET doesn't anthropomorphize humans. ET only assigns values to activities based on 1) what the individuals under observation demonstrate are assignable to the activity their engaged in and 2) what values it has learned from previous human ethology studies are to be equated to a given activity.[348] The only time ET asks for help is when it encounters a behavior it has never experienced before (within a certain statistical degree). Even then, ET is quite specific as to the type of help it requires (another behavior seed, for example).[150,h]

Second, ET is unlike traditional methods in which watching someone engage in a behavior will almost always influence that behavior[i]. Watching someone engage in a behavior via a blind neither causes that person to perform a behavior nor alter their demonstrated behavior, just as watching paint dry does not cause the paint to dry on the wall. However, watching someone watch paint dry will cause them to behave differently as the paint dries on the wall. In the case of the latter, ET is the wall because what people are watching (their browser) is what's watching them.

Third, ET is aware of both biological, social and cultural constraints on those it observes. Humans can only act "within the range of human possibility, constrained by heredity and environment, past experience, inner needs and goals, available strategies, current options offered by physical and social contexts and so on."[330]

---

[h] – ET makes many of its internal decisions based on two basic rules, the first of which is the Principle of Structural Coherence; ie, if there is some stimulus, X, which produces experience A in subject B, and this same X produces experience C in D, then there is a 1:1 coherence in the structures in B and D which produce experiences A and C. However, there is no such coherence in the experiences A and C themselves, only a statistical probability that actions based on those experiences will come to pass.
The second rule is the Principle of Organizational Invariance. Because all humans are organically designed the same way we will have the same non-subjective experiences; ie, if two humans are shown light of wavelength η they'll both have the experience of η even though one may call it "gold" and the other call it "blue" (see "Hues and cry", http://nlb.pub/y, for an interesting visual perception read on this).
[i] – As noted in footnote e in this chapter.

All I was doing was trying to get home from work.
— Rosa Parks

VI – The Long Road Home

Yes, I started writing this book in 2003. I kept at it long and hard until I realized that I kept on rewriting it as new information and new research augmented what I'd already written or done.

So I stopped writing the book. Obviously, I wasn't quite sure what I really wanted to write about.

Meanwhile, both our (Susan's and my) family and the greater NextStage family suffered major losses.

And during the whole process, I was learning about business. I could write another book about business (and probably will). I sometimes wonder if I'm bitter about what I've learned – we encountered people that could easily be bifurcated into

- those who didn't have a clue what ET or we were about, didn't actually care yet were convinced we and/or ET could be their (often personal) pot o' gold and
- those who had some idea what ET was about and gave according to their time, energy, resources, etc., to make it happen.

There were less than five who fell in between and eventually they chose a group to fall into.

And I'm not bitter. I can't be. I could only be bitter about the former and being so would force me to waste time better spent glorying in the latter. I realize that business, for those not inclined or involved, is a true case of "be wise as serpents", period. Forget that "harmless as doves" part. It ain't out there in the majority of cases. Yet I will offer that in all experiences I learned something. Often I wish I hadn't learned what I did[a] and part of my training is that all learning can do is bring out what's already there. Don't like what manifests? Then change it. It's the one power all people have and few are willing to use.

---

[a] – see Appendix C.6 – From Later in 2008 for more on this. I hope what was written is true. Especially the tranquility, solitude and wife and close friends and peers parts.

In my case (feel free to tell me I'm mistaken), it's made me more resolute and more confident in myself (others have told me I've become increasingly "arrogant, obnoxious and disliked"). A social system lesson I learned long ago can be paraphrased as "If the butchers, the bakers and the candlestick makers think you're a prick, then you're a prick. But if the butchers and the bakers think you're okay and only the candlestick makers think you're a prick then the problem is with the candlestick makers because everybody else thinks you're just fine."

Back in 2003, at that MIT Enterprise Forum I mention in the **Author's Foreword** (page 24), when asked what I really wanted to do with NextStage after I'd finished my presentation, I said "I want to go home to Nova Scotia. I'm not designed to run a business. I'm designed to do research." The uniform response was "No, **you** have to run the business. You're the only one who understands what your technology does."

I replied, "No, making me run a business is like making me ride a racehorse around a track. I won't like it, the racehorse won't like it and we definitely won't win the race."

And they replied sternly, "No, **you** must run the business."

It was kind of like Johnny Weissmuller's Tarzan telling his elephants to go for help, "Uen-gow!"

I mean, I think that's what they expected as a response, that I would simply go off in the direction they were pointing and get things done.

Did I mention most of the people were serial entrepreneurs or investors and most of them had what I would call miserable track records? I mean, anything less than a 3% success rate is spitting into the wind and trying to dodge what comes back at you. A 3% error rate is something I could live with, but a 3% *success* rate?

I'm guessing these folks didn't know much about elephants. Like the fact that elephants won't do what they know they can't do. Funny that elephants are smarter than investors and serial entrepreneurs, ain't it?

What I think is that those original folks simply wanted me to screw up as badly as they did.

Well, I'm sorry, I'm not designed that way.

Oh, I screwed up, a lot and badly, just not as they did. I learned enough from their mistakes to go out and make a whole new set of mistakes that were all my own.

Don't get me wrong. NextStage has had a string of CEOs, all of whom I learned from. What did I learn? Do the opposite of what they were doing. What I really want to know is why people who knew these individuals were massive screwups didn't come forward and warn me or at least share their experiences and concerns. Had this community never learned Edmund Burke's "The only thing necessary for evil to thrive is for men of good conscience to do nothing"?

And the list of people who were happy to charge us lots of money with absolutely no promise of anything in return is equally as long. One fellow offered to help us market our products for a "mere 20% of the company". I asked for a list of clients. He had none. I asked for names of people he'd worked with. Nada. Then I started asking people about him. The universal reply? If he was such a good marketer, how come his site sucks?

Or another fellow early on who offered to write a business plan for us for only US$5,000. He offered that with the right business plan we could get funding (did I mention he worked with investors?). So I asked, "If you write a business plan for us, will we get funding?" and he said that he couldn't guarantee that, only that he would write a *fundable* business plan. And did I mention that he worked with investors, that he was in daily contact with them? So I then asked, "How many of these business plans you've written actually led to companies getting funding?" and he said that if I wasn't going to take his offer seriously then he didn't have time to talk with me anymore.

Or how about the fellow who was willing to be our CEO for a mere 33% of the company. "How many companies have you run previously?" "Three." "How many have been successful?"

One company died but he saw the death coming and managed to sell his interest in it before it died. He didn't tell the investors, board, employees or anybody else that he knew death was coming but he managed to get out in time. A second company went bankrupt, a third company he couldn't talk about because he and the board were in litigation.

Oh, yeah. Sign me right up for that one. Or the folks who said we weren't "demonstrating the proper amount of enthusiasm" for what they were proposing?

There were lots of people who kept telling us they knew better when evidence – good old, objective evidence – repeatedly demonstrated they didn't know anything at all.

Yet all were perfectly happy to take our money to demonstrate their ignorance to us.

Remind me some time to explain "If I am a thief then you must steal" to you. It fits these people sooooo perfectly... Or about "I don't know how to help you, Joe". It's an excellent example of people using the same words and not speaking the same language at all, not to mention the psycholinguistic concept of *congruency*, something politicians worldwide need to learn about. Or "We could really use your technology" "Then let's sign a contract" "No, but we could really use your technology".

And we learned from them all.

Really!

Meanwhile, there were people from the other group who also offered to help us, people who have never asked for pay in any way, shape or form. These include our researchers, people who did programming, provided legal advice, people who gave us space on their servers, who made connections for us, who provided tools, gave us office space, ... The original offer was that they need only stay with us until the original patent was awarded and that would only take 3-4 years. It took seven in the end. And all of us were exhausted. I described it as winning a race in which I was the only runner. Why did it take so long? According to the USPTO examiner assigned to our patent, "You've created a new field of technology and if I award you the patent you'll own that field completely."

Our IP attorney replied, "Isn't that what a patent's all about?"

The people in this group were rewarded and I'm not talking pie-in-the-sky, we'll-make-it-good-when-we-can types of rewards. All the money that NextStage ever netted from 2001-2008 was distributed to all those who helped.

So now it's 2009. The clans are gathering again. When people ask me what I want to do with this company, I answer that I want to go home to Nova Scotia (I mentioned I became resolute? I was probably always resolute).

I've come to realize *Reading Virtual Minds* is not a book, it's a series. Something for trainings, I think. To help people understand.

That I'm obnoxious, arrogant and disliked.

*Je m'en vay chercher
un grand Peut-etre.
— Rabelais*

VII – The End

Remember what I wrote way back in the beginning of this book, that I was in a fiction writing program at the time I started investigating these fields? One of the teachers in that program was a man by the name of Algis ("AJ") Budrys. He's the AJ in my dedication.

AJ was a bull of a man. He was also an incredibly compassionate and passionate teacher from whom I learned many things. One of the ways I paid the mortgage while doing my research was by writing, and AJ, an editor for several publications and publishing houses, had the pleasure of rejecting much of my work.

But AJ's rejections were vastly different from the majority of the other editors I submitted my work to. AJ gave details as to *why* something wasn't working, suggestions on how to change it, and always ended his rejections with "...and it's your story, you decide." NextStage clients have AJ to thank for ET's suggestion and recommendations system being both direct and gracious. AJ taught me to be so.

AJ started buying my stories and eventually became my agent, and we had great success until I decided I needed time.

To do what?

To learn how to write, of course.

AJ was also an incredible author in his own right. Reading his work was one of the reasons I wanted to get into that particular writing program. I well remember, as a child sitting in a family cottage in northern Maine, spending my evenings reading (there was no TV in that time or place). One of the stories I read was AJ's novella, *Wall of Crystal, Eye of Night* in the December 1961, GALAXY magazine.

> ... EmpaVid," Sollenar agreed. "Various subliminal stimuli are broadcast with and keyed to the overt subject matter. The home receiving unit contains feedback sensors which determine the viewer's reaction to these stimuli, and intensify some while playing down others in order to create complete emotional rapport between the viewer and the

subject matter. EmpaVid, in other words, is a system for orchestrating the viewer's emotions. ...

Long after I started work on ET I reread AJ's novella and thought, *Whoa!* I shared my discovery with him and he guffawed like only a long-time chain smoker could.

If I've seen further than other men, it's because AJ let me become a giant. There is nothing new under the sun. All that's required is that men of great vision share it and allow others to have visions of their own. As my dedication indicates, in The End you'll discover that it was his idea at the beginning.

Thank you, AJ. Rest well, Old Friend.

Algis Budrys at the 1985 Clarion Science
Fiction Writing Workshop -
http://nlb.pub/I

Appendix A – Anecdotal Correspondence

With the exception of two anecdotes ("The Investors Heard the Music" on page 95 and "People Aren't the Same Everywhere" on page 112) all anecdotes are used with the full knowledge of the individuals named therein. Correspondence about those anecdotes follows.

A.I – Dave Nelson was Hungry (2002)

From: Dave Nelson
Sent: Monday, January 03, 2005 8:17 PM
To: jcarrabis@nextstagevolution.com
Subject: Re: The other email I mentioned

Feel free to use this anecdote for any purpose

Your friend
David

From: Joseph Carrabis [jcarrabis@nextstagevolution.com]
Sent: Thursday, December 23, 2004 11:15 AM
To:
Subject: The other email I mentioned

Hello again,
As I mentioned on the phone, I'd like to include the anecdote about the first time we met. You started browsing the site and ET reported that you were highly visual and thinking about something in the near future, 1-3 hour time frame I think it was, and we were meeting at 10:30am. You said that your wife always comments on how visual you are and that you were wondering what you were going to have for lunch.
Anyway, I'd like to use the anecdote.
Hope all is well. Enjoy your holidays.
Joseph

... the modality of novelistic enunciation is inferential; it is a process within which the subject of the novelistic utterance affirms a sequence, as conclusion to the inference, based on other sequences (referential - hence narrative, or textual - hence citational), which are the premises of the inference and, as such, considered to be true. - Julia Kristeva, Desire in Language

Joseph Carrabis, Chairman, CRO and Founder
NextStage Evolution/NextStage Analytics
The Behavioral Analytics You Really Wanted
http://www.nextstagevolution.com
http://www.nextstageanalytics.com
49 Brinton Dr
Nashua, NH 03064-1274
603 577 4575 voice
603 577 9636 fax

A.II – The Investors Heard the Music (2002)

No correspondence available

A.III – The Toddness Factor (2002)

From: Todd Sullivan
Sent: Friday, December 17, 2004 2:23 PM
To: Joseph Carrabis
Subject: Re: Don't know if I asked your permission for this or not

absolutely. And, for what its worth, I think its a good idea to get the written (and email counts) acquiescence of anyone else you are referencing in the book. You never know who may try to change their mind after the book is published.

   Joseph Carrabis <jcarrabis@nextstagevolution.com> wrote:
      Howdy,
      I think I told you I'm using the Toddness Factor story in the book. Just to make sure, do I have your permission to use it?
      Thanks.
      Joseph

      It was as easy as shoving smoke into a closet.

      Joseph Carrabis, Chairman, CRO and Founder
      NextStage Evolution/NextStage Analytics
      The Behavioral Analytics You Really Wanted
      http://www.nextstagevolution.com
      http://www.nextstageanalytics.com
      49 Brinton Dr
      Nashua, NH 03064-1274
      603 577 4575 voice
      603 577 9636 fax

A.IV – Hans Reimar Gets Offered a Job in Sales (2002)

   Hi Joseph,
   By all means, use that anecdote in your book, it was rather funny (and incredible) at the time. In the interest of journalistic integrity, my actual title at Marketreach was Director of Business Development, but everybody knows that means "glorified sales rep."
      ...
   All the best to you and your wife.

-Hans-

-----Original Message-----
From: Joseph Carrabis [mailto:jcarrabis@nextstagevolution.com]
Sent: Wednesday, December 15, 2004 7:24 PM
To: Hans J. Riemer
Subject: Hey There! Long Time No Write!

Howdy, Hans,
...I'm writing a book about my research and what we've learned working with people over the past four years. I'm including some anecdotes in the book and I was wondering if I could use the anecdote about you looking for a job on the site and the site offering you a sales position, which gave you a laugh because you were VP of Sales (I think that was it) at the time.
Anyway, I hope all is well.
Have safe and enjoyable holidays.
Joseph

How long is a rope?

Joseph Carrabis, Chairman, CRO and Founder
NextStage Evolution/NextStage Analytics
The Behavioral Analytics You Really Wanted
http://www.nextstagevolution.com/
http://www.nextstageanalytics.com/
49 Brinton Dr
Nashua, NH 03064-1274
603 577 4575 voice
603 577 9636 fax
This email message and any attachments are confidential and may be privileged. If you are not the intended recipient, please notify NextStage by replying to this message or by sending an email to support@nextstagevolution.com and destroy all copies of this message and any attachments. Thank you.

A.V – Mark Broth, Esquire, Discovers What Makes a Lawyer a Lawyer (2002)

Joseph- Great to hear from you. You certainly have my permission. I hope all is well with you and the business. The websites are impressive. Regards.

From: Joseph Carrabis
[mailto:jcarrabis@nextstagevolution.com]
Sent: Wednesday, December 15, 2004 8:59 AM
To: Mark T. Broth
Subject: Howdy
Hello!
Long time no correspond. How're things up there at DMB?
Ok, so what am I writing about?
I've been asked to write a book about my research and what we've learned by working with clients for the past four years. I'm including anecdotes in the book, and one which I'd like to use is when I was talking about the dogsled ad up at a lunch meeting at DMB. I showed some graphs about how different people responded to the ad and, when I got to the responses of the lawyer, commented that I'd never seen that spike before so I (jokingly) guessed that it was the "attorney" marker. You asked what the spike indicated and I said "a high preference for order and structure, a need for logical flow" or something similar. You said that that was pretty much how attorneys are taught to think, which made me laugh because my joke was then on me.

Anyway, I think it's a good anecdote for the book and I'd like to use it, hence I'm writing for your permission to do so.

Again, hope all is well.
Joseph Carrabis

Conversation is a meeting of minds with different memories and habits. When minds meet, they don't just exchange facts: they transform them, reshape them, draw different implications from them, engage in new trains of thought. Conversation doesn't just reshuffle the cards: it creates new cards. That's the part that

interests me. That's where I find the excitement. It's like a spark that two minds create. And what I really care about is what new conversational banquets one can create from those sparks. - Theodore Zeldin

Joseph Carrabis, Chairman, CRO and Founder
NextStage Evolution/NextStage Analytics
The Behavioral Analytics You Really Wanted
http://www.nextstagevolution.com/
http://www.nextstageanalytics.com/
49 Brinton Dr
Nashua, NH 03064-1274
603 577 4575 voice
603 577 9636 fax
This email message and any attachments are confidential and may be privileged. If you are not the intended recipient, please notify NextStage by replying to this message or by sending an email to support@nextstagevolution.com and destroy all copies of this message and any attachments. Thank you.

A.VI – People Aren't the Same Everywhere (2003)

No correspondence available, however John Hargreaves, mentioned on page 143, was a witness to these events and the conversation with the SEO company's CTO which ensued.

A.VII – Politics Aren't Horse Races Anymore (2004)

Matt van Wagner's quote was approved during a phone conversation on 27 June 05. Rob Graham's quote has appeared numerous times in the press.

A.VIII – The Progress Software 2005 Kickoff and Picking Winners

Progress Software sent out a press release to showcase our results. A copy is available at http://nlb.pub/t

A.IX – John Hargreaves Listened More Than He Looked (2005)

From: John Hargreaves
Sent: Sunday, December 19, 2004 7:49 PM
To: Joseph Carrabis
Subject: Re: Another favor

Go for it Joseph, it's ok with me.
Cheers mate,
John

--- Joseph Carrabis <jcarrabis@nextstagevolution.com> wrote:

> Howdy,
>
> ...I'm using some anecdotes in the book and there's one involving you and Danny which I'd like to use.
>
> Do you remember when I had the demo site up, the one which modified itself based on how people were thinking while they were navigating? You, Danny and I were on the phone and I said that the ET would modify the presentations to each of us a little differently because each of us was thinking a little differently. Originally what ET showed you was different than what it was showing Danny, but he kept on saying to you "Look at this" "Look at that" and ET, recognizing you were going into a visual mode, started showing you the same thing it was showing Danny (who was being very visual). When I was talking to you ET created a different presentation from Danny's because, by paying attention to what you were hearing, ET recognized you were being auditory and presented you a more audially=based presentation.

>
> Anyway, it turns out I need your permission to use this anecdote, hence I'm asking. Thanks in advance.
>
> Joseph
>
> ---
>
> It was as easy as shoving smoke into a closet.
> Joseph Carrabis, Chairman, CRO and Founder
> NextStage Evolution/NextStage Analytics
> The Behavioral Analytics You Really Wanted
> http://www.nextstagevolution.com
> http://www.nextstageanalytics.com
> 49 Brinton Dr
> Nashua, NH 03064-1274
> 603 577 4575 voice
> 603 577 9636 fax
> This email message and any attachments are confidential and may be privileged. If you are not the intended recipient, please notify NextStage by replying to this message or by sending an email to support@nextstagevolution.com and destroy all copies of this message and any attachments. Thank you.

A.X – Charles Wentworth was Greeted Based on His Browsing Behavior (2003)

From: Charles Wentworth
Sent: Friday, December 17, 2004 11:22 AM
To: Joseph Carrabis
Subject: Re: I think this might be most of them.

Why sure that's fine to use my quote from the day I was browsing your site and called about a typo and you answered the phone by saying, "What are you doing on the site?"

Charles

From: Joseph Carrabis [jcarrabis@nextstagevolution.com]
Sent: Friday, December 17, 2004 9:12 AM
To: Charles Wentworth
Subject: RE: I think this might be most of them.

... do you remember when you were navigating our site and ET notified me you were browsing because it recognized your browser behavior? I called and asked, "How do you like the site?" or something like that? We both got a chuckle out of it. Do you mind if I use that as an anecdote in the book I'm writing about online behaviors?
Thanks,
Joseph

It was as easy as shoving smoke into a closet.

Joseph Carrabis, Chairman, CRO and Founder
NextStage Evolution/NextStage Analytics
The Behavioral Analytics You Really Wanted
http://www.nextstagevolution.com
http://www.nextstageanalytics.com
49 Brinton Dr
Nashua, NH 03064-1274
603 577 4575 voice
603 577 9636 fax

Appendix B – Proofs

Sharing the entirety of ET's proofs would require several texts in themselves as the core system pulls from over 120 separate disciplines. This appendix shares two proofs (the full papers are available to NextStage Members[a]) and a demonstration of ET's abilities determining how well different entities – be they people, products and people, companies, executives, politicians and constituents, etc. – will get along.

B.I – Susan's Proof of Concept

Susan developed the following material for investors circa 2001. Investors circa 2001 proved interesting. Forget the following material, we did live demonstrations of ET's accuracy and its abilities were so foreign to them they simply refused to accept its capabilities. One investor in particular told us that he wasn't going to invest because he didn't want it to work. "It doesn't matter what we demonstrate or how accurate it is," I said, "you just aren't going to believe it's doing what it's doing."

He responded angrily, "It can't do what it's doing. Nothing can, and I'm not going to believe it *no matter what you show me.*"

'Nuff said. We stopped looking for investors. Now they're coming to us each quarter.

Anyway, Susan's proof...

Evolution Technology's accuracy was built through a series of research projects which were conducted over the course of several years starting in 1991. These research projects were in the following areas:

- Gender Linguistic Modeling
- LexicoStatistical Modeling
- Memetic Recognition Modeling

---

[a] – http://nlb.pub/4

- Presentation Format Preference
- Sensory to Δt Mapping
- Teleology
- Time Normalization Studies
- Ungoaled Persistence

The tests were performed in two stages. The first stage was with a small world model (15-20 participants). Second stage testing involved a larger participant populations (400+ participants, "large world model"). In some cases intermediate tests were involved and are documented as such.

B.I.1 – Gender Linguistic Modeling

A key and obvious physiologic metric is gender. The goal of the Gender Linguistic Modeling test was to determine if *neurologic gender* could be determined.

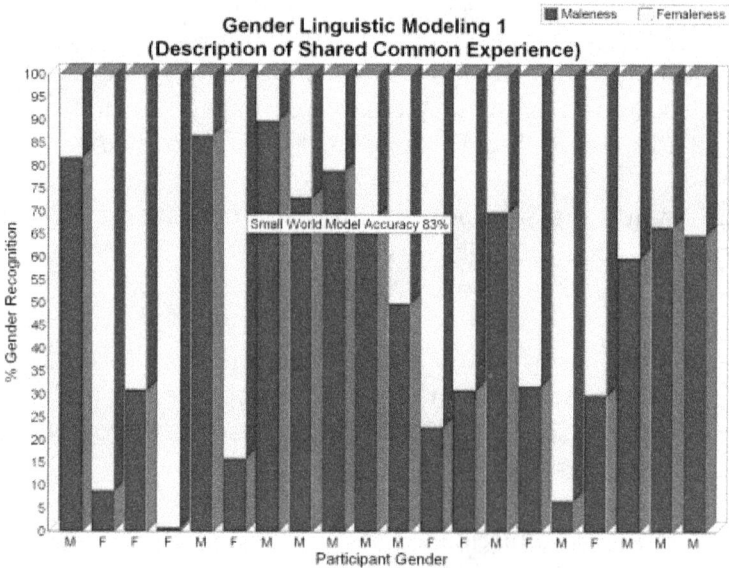

B.I.1 – Gender Linguistic Modeling 1 - Small World Model

h e
test
i   n   v   o

lved males and females being given a shared, common experience, inviting them to write a synopsis of the experience then performing a psycholinguistic analysis on that written synopsis. The interaction was fairly mixed with the description of the interaction being highly segmented along sexual identity lines resulting in 83%, as shown in figure B.I.1 on page 188.

This method was extended to an intermediate test involving some 100 students from classes the author was teaching at the time. The purpose of extending the test to this specific group of participants was to secure any variations which might arise from an individual's chosen sexual orientation. This test extension resulted in 86% accuracy along orientation.

After this, a large world model analysis was performed on 430 individuals. This large world model resulted in 71% accuracy as shown in figure B.I.2 on page 189.

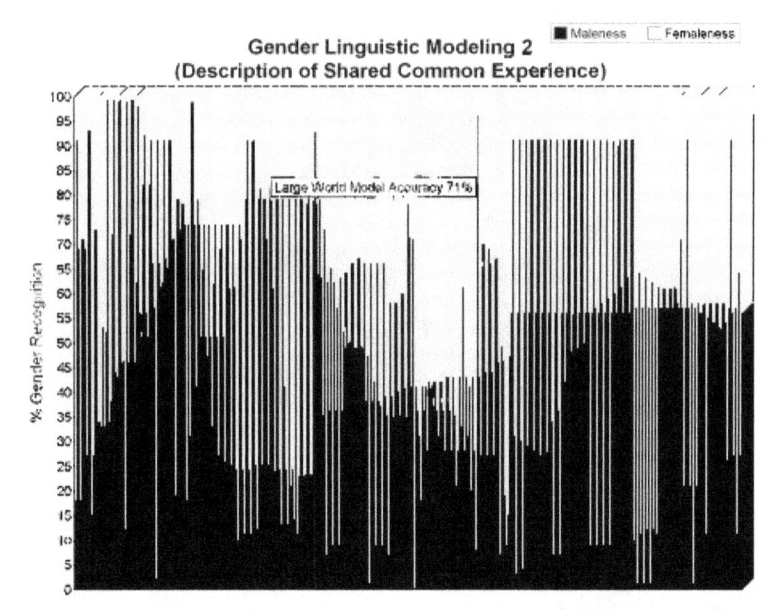

B.I.2 – Gender Linguistic Modeling 2 - Large World Model

Given that the 90% accuracy in physical gender is an assumption in the large world model and that the extended test indicated a 2-11% gender orientation shift, we state that the above accuracy is conservative and true accuracy could be from 73-83%.

B.I.2 – NeuroLexical Scoping by Gender

Coexistent with Gender Linguistic Modeling is the concept of *NeuroLexical Scoping by Gender*. The previous tests determined psycholinguistic differences between the genders. These next tests determined neurolinguistic differences between the genders by using the conceptual-primitives revealed in the above.

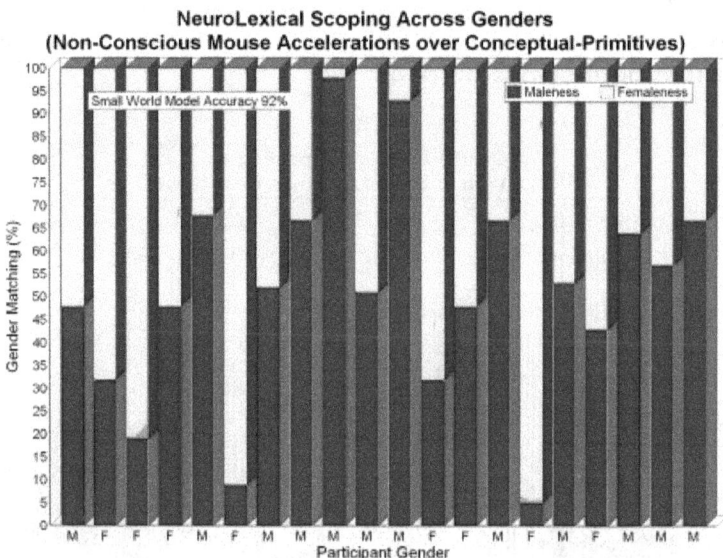

B.I.3 – NeuroLexical Scoping by Gender - Small World Model

NeuroLexical Scoping was determined by tracking cursor accelerations across conceptual-primitives in the test material itself. It is assumed and unproven that cursor accelerations are non-conscious when the acceleration does not result in bringing the cursor to some target (button, link, etc). Measurements were taken of all cursor activity and the resulting measurements were superimposed on the presentation itself. This showed that the genders non-consciously responded to gender-specific conceptual-primitives in the presentation itself with a 92% accuracy. The result of the small world test is shown in figure B.I.3 on page 190.

Using this small world model as a basis, the test was performed on a large world model. This large world model had a similar number as the previous large world model test although the participants were different individuals. The results of the NeuroLexical Scoping large world model test are shown in figure B.I.4 on page 191.

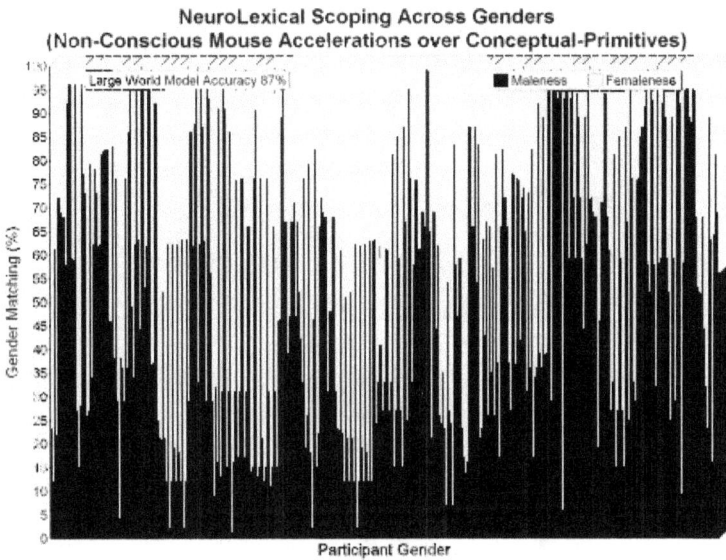

B.I.3 – NeuroLexical Scoping by Gender – Large World Model

There was no way to determine gender orientation during this test so the 11% figure from previous testing was arbitrarily assumed to carry through. Thus the NeuroLexical Scoping test probably has a realistic accuracy of 76%.

B.I.3 – Marketing Application of Gender Modeling

Say that a media buyer wants to buy 15,000 impressions of a male-oriented ad. Previous media buys cost US$1 per impression. Previously there was no way to insure that the ad would actually be seen by males.

Using Evolution Technology™, the web-sales team can tell the media buyer that there's a 76% chance each impression will be seen by a male. The cost for this increased certainty is US$0.75 per impression, bringing the total to US$1.75 per impression. the web-sales team has just increased their profit by 75% using Evolution Technology™.

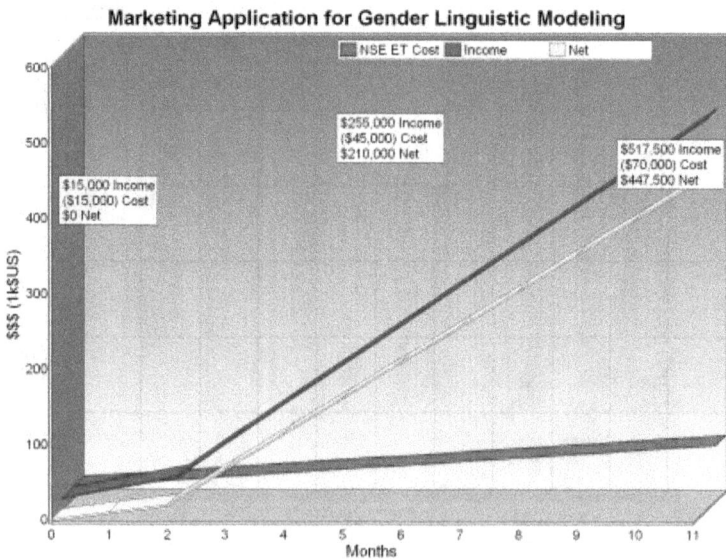

B.I.5 – Typical Marketing Gains for Gender Linguistic Modeling

The web-sales team also knows that there will now be free impression space when a female is on the site. They contact another media buyer and sell that individual the same deal this time directed at female-oriented ads. The previous media purchase would have resulted in a single sale of US$15,000. The

Evolution Technology™ enhanced site has brought in two sales for a total of US$52,500.

Assuming Evolution Technology™ had been on the site for three months prior to the sale, that the media buys were for simultaneously consecutive one month durations, and that the site falls into the NextStage Evolution pricing category of a "medium business", the web-sales team revenue curve would look figure B.I.5 on page 192.

B.II – Machine Detection of Website Visitor Age and Gender via Analysis of Psychomotor Behavioral Cues

First, some background.

NextStage's first CEO decided we needed to validate our technology. He elected to do this by offering 51% of NextStage to the company that would perform the validation study. Without telling us what he was doing.

Susan and I explained that you can't unbiasedly validate something when you have a stake in the outcome. Then we fired him.

Flash forward to 2008. Several companies have come forward between 2001 and 2008, each willing to prove ET did what we claimed, and all of them wanted a better than 50% stake in the company for doing so.

Each time Susan and I responded that you can't perform a validation study when you have a stake in the outcome. That's unethical.

As I've written before, we don't understand business. We didn't know (and still don't truly understand) that truth is the greatest fiction in business. We believe there's things like ethics involved. We are maroons and nin-cow-poops (to quote one of the great sages, Bugs Bunny[b]).

But now it is 2008 and another test is requested, a test we know will never result in business because we know the people requesting the test have no desire to move forward regardless of

---

[b] – http://nlb.pub/z

the outcome of the test. Ask me the details sometime and I'll tell you.

But we went ahead with the test. We just needed to find some group that would honestly tell us if ET failed. We knew ET would succeed, and that didn't matter. Unless whoever was doing the test was willing to tell us that ET failed, there'd be no point in doing the test at all.

We hired two people who were trained skeptics to conduct the test. To them, it would be nice if ET worked and a damn shame if it didn't, but they were curious themselves and also wanted a definitive proof. What follows details the test we devised and its results.

B.II.1 – Abstract

This paper describes one methodology and a technology[c] designed to overcome a specific deficit in current human-machine interfaces, particularly as they apply to the world of online information exchange but applicable to all human-machine interactions: the determination of human age and gender based entirely on human interaction with the machine.

Overcoming this deficit and related challenges would allow machine systems to determine individuality as a function of several factors. This paper focuses on neurologic age[103] and gender.[60,155] The technology described in this paper determines these factors by analyzing psychomotor behavioral cues[15,73,77,78,80,117,156,199,207,213,215,229,297,350] that have been collectively recognized as indicative of a given user's non-conscious,[6,8,10,11,55,151,159,160,187,189,190,193,197,222,240,253,271,281,303,313,320] cognitive, behavioral/effective and motivational processes and methodologies (collectively called "the {C,B/e,M} matrix"[51,122,124,126,127,137,236]). The end result of these determinations is that a given individual is a) known and b) demonstrates a {C,B/e,M} state of existence that is itself recognized as in keeping with this known individual's history,

---

[c] – Evolution Technology™ or *ET*. see http://nlb.pub/A

regardless of any boundary issues while being able to respond to both in-bounds and out-of-bounds responses to the immediate interaction.

Such machine capabilities are currently in use in web-based systems[d] and are intended for a much more diverse employment.

B.II.2 – Introduction

Commerce (intellectual, financial, etc) is increasingly becoming an online experience. Several businesses use cookie-based systems to provide content that they believe will best match visitor goals and experience for a given commerce interaction.

All of these systems make use of aggregated historical statistical data (Amazon.com's "People who chose this ... also chose ..." is an example). Such systems are good at placing individuals in very large buckets. These buckets are large because individuals are rarely recognized as individuals "in the moment" and instead are recognized as an average of their historical interactions at best.

The challenge presented by such systems is that present visitor detection methods do not guarantee that each session is unique to a given individual, nor that one set of cookies is uniquely tied to a given individual. A major flaw in these systems is that they do not recognize individuals in the moment as the sum of all previous moments of interaction, only averages over all interactions tied to a given set of cookies, thus recognition of an individual user's immediate (present[328]) state of being (anxiety, jubilation, inattentiveness due to external stressors, exhaustion, ...) is not considered as part of the machine's response set during the interaction. Even systems with advanced password and biometric capabilities might reject a known user who is "having a bad day" or have the bad day's interaction data throw off the system for future acceptance and interactions.

-----

[d] – NextStage's Onsite web tracking tool and several of its online tools – NextStage Gender Agent, NextStage Age Agent, for example – use these capabilities. See http://nlb.pub/s

B.II.2.a – For Researchers

Researchers need to be aware that the data presented in this paper actually represents a single meta-data point. The authors' view is that some 100 (minimum) more tests would need to be performed as that would produce a meta-data sampling error of 9.8% (just within the scientific research standard). Ideally some 300-500 more tests should be run and the cost of doing so is recognizably prohibitive.[e] The sampling error in this test is estimated at 5.7%.[345]

The above recognized, a similar test was performed in the 1999-2001 timeframe and reported in 2003. Much of that report is shared in **B.I – Susan's Proof of Concept** (page 187). Noted in there is that the realistic results of that test were approximately 76%. This is close enough to this test's similar result of 75.29% to form a basis of comparison although not necessarily standard for definition. In all cases it must be remembered that ET and its conclusions are part of an evolving system, one in which the rules of determinism change with the environment.[225]

B.II.2.b – For Marketers

Marketers are encouraged to use the results shared in this paper with caution. It is our suggestion that the lower results numbers be used when describing ET's capabilities and accuracy. Much as is stated in car ads, remember that this test was "performed by a professional driver on a closed course" and that "your mileage may vary".

B.II.3 – History

The ubiquity of the internet can be thought of as a good or bad thing. Good in the sense that more information is available to a wider population than ever before, bad in the sense that the

---

[e] – Current estimates indicate a reasonably complete test would cost US$2,000,000.

quality of the information available has decreased as everyone now has a voice and a means of quick and easy publication.[105,195] Another well-recognized good is that the internet provides social scientists with access to much larger populations for their studies.[38,39,46,196,211,236,242,318,329,340] The bad side of this is that much of the baggage from traditional, non-internet survey methods have been carried onto this new medium. The ideal would be to have a research tool that acts over the internet much like the anthropologist's *blind*,[52,61,79,116,119-121,126] gathering metrics non-invasively, totally passively, never interfering in the test subject's (visitor, user, student, ...) experience, never asking questions, never intruding on the subject in the act of being his or herself, monitoring and reporting how people interact with the information in their environment both on and off screen, and this blind should work with any existing technology that conforms to W^3C^f standards.

Such a system was developed and initially deployed in educational settings as early as 1991 (pre-web), then deployed through business websites starting in 1997. Consider the following quote:

> Marketing research methodologies that rely on questionnaires and standard surveys are inherently loaded with biases and errors related to the sampling frame, the survey instruments, the interviewers and the fact that the respondents know that they are being evaluated. NextStage is truly a non-biasing research tool with a lot of validity and reliability because it is based on non-conscious responses to information. This methodology offers a lot of advantages over traditional methods to evaluate the appeal and the benefits of a website. - Eric Drouart, Former VP, International Operations, Bristol-Myers Squibb

The author's recent patent acquisition[g] teaches the method described above.

---

[f] – The World Wide Web Consortium, http://www.w3.org/.
[g] – http://nlb.pub/B

B.II.4 – About Evolution Technology

ET is a patented technology (as noted above) that matches human psychomotor behavioral cues – non-conscious somatic movements – to the conscious and non-conscious neural activities that spawn those movements. These types of movements are recognized in the literature as defining states of consciousness, behavior and body-awareness. Further, analyzing these states as mathematical variables has a long history ("...a possible beginning point for the needed task of controlling for state of consciousness as a variable in each and every method of inquiry, ...").[209,311] All ET does is identify with a high degree of accuracy the neural states involved.

B.II.5 – Research Protocol

The initial conditions for this study were as follows:

1) Four websites were used for the study; W_0, W_1, W_2 and W_3.

2) All four websites were designed by NextStage Evolution (NSE).

3) W_0 was maintained and housed by NSE. The purpose of W_0 was to get responses from people versed in the field regarding changes and modifications to achieve the desired result.

4) Sites W_1, W_2 and W_3 were maintained and housed by an independent internet marketing consultant[h] (MC).

---

[h] – All independent contractor businesses and names are held in confidence by NextStage Evolution for future research and data integrity purposes. The names and addresses of the marketing consultant (MC), marketing research firm (MRF) and independent auditing group (IAG) are available to fully vetted partners for due diligence purposes and on an as needed basis only.

MC – The marketing consultant has over 20 years in the field and served as Director of Research in a nationally recognized firm for twelve years before going independent.

MRF – The market research firm used was founded in 1985, has a national presence and a worldwide reputation for comprehensive research services. Their staff includes members of the Marketing Research Association (MRA), the American Marketing Association (AMA) and the Council of American Survey Research Organizations (CASRO).

IAG – The independent auditing group consisted of a lawyer-accountant partnership skilled in technological evaluations.

5) W_1 was used to gather small world ControlGroup data (20 individuals).

6) W_2 was used to gather TrainingGroup data (300 individuals).

7) W_3 was used to gather TestGroup data (300 individuals).

8) The small world ControlGroup (W_1) population consisted of individuals both known to and selected by NSE, and was used to confirm and proof the test methodology.

9) The MC and NSE worked together during the W_1 proof and testing phase to insure that the MC understood the test requirements and was comfortable and able to administer and monitor the test correctly.

10) The TrainingGroup (W_2) population consisted of individuals comprising a marketing research panel.

11) The TestGroup (W_3) population consisted of individuals comprising a marketing research panel that was wholly separate and unique from TrainingGroup (W_2) individuals.

12) The Test- and Training- Group's exact demographics were known only to the MRF and the MC.

13) The marketing research panels were contracted through a third-party marketing research firm (MRF).

14) The MRF was contracted through the MC.

15) NSE had no contact with the MRF or any of the marketing research panels.

16) Only the MC had contact with the MRF.

17) NSE had no knowledge of the Test- or Training- Group's exact demographics other than those specified in item 18 below.

18) NSE requested that the Test- and Training- Group demographics be:

- 17-75 years old
- mixed male and female
- diverse income groups
- diverse ethnicity
- continental USA geographic locations

19) The MRF had no knowledge of the Training- or Test-Group questionnaire's purpose or intention.

20) The MRF did have knowledge of the Training- and Test-Group questionnaire's elements, look and feel but not its intention.

21) Web page navigation for all groups was through a four page solicitation form:

> 21.a) an Introductory page followed by
> 21.b) a 1st level Survey page followed by
> 21.c) a 2nd level Survey page followed by
> 21.d) a Thank You page

22) The purpose of the individual pages was as follows:

> 22.a) The Introductory page was designed to create a baseline for psychomotor behavioral measurement and to determine a "neutral" $\{C,B/e,M\}$[51,52,116,119-121,124,126,127,135-137,236] matrix for each user.
> 22.b) The 1st level Survey page was designed to force specific personality aspects to dominate non-conscious neural activity.
> 22.c) The 2nd level Survey page was designed to demonstrate those specific personality aspects of non-conscious neural activity.
> 22.d) The Thank You page was designed to return visitors to their neutral $\{C,B/e,M\}$[51,124,126,127,137,236] matrix states.

23) All groups (W_1, W_2, W_3) interacted with identical Introductory pages (figure 1, page 215).

24) The entirety of the TrainingGroup (W_2) and select members of the small world ControlGroup (W_1) interacted with the 1st level Survey page shown in figure 2 (page 216). This page included two questions (age, gender) not included in the TestGroup (W_3) 1st Level Survey page to determine self-identification error rates for the final determination.

25) The entirety of the TestGroup (W_3) and select members of the small world ControlGroup (W_1) interacted with the 1st level Survey page shown in figure 3 (page 217).

26) The entirety of the TrainingGroup (W_2) and select members of the small world ControlGroup (W_1) interacted with the 2nd level Survey page shown in figure 4 (page 218).

27) The entirety of the TestGroup (W_3) and select members of the small world ControlGroup (W_1) interacted with the 2nd level Survey page shown in figure 5 (page 219).

28) All Groups (W_1, W_2, W_3) interacted with identical Thank You pages (figure 6, page 219) as part of the study.

29) All NSE access to W_2 and W_3 was removed before the study went live.

30) All Training- (W_2) and Test- Group (W_3) questionnaire results data, along with all marketing research panel demographic data, were maintained by the MC.

31) NSE delivered ET predictions based on the W_3 data collected by its "bug" to an independent auditing group (IAG) for final evaluation.

32) The MC delivered the W_3 data to the IAG.

33) After delivering the W_3 data to the IAG, the MC delivered the W_2 and W_3 data to NSE.

34) The IAG determined valid and invalid data points via a matched-pair algorithm between ET's W_3 gender and age predictions to the known W_3 demographic data supplied by the MC.

35) The IAG determined the accuracy of ET's W_3 gender and age predictions of collected data to the known W_3 demographic data supplied by the MC.

36) The accuracy determinations were then delivered by the IAG to NextStage Analytics (NSA).

37) NSE selected ten random W_3 data points and replaced them with ten randomly selected W_2 data points to provide internal controls on the TestGroup (W_3) data.

B.II.6 – Methodology

All fields of scientific research recognize the need to design a given test based on the desired outcomes.[43,50,202,240, 295,318,351] The concept is prevalent in modern physics when the detector is specifically designed to respond to a singular particle and in micro- and immuno-biology when the detecting mechanism is specifically designed to respond to a single (and often trace) signal. Rigorous parameters are required to ensure accurate results and highly controlled conditions are necessary to ensure the accuracy of data and maximize the information gathered.[221,293]

Step 22 (page 200) of the above protocol demonstrates first the creation of information specifically designed to force desired psychomotor behaviors ({C,B/e,M} matrices[51,117,124, 127,137,236]) to the fore for easier and more rapid identification. Questions 1 and 2 on both W_2 and W_3 1st Level Survey pages will exaggerate female-age behaviors, questions 1 and 3 on these same pages will exaggerate male-age behaviors. The images presented on both W_2 and W_3 2nd Level Survey pages will exaggerate age-based behaviors and attenuate male/female dominant behaviors.

In this research model, the questions, colors, font, logo image, etc., and a multitude of other variables were coded to maximize the probabilities of determining the desired information. For example, this test was performed only in the USA and during the first few weeks of April '09. At this time the USA and world were in a well recognized and publicized economic recession. All news outlets had daily reports of people losing jobs, losing homes and other assorted economic hardships. In addition, the first few weeks of April are "tax time" for the majority of USA citizens. Thus these questions were tied to the majority consciousness, the colors and logo image used on all but the 2nd Level Survey pages were used intentionally to isolate specific, desired traits and behaviors, and the sudden introduction of color images and higher reasoning question on the 2nd Level Survey pages to attenuate those traits and behaviors.[15,58,78,80,207, 229,257,299]

The NextStage term for these traits and behaviors when applied to these and similar information streams is *Priority Trees*. The human brain is designed to consciously process information via a step-wise methodology, non-consciously via a more distributed and integrative methodology.[77,156,213,240, 297,350] In this case, people create a decision about the information based on a series of micro-decisions made about the different elements of an object/image/situation as they come into our consciousness. What elements come into consciousness is determined by non-conscious filters that are created and internalized in response to the greater information environment (tax time, economic hardship, etc).

Steps 4 (page 198), 30 (page 201) and 34 (page 201) of the above protocol demonstrate that necessary and independent personnel were trained on various aspects of the test including and not limited to implementation, data collection and collation, and results calculation and presentation.

Steps 30 (page 201) and 31 (page 201) of the above protocol demonstrate that controls were applied to how the data was collected, and step 34 (page 201) demonstrates that only correctly formatted data was used in the study (all data due to internet transmission errors, incomplete data packets, communication losses between browser and server, etc., were eliminated before final determinations were made).

Specific to step 34 (page 201), the IAG determined that NSE's preferred method for determining age was too restrictive (an exact determination of age and a determination of age range, see the **Results** section starting on page 209). The progressions demonstrated in figures 7 (page 220) and 8 (page 221) demonstrate the IAG's analysis of the data sets.

Figure 7 shows ET's age estimate errors in years for ET's calculation of a given visitor's exact chronologic age. Figure 8 shows ET's age estimate errors by number of errors within a ± group.

Steps 5 (page 199) through 37 (page 201) of the above protocol address the need to run samples (small world and large world), isolate samples outside of a 2σ range, duplicate sampling for data outside 2σ, that no samples were above or below what ET could measure, etc.

For example, the W_2 and W_3 runs were necessary to determine self-identification errors – the panel participant answered the W_2 age and gender questions incorrectly according to demographic data supplied by the MRF – that might influence the final outcome as well as to isolate occurrences of *professional test-taker bias.*[119,120,122,135,136,336] Note that the average age estimate error is roughly ±3.18years, well within the 2σ of 14.96 years, and that there was a single data point outside the 2σ range, at +23 years. It was determined that this single data point (a possible self-identification error) didn't warrant further investigation. W_2 self-identification errors were 1%, equal to ET's calculation error.[i]

Note that the complete protocol described above need only be modified slightly to test for other {C,B/e,M} matrix states.[51,52,116,117,119-122,124,126,127,137,236]

Step 37 (page 201) of the above protocol demonstrates that known W_2 samples were randomly introduced into the W_3 data without affecting results (removing any ten randomly selected W_3 data points doesn't adversely affect the final determinations and definitely does not negatively impact the 2σ range).

Step 9 (page 199) of the above protocol demonstrates that the MC was properly trained in the administration, maintenance and protocol of the test.

Lastly, no outgroup testing was performed. Outgroup testing may be performed in the future (perhaps through person-to-person interviews in a social setting) to determine how public self-identification errors may affect private error placement.

---

[i] – If anything, this correlation between self-identification error and ET's calculation error would make a worthwhile study to determine how many panel participants had someone else take the survey. The implications to learning that 1% or greater of a given population isn't who they claim has eCommerce information value.

B.II.7 – Caveats

A) The test detailed in this paper was designed to capture point-to-point gender and age data points. Participants, MC and MRF were not informed ahead of time what the true purpose of the test was (this test used the Chinese General Solicitation information discovery methodology[61,72,82,96, 143,147]). No placebos were constructed or needed for this test as people did not know what they were actually being tested for.

B) This test should be considered a unique event; ET data was matched to unique individuals, normally a violation of NSE's privacy policies[j] and something that won't be repeated in the future.

C) It must be understood that normal eCommerce and related web exchanges are more significant using neurologic results rather than biologic results.

D) Different tests would need to be constructed, developed and run to measure other recognizable interaction elements such as engagement, attention, buying attitude, intender status, etc.

E) It must be understood that NSE does not claim to be able to produce the results demonstrated in this paper and by this test on a "standard" information piece (web page, print out, TV spot, etc.). Standard information exchanges are rarely if ever designed to isolate psychomotor, psycho- or emotional-cognitive or {C,B/e,M} matrix states.[51,52,79,90,116,117,119-122,124,126,127,137,236]

B.II.8 – The Role of Neurologic Age and Gender in Marketing

It is understood that nobody's brain and mind is exclusively male *or* female.[3,5,175,180,268,287,305] At least not people you want to know, to talk to, to have in your home, and definitely not anybody you want to sell anything to. People's brains are designed to express both male *and* female tendencies. How much of each depends on lots of factors (currently ET tracks over 90 separate factors to make its determinations). Recent studies have

[j] – http://nlb.pub/C

indicated that the brain's sexual development begins in utero and even before gender-basing hormones come into play.[173] Those studies are valid and only partially deal with what is being discussed in this paper.

Reproductive physiology (and what are known as primary and secondary sexual characteristics) don't play that much of a role in most marketing. The concept of "sex sells" and the facts of reproductive physiology are far removed from each other for all but a select few products and services.

What ET does is make predictions based on how populations interact with information in their environment[52,59, 116,119-121,123,125,126,128,129] (in the eCommerce case, a site visitor population, the presentation of information on that site and other environmental, horologic, cultural and related factors).

Consider someone interacting with an information presentation[53,54,59,84-86,125,136,212,240,274,301] (navigating a website). They traverse three pages, 1, 2 and 3 and demonstrate the following male/female cognitive patterns while navigating each page.

Page	Female %	Male %
1	46	54
2	50	50
3	52	48

Note that these percentages are measurements of psychomotor behavioral patterns (neurology, not biology). Average the above values out and you have someone whose neurologic gender[17,33,48,84-86,110,149,168,173,176,184,194,204,205, 209,211,212,216-218,228,231,244,292,325,333] (an element of their thinking pattern or {C, B/e, M} matrix[51,117,122,124,127,137,236]) is roughly 51% male, 49% female. This determination has nothing to do with biology or physiology and everything to do with how their brain fires as they're interacting with the information immediately in their environment.

The majority of people interacting with an information presentation (navigating a website) may be using male cognitive patterns during their interaction but this doesn't mean they are necessarily biologically male. What it does mean is that the information presentation and their immediate environment require male cognitive patterns in order to be incorporated into consciousness.

This information is extremely useful in education, marketing, any endeavor that requires subjects be able to respond correctly and as desired to an environmental stimulus (a conversion process, clicking through to a purchase, etc.). Material requiring male cognitive patterns can be incorporated by biologic females and vice versa depending on system, situational and environmental conditions, thus the information gathered by ET is best used to ensure that information is properly designed for the desired audience.

Where this really comes into play is when you're asking or inviting subjects to make some kind of decision.[29,124,127,156, 167,185,213,226,240,250,267,273,283,350] There are everyday decisions that biologic males and females make that require female cognitive patterns and every day decisions that require male cognitive patterns regardless of biologic gender.

Basic information design[53] and semantic information mechanics[54] can be described by the following simple formula:[121,132]

$$A + B = C$$

This formula takes the form:

The Subject + The Information = The Response

Consider how this concept can be used to determine neurologic gender and other factors of interest. Determining neurologic gender ratios in large populations is not difficult because all possible responses to the question "What gender are you?" is a remarkably small, countable set (the binary set $C \equiv \{M,F\}\ ||\ \{0,1\})^k$.

However, all possible As ("The Subject" in the above equation) is a very large, countably infinite set (there is a countably finite number of subjects available to interact with any information presentation, $S \equiv |_0{}^\infty s\ ||\ s \in S$). The simple formula becomes an equation when the only Bs ("The Information" in the above equation) used are elements of an extremely small, countably well-defined set, specifically a set that only contains elements that will isolate the Cs (in this case, neurologic gender) from all the given As^l. NSE has authored and published information as far back as the late 1990s (see **B.I – Susan's Proof of Concept** (page 187), originally published in 2003 and based on data collected from 1999 to 2002).

Specifically to marketing purposes, when someone is 99% of something neurologically but their neurology doesn't match their biology, how do you market to them? The safest move would be to market to their neurology (based on traditional psycho-therapeutic models). Any individual exerting that much energy to neurologically be something they're biologically or chronologically not is non-consciously screaming their preference and forcing an external reality on them can only be done at all parties' peril.[93] You want to market to their inner fantasy – not their external reality – because the concept of sexuality is not the same as the concept of gender. All marketing is based on fantasy and the willing suspension of disbelief.[170,342] Selling a 53-year-old male an "arrest-me-red" muscle car is often a sell to that male's fantasy concept of their sexuality and age, not to their biologic and chronologic identity. Thus testing for the client's self-concept (self-identification) rather than what society imposes on them ("act your age", "are you a man or not?") is the marketer's imperative.

The methodology used in this test was based on an advanced understanding of information design[53] and mechanics,[54] and

---

^{k} – ET actually recognizes five different genders in most populations we've studied.
^{l} – This is really nothing more than the Venturi Principle applied to information design and (semantic) information mechanics.

gender- and age-specific elements contained in the {C, B/e, M} matrix.[51,52,116,117,119-122,124,126,127,135,137,236]

B.II.9 – Technology Constraints – Spectacular Errors and Their Meanings

ET responds with the equivalent understanding and mentality of a 1½-2-year-old[m] to how individuals are "acting in the moment", what is known as *present-time consciousness*.[8,197,328] Children at that age don't differentiate male/female as adults do, they differentiate male/female by proto-conceptual patterns; principal care-giver, principal provider.[165,170,181,255,256,291,341,344,349] Also they have no conscious recognition of past or future unless cognitively forced to consider absent time situations. For the purposes of this paper, these two "principle" symbols can mix and overlap which is why early childhood (pre- and near-lingual) gender-identity confusion occurs more and more often in modern society and disappears as the child enters adolescence.

ET makes many of its gender determinations based on the demonstration of care-giving and providing behaviors. In very large numbers (real large-world studies such as suggested in **B.II.2.a – For Researchers**, page 196) these still tend to balance out to what adults recognize as male and female. In small numbers (real small-world studies, populations less than 10,000) extra care needs to be taken in the information environment to "force" the proto-conceptual male/female behaviors to manifest along traditional gender lines.

ET is capable of some spectacular errors, the determination that someone in their late 20s is neurologically in their 80s being an example, or a male demonstrating 99% female patterns another.

B.II.10 – Results, Example Data Sets and Explanations

The final evaluation as determined by the IAG is as follows:

---

[m] – As of ET v0 (1999-2009). Currently ET is being modified to have the equivalent understanding and mentality of a 3-7-year-old.

Evaluation	Accuracy
ET's accuracy determining exact chronologic age of survey participant	7.33%[i]
ET's confidence in its exact chronologic age determination	64.82%[ii]
ET's accuracy determining chronologic age range of survey participant	98.00%[iii]
ET's confidence in its chronologic age range determination	**68.33%**[iv]
ET's accuracy determining physical gender of survey participant	99.33%[v]
ET's confidence in its physical gender determination	**75.29%**[vi]

[i] - ET was neither designed nor intended to determine exact chronologic age. The fact that we got 7.33% "dead-on" correct (22 out of 300) demonstrates the accuracy of this statement.

[ii] - As noted above, ET was designed to determine approximate neurologic age, not chronologic age. Its method can be conceptualized as someone sitting in a mall, watching people walk past and being asked 1) "How old do you think that person is?" ET answers some number and the follow-up is 2) "How sure are you that you're correct?" The number given here is the average surety (certainty) ET has that its estimate of chronologic age is correct. The fact that ET thought it was correct approximately 65% of the time and had a real accuracy of 7.33% demonstrates it should not be used for this purpose.

[iii] - ET's approximation of neurologic age is actually a determination of neurologic sophistication and maturity of information processing and retention. These roughly match out to the age groups -19, 19-24, 25-34, 35-44, 45-54, 55-59, 60-64, 65-74, 75+ years old. Here ET was able to match these elements to chronologic age groups with a 98% accuracy (an average error of ±3.18 years). This test was highly exceptional in that the

information presentation and cultural environment allowed for exceptional accuracy in matching neurologic to chronologic age range. However, it must be noted that rarely are information presentations so well-designed and cultural environments shift on a daily if not more frequent basis.

[iv] - Following on items i and ii above, ET's confidence in its ability to determine neurologic age is approximately 68%. It is worth noting that this is only less than four points from its totally erroneous confidence in exact age determination, proving you can trust its confidence in the latter and not the former.

[v] - ET is designed to determine neurologic gender, not biologic gender. As noted in item iii above, this test was highly exceptional. The caveats presented in item iii above and throughout this paper must be applied in a real-world situation.

[vi] - Using the example described in item iii above, ET is asked 1) "Do you think that person's a male or a female?" and the answer is followed up with 2) "How sure are you?" The 75.29% value indicates that ET is confident 3/4 of the time when calculating neurologic gender.

B.II.11 – Results TakeAway

While it is accurate to say that ET can sometimes predict biologic gender and chronologic age to an accuracy in the high 90%s, it is much more realistic to state that ET can most often predict neurologic age and gender to about 75% accuracy. This latter value is in accord with previous age and gender tests of the technology (see *B.II.2.a For Researchers*, page 196, and *B.I – Susan's Proof of Concept*, page 187).

B.II.12 – Sample Data

NSE ID	Demographic Data Provided by market research firm			Age Estimate (years)	Age Range Low (years)	Age Range High (years)	Age Estimate Confidence (%)	Gender Estimate	Gender Estimate Confidence (%)
	Age	Gender							
jdchfcagfdhdf	29	Female	f	30.8	25	34	64.75	F	60.75
jdchfcaijfodc	48	Male	m	50	45	54	78	M	70.5
jdchfcaiaehie	28	Male	m	24	0	24	62	M	59
jdchfcaigcffi	39	Female	f	44	35	44	50	F	92
jdchfcbjdddec	66	Female	f	67	65	74	50	F	89
jdchfcbadahda	38	Female	f	40	35	44	50	F	56
jdchfcbcibfej	55	Male	m	48	45	54	50	M	79
jdchfcbdbacge	78	Male	m	78.3	75	125	67.17	M	76.83
jdchfcbfibjgh	61	Male	m	58.8	55	64	66.25	M	71.5
jdchfcbgfieca	50	Male	m	48	45	54	91	M	99
jdchfccjagjih	41	Female	f	37	35	44	67.25	F	77
jdchfccaciija	62	Male	m	58	55	64	50	M	84
jdchfccdeacdb	44	Male	m	39	35	44	50	M	91
jdchfccfgafef	61	Male	m	60.3	55	64	75.75	M	75.5
jdchfcdahghij	41	Male	m	40.5	35	44	71	M	65
jdchfcdoeebbf	61	Female	f	58.8	55	64	68.75	F	82.75
jdchfcdeefjgh	47	Male	m	54	45	54	54	M	98
jdchfcecegej	70	Male	m	65	65	74	88	M	95
jdchfceeeacij	57	Female	f	63	55	64	50	F	94
jdchfceeehoeb	66	Male	m	71	65	74	50	M	81
jdchfcefhichi	62	Female	f	60	55	64	50	F	70
jdchfceidddfh	42	Male	m	41.5	35	44	86.5	M	89.75
jdchfcfajhjqf	66	Male	m	68	65	74	75	M	81
jdchhiajgibdb	59	Female	f	59.3	55	64	81.5	F	81.75
jdchhigggfjgh	54	Male	m	52	45	54	50	M	88
jdchijbhabfff	23	Female	f	23	0	24	68	F	88
jdchijfafifhg	53	Female	f	51	45	54	50	F	78
jdchijfbhebcd	38	Male	m	41	35	44	65.5	M	69.5
jdchiajdhhbda	54	Female	f	52	45	54	85	F	100
jdchichhbabjj	28	Female	f	30	25	34	73	F	83
jdchidecehjdf	56	Male	m	55	55	64	88	M	95
jdchiedjajaii	70	Male	m	70	65	74	50	M	70
jdchifbiiejjj	61	Female	f	60.5	55	64	67	F	80.25
jdchifdbihhec	61	Female	f	56	55	64	52	F	96
jdchifgibeeic	57	Female	f	58	55	64	50	F	77
jdchifijcjagc	64	Female	f	57	55	64	78.75	F	74.75
jdchifigeajba	23	Female	f	23	0	24	64	F	70
jdchigaebadce	63	Male	m	64	55	64	50	M	100
jdchigdiiboei	51	Male	m	45	45	54	67	M	53
jdchigeiejbeh	24	Female	f	21.5	0	24	83.25	F	82.75
jdchighbiahbh	29	Male	m	34	25	34	50	M	77
jdchihabggech	45	Female	f	38	35	44	85.5	F	72.25
jdchiheejbhib	51	Male	m	49.8	45	54	70.5	M	64.25
jdchiijaejfbd	61	Female	f	61	55	64	50	F	73
jdchiiiabgdca	26	Female	f	29	25	34	68.5	F	79

| | 49.58 | | | 48.543667 | | | 65.776367 | | 75.5554 |

NSE ID	Demographic Data Provided by market research firm			Age Accuracy	Age Accuracy within one year	Age Prediction Proximity	Age Range Accuracy	Age Estimate Confidence Accuracy	Gender Accuracy	Gender Confidence Accuracy
	Age	Gender								
jdchfcagfdhd	29	Female	f	0	0	1.8	1	64.75	1	60.75
jdchfcaijfodo	48	Male	m	0	0	2	1	78	1	70.5
jdchfcaiaehie	28	Male	m	0	0	4	0	38	1	59
jdchfcaigdfi	39	Female	f	0	0	5	1	50	1	92
jdchfcbjdddec	66	Female	f	0	1	1	1	50	1	89
jdchfcbadahda	38	Female	f	0	0	2	1	50	1	56
jdchfcbcibfej	55	Male	m	0	0	7	1	50	1	79
jdchfcbdbacge	78	Male	m	0	1	0.3	1	67.17	1	76.83
jdchfcbfibjgh	61	Male	m	0	0	2.2	1	66.25	1	71.5
jdchfcbgfieca	50	Male	m	0	0	2	1	91	1	99
jdchfccjagjih	41	Female	f	0	0	4	1	67.25	1	77
jdchfccaciija	62	Male	m	0	0	4	1	50	1	84
jdchfccdeacdb	44	Male	m	0	0	5	1	50	1	91
jdchfccfgafef	61	Male		0	1	0.7	1	75.75	1	75.5
jdchfcdahghij	41	Male	m	0	1	0.5	1	71	1	65
jdchfcdoeebbf	61	Female	f	0	0	2.2	1	68.75	1	82.75
jdchfcdeefgh	47	Male	m	0	0	7	1	54	1	98
jdchfcecegejj	70	Male	m	0	0	5	1	88	1	95
jdchfceeeacij	57	Female	f	0	0	6	1	50	1	94
jdchfceeehoeb	66	Male	m	0	0	5	1	50	1	81
jdchfcefhichi	62	Female	f	0	0	2	1	50	1	70
jdchfceidddfh	42	Male	m	0	1	0.5	1	86.5	1	89.75
jdchfcfajhjgl	66	Male	m	0	0	2	1	75	1	81
jdchhiajgjbdb	59	Female	f	0	1	0.3	1	81.5	1	81.75
jdchhigggfjgh	54	Male	m	0	0	2	1	50	1	88
jdchijbhabff	23	Female	f	1	1	0	1	68	1	88
jdchijfafifhg	53	Female	f	0	0	2	1	50	1	78
jdchijfbhebod	38	Male	m	0	0	3	1	65.5	1	69.5
jdchiajdhhbda	54	Female	f	0	0	2	1	85	1	100
jdchichhbabj	28	Female	f	0	0	2	1	73	1	83
jdchideoehjdf	56	Male	m	0	1	1	1	88	1	95
jdchiedjajai	70	Male	m	1	1	0	1	50	1	70
jdchifbiiejj	61	Female	f	0	1	0.5	1	67	1	80.25
jdchiidbihheo	61	Female	f	0	0	5	1	52	1	96
jdchifgibexic	57	Female	f	0	1	1	1	50	1	77
jdchiiijdjago	64	Female	f	0	0	7	1	78.75	1	74.75
jdchiiigeajba	23	Female	f	1	1	0	1	64	1	70
jdchigaebadoe	63	Male	m	0	1	1	1	50	1	100
jdchigdiboei	51	Male	m	0	0	6	1	67	1	53
jdchigeiejbeh	24	Female	f	0	0	2.5	1	83.25	1	82.75
jdchighbiahbh	29	Male	m	0	0	5	1	50	1	77
jdchihabggech	45	Female	f	0	0	7	1	85.5	1	72.25
jdchiheejbhib	51	Male	m	0	0	1.2	1	70.5	1	64.25
jdchiiaejfbd	61	Female	f	1	1	0	1	50	1	73
jdchiiiabgdoa	26	Female	f	0	0	3	1	68.5	1	79
				22	74		294		298	
	49.58			7.33%	24.67%	3.177667	98.00%	64.77%	99.33%	75.29%

B.II.13 - Images and Charts

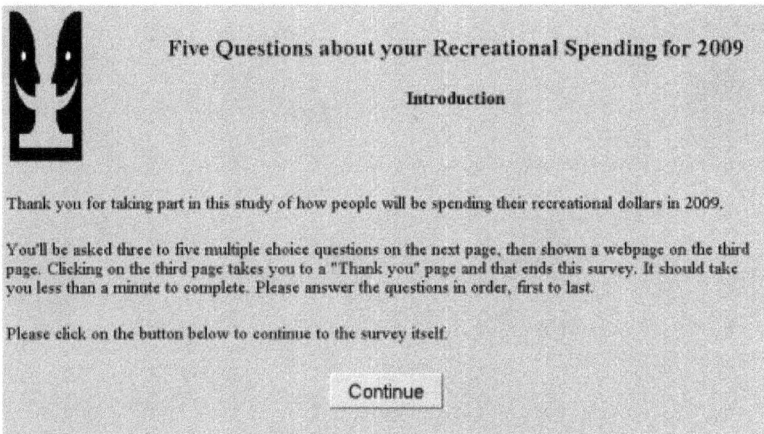

Five Questions about your Recreational Spending for 2009

Introduction

Thank you for taking part in this study of how people will be spending their recreational dollars in 2009.

You'll be asked three to five multiple choice questions on the next page, then shown a webpage on the third page. Clicking on the third page takes you to a "Thank you" page and that ends this survey. It should take you less than a minute to complete. Please answer the questions in order, first to last.

Please click on the button below to continue to the survey itself.

Continue

Figure B.II.1 - All Groups (W_1)(W_2)(W_3) interacted with this
Introductory page

Figure B.II.2 - The entirety of the TrainingGroup (W$_2$) and select members of the small world ControlGroup (W$_1$) interacted with this 1st Level Survey page

Five Questions about your Recreational Spending for 2009

Survey

1) How will you be spending the majority of your recreational dollars in 2009?

Travel ⚬   Music ⚬   Movies/ Theater ⚬   Dining Out ⚬   DVDs/ Videos ⚬   None of these ⚬

2) What portion of your 2009 budget is for recreation?

0% ⚬   0-10% ⚬   10-25% ⚬   25-50% ⚬   50% or more ⚬

3) Do you believe your financial situation will improve in 2009?

Yes ⚬   No ⚬   Stay the same ⚬

Submit Form

Figure B.II.3 - The entirety of the TestGroup (W₃) and select members of the small world ControlGroup (W₁) interacted with this 1st Level Survey page

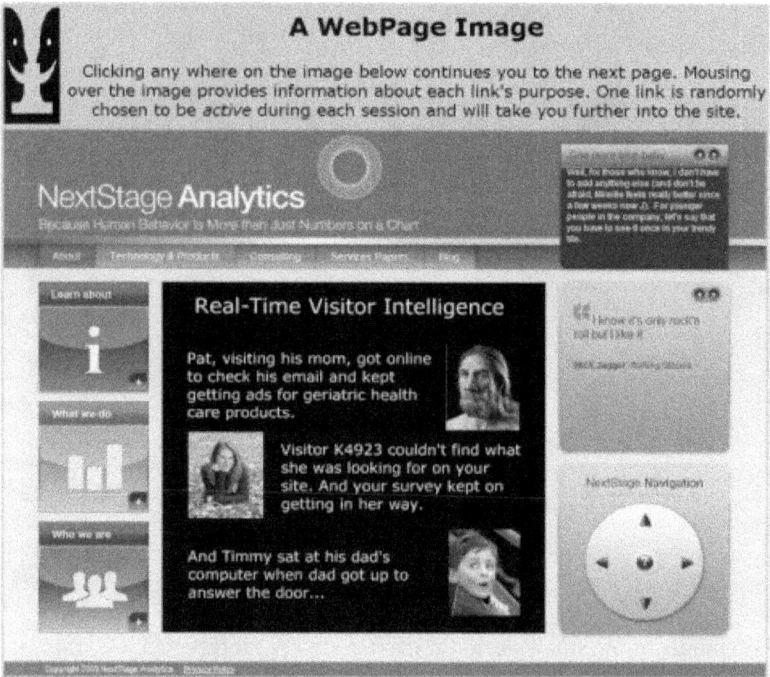

Figure B.II.4 - The entirety of the TrainingGroup (W₂) and select
members of the small world ControlBroup (W₁) interacted with this as
the 2nd level Survey page

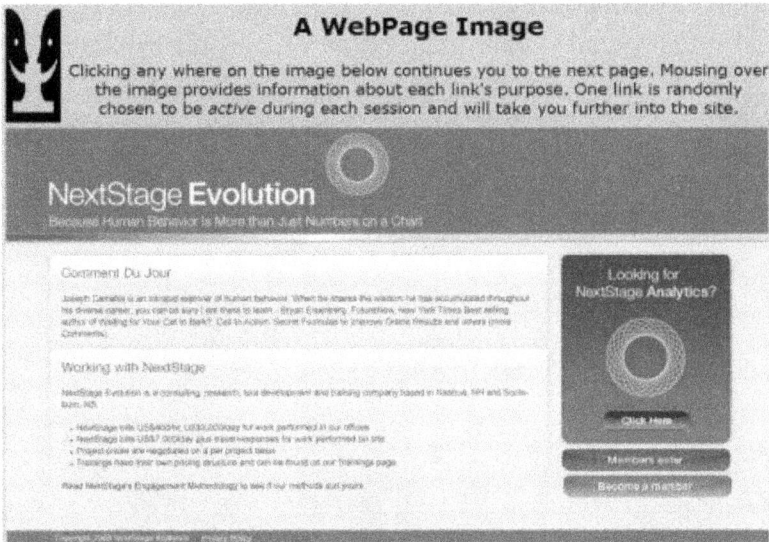

Figure B.II.5 - The entirety of the TestGroup (W₃) and select members of the small world ControlGroup (W₁) interacted with this 2nd Level Survey page

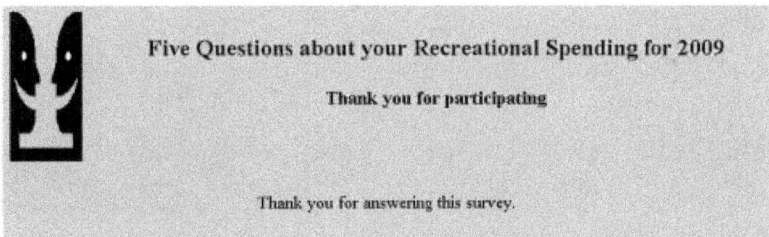

Figure B.II.6 - All groups (W₁, W₂, W₃) saw the same Thank You Page

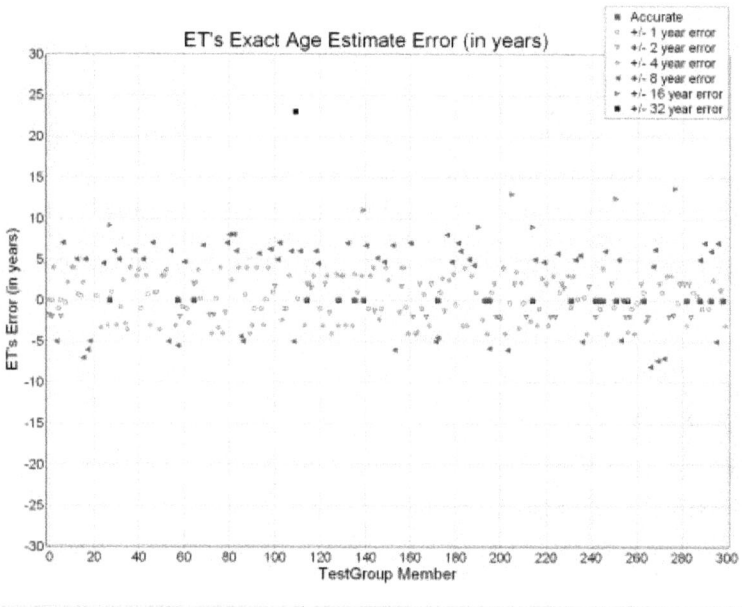

Figure B.II.7 - ET's chronologic age guesses will never be completely
accurate as ET determines neurologic age and people never think (or
act) their age

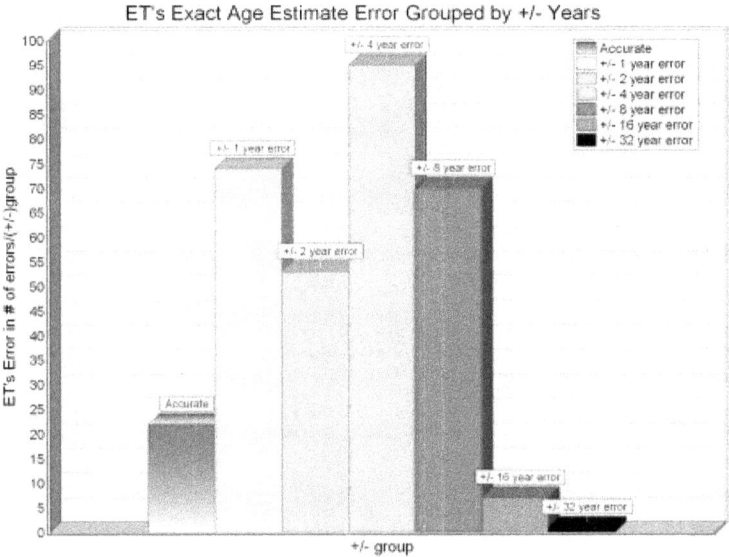

Figure B.II.8 - ET's chronologic age estimate errors by ±groups. The roughly bell shape of this curve is a byproduct of ET's use of probability solids to determine the meanings of psychomotor behavioral cues

Human learning is rooted in conversations. Learning conversations are collaborative inquiries between people and among groups of people in which the possibilities for breakthrough thinking, insight, and innovation are enhanced. Learning conversations are a way of generating questions that matter.

— Brown and Isaacs, 1997

B.III – I Am the Intersection of Four Statements[n]

I've previously mentioned Evolution Technology's *Language Engines* (see ***IV.9 – Teaching ET to Grow Older (Politics 2008)***, page 143ff) without really going into detail on what the Language Engines actually are. In a nutshell, they emulate the brain's language centers. The original *I Am the Intersection of Four Statements* explained about the Language Engines and how they function, and a-high level understanding of them may help readers better understand some of ET's capabilities.

We're going to get into *Modality Engineering*, something that NextStage's Language Engines do when they do...well...anything. Our "sentiment analysis[o]" tool uses equations derived from Modality Engineering to make its determinations. We've written a whitepaper, *A Primer on Modality Engineering*, which is available to NextStage Members[p] as part of their membership benefits.

A long time ago (mid to late 1980s) I studied mathematical linguistics (I still do, as much as one can).

Unfortunately, mathematical linguistics no longer exists as a discipline (as far as I know). The late 1980s was when recognizable computing power moved from computer rooms to desktops and cycle time became cheap. *Mathematical* linguistics quickly became *computational* linguistics because it was easier (I'm guessing here) for people to use software than to actually understand the underlying principles of what they were doing.

This week four different individuals made four different statements about me based on their personal experience of me. My mathematical linguistics nerves tingled because I recognized the four statements as mathematically orthogonal and that "I" was the intersection of their four statements.

---

[n] – This is an abridged version of the "I Am the Intersection of Four Statements" blog post. The charts presented here are different from the originals as ET is now incorporating cultural variants immediately. You can read the full, original post at http://nlb.pub/D
[o] – http://nlb.pub/E
[p] – http://nlb.pub/F

This means one could mathematically determine how well the five of us would get along together should the situation ever arise. Mathematically, are there certain conditions such that all four statements must be simultaneously true?

Whoa!, don't you think?

The four statements are:

1) You are somebody that transmits confidence. And I have to admit that sometimes I'm concerned when I want to convince you of something as I know you'll know more facts than I will and it won't matter what we're talking about.

2) You have a knack for bringing out people's lack of self-confidence. People don't like to be corrected, even in private (I've never seen you publicly correct anybody) and when *you* correct someone (even in private) it's like being hit by a firehose. "How does he know all this stuff?" People have faith in your being correct and in their being wrong.

3) Your commitment to the truth outweighs your commitment to people's feelings – particularly when dealing with idiots or assholes – but it's a close race.

4) Everybody I know thinks you're a great guy. Everybody likes you. But everybody's intimidated by you, too, because they go around saying they're experts in something, you say you're not an expert in anything and you always know more about their field than they do so they end up feeling like impostors.

I was particularly taken by the use of the term "impostor". I've met lots of people whom I recognize as dealing with what's called "The Impostor Syndrome" -- a core belief that they are not able to do what they claim to be able to do, basically not who they say they are or that what they do doesn't do what it claims to do (see **Section II.3 – Core, Identity and Personality**, page 67). I'll point them out to you the next time we're at a conference together.

Most people don't recognize that language and mathematics are both symbolic representations of internal reality. Mathematics is nothing more than a language itself, merely a specialized language. For that matter, English is a specialized language. Only people who "know" English can understand it or even recognize it when spoken. The same is true for French, Mandarin, Lakotah, ... Want to have fun sometime? Listen to a native speaker of some language you've never heard before. Most people can't even figure out where words start and stop, it's all gibberish (someday let's talk about glossolalia).

So language – any language – is just as symbolic a representation of reality as mathematics is. The symbols may be different ("±" rather than "plus or minus") and that's just a matter of translation.

So it occurred to me long, long ago that language – any language – could be symbolically represented by mathematical forms (and this gets into our first patent[q], a fun read in itself). All you needed was to know what mutually understandable information language – any language – was communicating.

Read that last sentence as "Determine the variables involved" and the mathematical forms pretty much reveal themselves to you.[r]

That first statement, "You are somebody that transmits confidence. And I have to admit that sometimes I'm concerned when I want to convince you of something as I know you'll know more facts than I will and it won't matter what we're talking about." becomes an equation that generates the graph shown in figure B.III-1 (page 226).

---

[q] – http://nlb.pub/B
[r] – *Note*: I've done lots of simplifying on the following graphs. Our current Modality Engineering system does calculations in a 92 dimension Hilbert space and collapses that space as necessary. These statements could be collapsed to about a 30 dimension Hilbert space. Colors, directions, placement, angle, shape, ..., everything has meaning in the following charts.

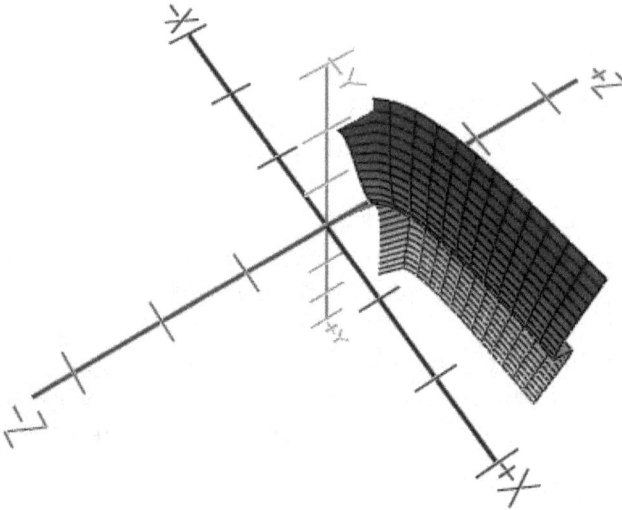

Figure B.III-1 A mathematical representation of "You are somebody
that transmits confidence. And I have to admit that sometimes I'm
concerned when talking with you as I know you'll know more facts than I
will and it won't matter what we're talking about."

The second statement, "You have a knack for bringing out
people's lack of self-confidence. People don't like to be corrected,
even in private (I've never seen you publicly correct anybody)
and when *you* correct someone (even in private) it's like being hit
by a firehose. 'How does he know all this stuff?' People have faith
in your being correct and in their being wrong." produces the
graph shown in figure B.III-2 (page 227).

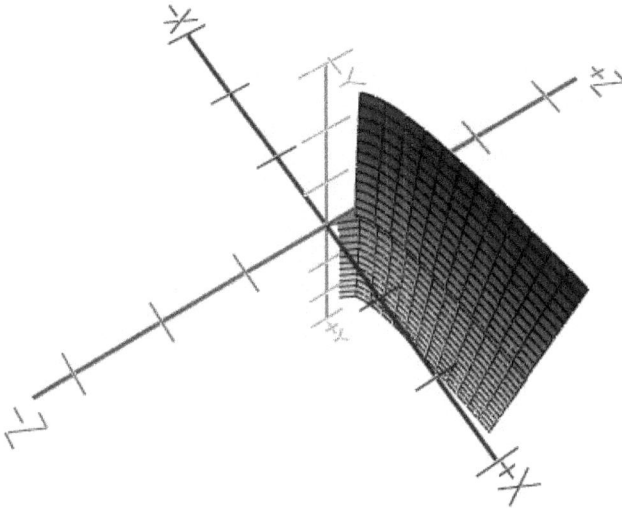

Figure B.III-2 A mathematical representation of "You have a knack for bringing out people's lack of self-confidence. People don't like to be corrected, even in private (I've never seen you publicly correct anybody) and when you correct someone (even in private) it's like being hit by a firehose. 'How does he know all this stuff?' People have faith in your being correct and in their being wrong."

Statement three, "Your commitment to the truth outweighs your commitment to people's feelings – particularly when dealing with idiots or assholes – but it's a close race." generates the graph shown in figure B.III-3 (page 228). Figures 1-3 may look similar and they're not. But let's finish with the basic charts first.

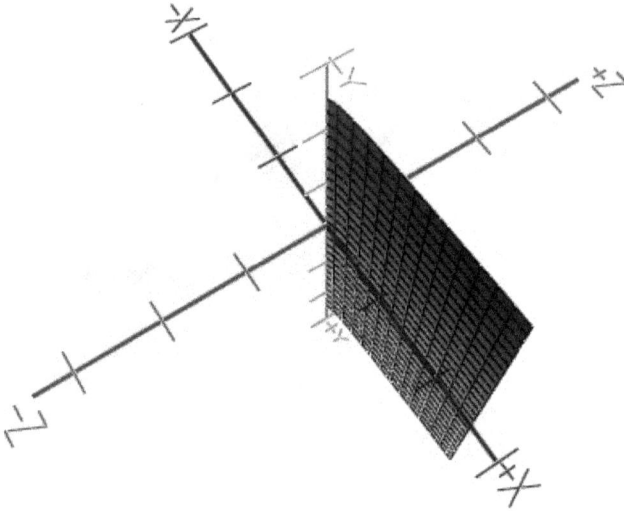

Figure B.III-3 The mathematical representation of "Your commitment
to the truth outweighs your commitment to people's feelings –
particularly when dealing with idiots or assholes – but it's a close race."

And finally, statement four, "Everybody I know thinks you're a great guy. Everybody likes you. But everybody's intimidated by you, too, because they go around saying they're experts in something, you say you're not an expert in anything and you always know more about their field than they do so they end up feeling like impostors." looks like figure B.III-4 (page 229).

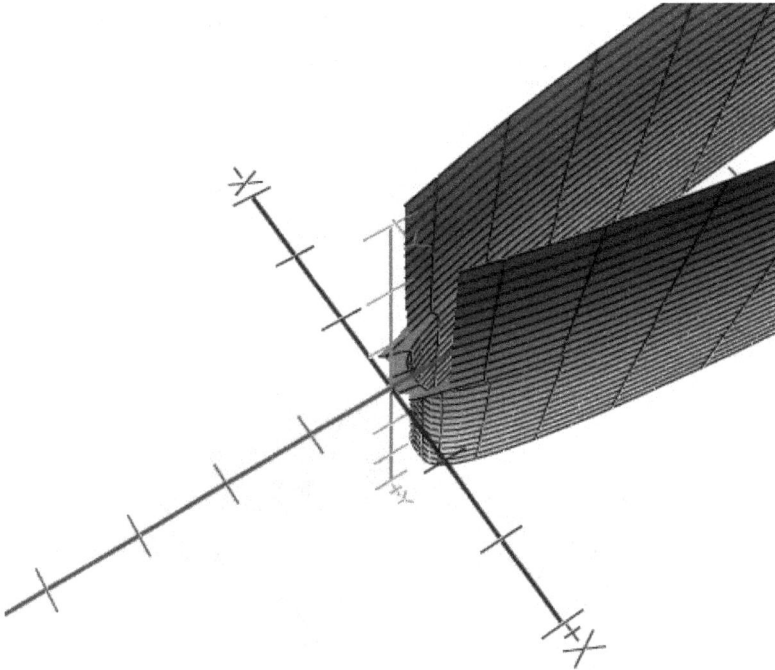

Figure B.III-4 The mathematical representation of "Everybody I know thinks you're a great guy. Everybody likes you. But everybody's intimidated by you, too, because they go around saying they're experts in something, you say you're not an expert in anything and you always know more about their field than they do so they end up feeling like imposters."

These four charts are mathematical representations of people's experiences. In this case, of me. Let's start putting these people in the same room. Let's match people to the statements. Statement 1 is made by "A", statement 2 by "B", statement 3 by "C" and statement 4 by "D".

What happens when A, C and I get together (figure B.III-5, page 230)? A and C have similar and not identical "concepts" of me (this is demonstrated by colors, distance and relative positions from the axes, planar presentations, ...). But – and this is the important *But* – if you were to change the scale of that image those two representations would intersect.

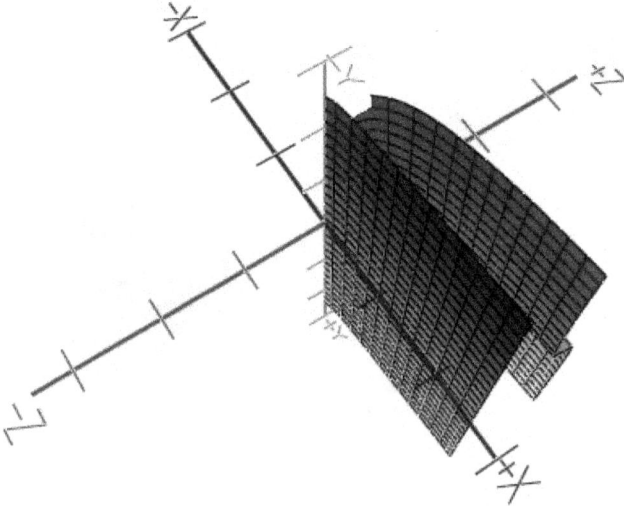

Figure B.III-5 A, C and I walk into a bar...

In other words, there would be certain topics, certain areas of discussion, certain activities that the three of us could participate in and have a great time.

But only certain topics, discussions or activities. And this is for A, C and me. Not A and me, not C and me, not A and C. It's only for A, C and me. Vary from those certain topics, etc., and things get uncomfortable. The further things stray the more uncomfortable (because the wider the separation between the two manifolds (or *concept spaces*)).

Let me give you a real-life example; you get together with a friend and a friend of that friend (anybody picking up the social implications of this?). You're all talking and chatting, maybe playing pool or darts, maybe in a theater line or at a game. Everything's going great. Then your friend or your friend's friend references something that was just between them and they laugh but you can't because you're not in on the joke.

They either have to bring you in on the joke to reestablish the social connectivity or they can continue down their road and you'll feel more and more astray. Needing to stay "on topic" so that the social connectivity remains in tact is a real-life example of the meaning of the A and C charts intersecting.

What happens when B, D and I get together (figure B.III-6, page 232)? The first thing to notice is that B and D do a lot more intersecting near the origin point. This means both of their concepts of me share quite a bit and only up to a point, literally points (actions, statements, activities, beliefs, ...) beyond which neither of them would believe me capable. What B completely accepts me capable of, D couldn't conceive of me doing and so on. It's not so much a question of limits and boundaries as it is "I couldn't imagine Joseph doing something like that". A and C could easily imagine me doing anything on their planes of my existence but I couldn't do anything off those planes of existence. B and D can imagine me doing lots more things than A and C can but there are things I'd do with B that D would find completely off the "Joseph map" and vice versa.

The next thing to notice is that B and D by themselves have similar colors in their charts of me (the areas at the bottom of both charts). This means they both and independently of each other have similar concepts of me. The fact that their charts merge and blend, some colors extending their range, some colors merging, is an indication that there's a great deal we could discuss in common, do in common, but if I "leaned" too much toward B-ish activity while D was around or too much toward D-ish activity while B was around, I'd probably lose one or the other as friends.

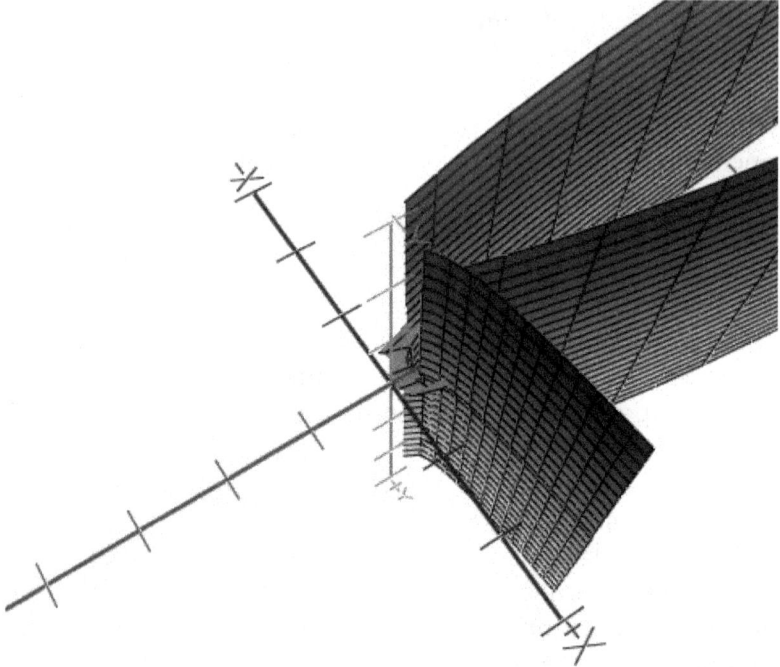

Figure B.III-6 B, D and I walk into a bar...

An example of this would be you, a friend and that friend's friend getting together and truly hitting it off. Private or in-jokes don't matter because there's enough shared concepts that everybody laughs and laughs harder when details are explained. The comfort level always remains high. But then B starts talking about a time B and I intentionally caused someone trauma. D is shocked, appalled and repulsed. They beg me to say it's a joke, that B is kidding. But when I confirm B's statement, D can't put that "territory" into D's "Joseph map" (can't accept the information into their "Joseph concept space") and our friendship ends.

What happens when the five of us go out for drinks or some such (figure B.III-7, page 233. Note that I've changed each chart to a single color for clarity)? Well, we shouldn't. It's as simple as that. A, B, D and I or B, C, D and I, yes, but the five of us – A, B, C , D and I – together?

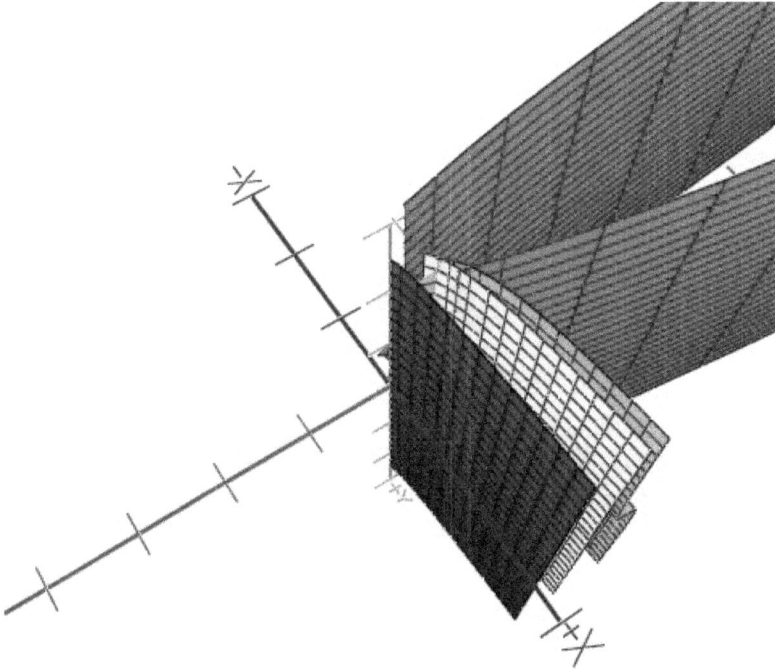

Figure B.III-7 A, B, C, D and I walk into a bar...and nobody comes out alive

Don't even attempt it. Oh, we'll be civil with each other, of course, but sooner rather than later A or C would find a reason to leave. Sadly, once A or C left the four remaining would suddenly get together fine. A or C, whoever was left, would put the blame on whomever left (non-consciously, of course), thinking the reason things picked up after the other left was because they were a poop of some kind.

The only other possibility is that A and C will focus on each other, B and D will focus on each other and I will have to "move" conversationally between them as both groups will want to pull me (again non-consciously) more in their direction.

Why is this so? Because the representations of A, B, D and I or B, C, D and I intersect but A, B, C, D and I don't. The intersection of A, C and I isn't even on the same scale as B, D and I, therefore such an encounter (in this limited scenario) would be doomed to fail.

B.III.1 – Using These Concepts

Let's say we're not a bunch of people going out for drinks or dinner or to the theater or even negotiating a contract (although using these principles for that makes things very fast and simple). Let's say you're putting up some marketing material (web page, TV spot, YouTube video, social campaign, radio spot, print, ...) and you know lots about your target audience...

...except *how they'll respond to it.*

Oh, you have an idea, an opinion maybe, and as John Erskine said, "Opinion is that exercise of the human will that allows us to make a decision without information."

But now you do know. With as much precision as you care to have (mathematically the 2nd and higher order elements can be forced to 0). All you need is some material from that target audience. Letters to the editor if you're going for a newspaper ad on or offline, blog entries (comments and posts) they've written if you're going purely online, snippets from a podcast or two if you're going for radio time or snatches from a call-in show. Same for video and TV. You get the idea.

Want to sell a car to A and C? You now can know the single selling point – the intersection of the two planes – that will motivate them both. Or to B and D? You now know the constellation of factors – the merged colors in their projections – that will sway them.

Or to sell bleach. Or TV sets. Or cell phone plans. Or jams and jellies. Or new products they've never seen before.

So now you can know with mathematical precision and certainty how well your marketing efforts will be received (something NextStage calls *Acceptance*, how long it will be remembered (branding), how often it will be talked about and passed on (something NextStage calls *Viral Capacity*), ... and probably more importantly what, *if anything, needs to be changed, by how much, in which direction,* ...

Probably the truly best part about all of this is that you never have to study these things, understand Modality Engineering beyond nodding appreciatively when I use the term, or even look at the types of charts I included above because ET will do it all for you.

Appendix C – Further Readings

People ask why I have so many references in my writings. Simple. Should anyone want to follow my reasoning, here you go. Some have claimed my long reference lists are an "appeal to authority". People who know me laugh every time they hear that[a].

1.   Abbott, A. (2002, 7 Mar). Music, maestro, please! *Nature, 416*(6876), 12–14. (Http://www.nature.com/nature/journal/v416/n6876/pdf/416 012a.pdf)
2.   Abbott, A. (2009, 27 Apr). Brain imaging skewed. *Nature, 458*(7242), 1087. (Http://www.nature.com/news/2009/090429/full/4581087a. html)
3.   Afraz, A., Pashkam, M. V., & Cavanagh, P. (2010, 7 Dec). Spatial Heterogeneity in the Perception of Face and Form Attributes. *Current biology: CB, 20*(23), 2112–2116. (Http://download.cell.com/current-biology/pdf/PIIS0960982210014429.pdf)
4.   Aho, A. V. (2004, 27 Feb). Software and the Future of Programming Languages. *Science, 303*(5662), 1331–1333. (Http://www.sciencemag.org/cgi/reprint/sci;303/5662/1331. pdf)
5.   Ainsworth, C. (2015, 15 Feb). Sex Redefined. *Nature, 518.* (Http://www.nature.com/polopoly_fs/1.16943!/menu/main/t opColumns/topLeftColumn/pdf/518288a.pdf)
6.   Aleksander, I., & Dunmall, B. (2003). Axioms and Tests for the Presence of Minimal Consciousness in Agents I: Preamble. *Journal of Consciousness Studies, 10*(4–5), 7–19. (Http://docserver.ingentaconnect.com/deliver/connect/imp/1 3558250/v10n4/s2.pdf?expires=1176670652&id=36910604& titleid=3956)

---

[a] – See "I'm the Intersection of Four Statements" http://nlb.pub/D

7.   Andersen, P. B. (1998). WWW as self-organizing system. *Cybernetics & Human Knowing, 5*(2).
8.   Arvidson, P. (2000). Transformations in consciousness: Continuity, the self and marginal consciousness. *Journal of Consciousness Studies, 7*(3), 3–26. (Http://www.ingentaconnect.com/search/article?title=Transfo rmations+in+Consciousness&title_type=tka&year_from=199 8&year_to=2009&database=1&pageSize=20&index=25)
9.   Aunger, R. (2002). *The Electric Meme: A New Theory of How We Think.* Simon&Schuster.
10.   Baars B.J. (1999, Feb/Mar). There is already a field of systematic phenomenology, and it's called 'psychology'. *Journal of Consciousness Studies, 6*(s 2–3), 216–218.
11.   Bailey A.R. (1999, Feb/Mar). Beyond the fringe: William James on the transitional parts of the stream of consciousness. *Journal of Consciousness Studies, 6*(s 2–3), 141–153.
12.   Bakan, D. (1980). On the effect of mind on matter. In R. Reiber (Ed.), *Body and Mind: Past, Present and Future.* Academic Press.
13.   Balter, M. (2004, 27 Feb). Search for the Indo-Europeans. *Science, 303*(5662), language; linguistics; psycholinguistics; sociolinguistics; neurolinguistics; semantics; semiotics; community; sociology;. (Http://www.sciencemag.org/cgi/reprint/sci;303/5662/1323. pdf)
14.   Balter, M. (2004, 27 Feb). Why Anatolia? *Science, 303*(5662). (Http://www.sciencemag.org/cgi/reprint/sci;303/5662/1324. pdf)
15.   Barinaga, M. (1995, 23 June). Remapping the motor cortex. *Science, 268*(5218), 1696–1698. (Http://www.sciencemag.org/cgi/reprint/sci;268/5218/1696. pdf)
16.   Barinaga, M. (1999, 2 Apr). Shedding Light on Visual Imagination. *Science, 284*(5411), 22. (Http://www.sciencemag.org/cgi/content/full/284/5411/22a)

17.   Baron-Cohen, S., Knickmeyer, R. C., & Belmonte, M. K. (2005, 4 Nov). Sex Differences in the Brain: Implications for Explaining Autism. *Science, 310*(5749), 819–823. (Http://www.sciencemag.org/cgi/reprint/310/5749/819.pdf)

18.   Barrs, B. (1997). *In the Theater of Consciousness: The Workspace of the Mind.* Oxford University: Oxford University Press.

19.   Belkin, N., Oddy, R., & Brooks, H. (1982, Sep). Ask for Information Retrieval Part 2 - Results of a Design Study. *The Journal of Documentation, 38*(2). (Http://comminfo.rutgers.edu/~belkin/articles/Belkin%20AS K%20p2.pdf)

20.   Benson J., Greaves W., O'Donnell M., & Taglialatela J. (2002). Evidence for Symbolic Language Processing in a Bonobo (Pan paniscus). *Journal of Consciousness Studies, 9*(12), 33–56.

21.   Berger, A., & Posner, M. (2000, January). Pathologies of brain attentional networks. *Neuroscience and Biobehavioral Reviews, 24*(1), 3–5. (Http://www.ingentaconnect.com/search/article?title=Orienti ng+of+attention&title_type=tka&author=Posner&year_from= 1900&year_to=2003&database=1&pageSize=20&index=5)

22.   Berger, D., & Schneck, D. (2003, Winter). The Use of Music Therapy as a Clinical Intervention for Physiologic Functional Adaptation. *Journal of Scientific Exploration, 17*(4), 689.

23.   Bernard, M. L. (2002, July). Examining the Effects of Hypertext Shape on User Performance. *Usability News (Software Usability Research Laboratory (SURL) at Wichita State University), 4*(2). (Http://www.surl.org/usabilitynews/42/hypertext.asp)

24.   Bernard, M., Liao, C., & Mills, M. (2001, Jan). Determining the Best Online Font for Older Adults. *Usability News (Software Usability Research Laboratory (SURL) at Wichita State University), 3*(1). (Http://www.surl.org/usabilitynews/31/fontSR.asp)

25.   Bernard, M., Mills, M., Frank, T., & McKown, J. (2001, Jan). Which Fonts Do Children Prefer to Read Online? *Usability News (Software Usability Research Laboratory (SURL) at Wichita State University), 3*(1). (Http://www.surl.org/usabilitynews/31/fontJR.asp)

26.   Bernard, M., Mills, M., Peterson, M., & Storrer, K. (2001, July). A Comparison of Popular Online Fonts: Which is Best and When? *Usability News (Software Usability Research Laboratory (SURL) at Wichita State University), 3*(2). (Http://www.surl.org/usabilitynews/32/font.asp)

27.   Bernard, M., & Mills, M. (2000, Jul). So, What Size and Type of Font Should I Use on My Website? *Usability News (Software Usability Research Laboratory (SURL) at Wichita State University), 2*(2). (Http://www.surl.org/usabilitynews/22/font.asp)

28.   Bernard, M. (1999, Jan). Preliminary Findings on the Use of Sitemaps. *Usability News (Software Usability Research Laboratory (SURL) at Wichita State University), 1*(1). (Http://www.surl.org/usabilitynews/11/pdf/Usability%20New s%2011%20-%20Bernard.pdf)

29.   Berns, G. S., Chappelow, J., Cekic, M., Zink, C. F., Pagnoni, G., & Martin-Skurski, M. E. (2006, 5 May). Neurobiological Substrates of Dread. *Science, 312*(5774), 754–758. (Http://www.sciencemag.org/cgi/reprint/312/5774/754.pdf)

30.   Bhattacharjee, Y. (2004, 27 Feb). From Heofonum to Heavens. *Science, 303*(5662), 1326–1328. (Http://www.sciencemag.org/cgi/reprint/sci;303/5662/1326.pdf)

31.   Bickerton, D. (1995). *Language and Human Behavior.* University of Washington: University of Washington Press.

32.   Bicknell, J. (2007). Explaining Strong Emotional Responses to Music. *Journal of Consciousness Studies, 14*(12), 5–23.

33.   Blinkhorn, S. (2005, 3 Nov). Intelligence: A gender bender. *Nature, 438*(7064), 31–32. (Http://www.nature.com/nature/journal/v438/n7064/pdf/438 031a.pdf)

34.   Bloj, M. G., Kersten, D., & Hurlbert, A. C. (1999, 23 Dec). Perception of three-dimensional shape influences colour perception through mutual illumination. *Nature, 402*(6764), 877–879. (Http://www.nature.com/nature/journal/v402/n6764/pdf/402877a0.pdf)

35.   Blood, A. J., & Zatorre, R. J. (2001, 25 Sep). Intensely pleasurable responses to music correlate with activity in brain regions implicated in reward and emotion. *Proceedings of the National Academy of Sciences of the United States of America, 98*(20), 11818–11823. (Http://www.pnas.org/content/98/20/11818.full.pdf+html)

36.   Bloom, P. (2001). Precis of How Children Learn the Meanings of Words. *Behavioral and Brain Sciences, 24,* 1095–1103.

37.   Bloom, P. (2004, 11 Jun). Can a Dog Learn a Word? *Science, 304*(5677), 1605–1606. (Http://www.sciencemag.org/cgi/reprint/sci;304/5677/1605.pdf)

38.   Bohannon, J. (2006, 10 Nov). Tracking People's Electronic Footprints. *Science, 314*(5801), 914–916. (Http://www.sciencemag.org/cgi/reprint/314/5801/914.pdf)

39.   Borgatti, S. P., Mehra, A., Brass, D. J., & Labianca, G. (2009, 13 Feb). Network Analysis in the Social Sciences. *Science, 323*(5916), 892–895. (Http://www.sciencemag.org/cgi/reprint/sci;323/5916/892.pdf)

40.   Bower, B. (1998, 5 Dec). Objective Visions. *Science News, 154,* 23. (Http://www.thefreelibrary.com/Objective+Visions-a053489706)

41.   Brader, T. (2006). *Campaigning for Hearts and Minds: How Emotional Appeals in Political Ads Work (Studies in Communication, Media, and Public Opinion).* Chicago: University of Chicago.

42.   Buchanan, M. (2009, 29 Jan). Secret Signals.
        Nature, 457(7229), 528–530. (Http://staging-
        www.nature.com/news/2009/090128/pdf/457528a.pdf)
43.   Buckling, A., Wills, M. A., & Colegrave, N. (2003, 19 Dec).
        Adaptation Limits Diversification of Experimental Bacterial
        Populations. *Science, 302*(5653), 2107–2109.
        (Http://www.sciencemag.org/cgi/reprint/sci;302/5653/2107.
        pdf)
44.   Burnett, S., & Blakemore, S.-J. (2009, 6 Mar). Functional
        connectivity during a social emotion task in adolescents and
        in adults. *European Journal of Neuroscience, 29*(6), 1294–
        1301. (Http://www3.interscience.wiley.com/cgi-
        bin/fulltext/122242982/PDFSTART)
45.   Burnham, D., Kitamura, C., & Vollmer-Conna, U. (2002,
        24 May). What's New, Pussycat? On Talking to Babies and
        Animals. *Science, 296*(5572).
        (Http://www.sciencemag.org/cgi/reprint/sci;296/5572/1435.
        pdf)
46.   Butler, D. (2009, 12 Mar). Web usage data outline map of
        knowledge. *Nature, 458*(7235), 135.
        (Http://www.nature.com/news/2009/090311/pdf/458135a.p
        df)
47.   Caggiano, V., Fogassi, L., Rizzolatti, G., Thier, P., & Casile,
        A. (2009, 17 Apr). Mirror Neurons Differentially Encode the
        Peripersonal and Extrapersonal Space of Monkeys.
        Science, 324(5925), 403–406.
        (Http://www.sciencemag.org/cgi/reprint/324/5925/403.pdf)
48.   Carlos David Navarrete, A. O., Arnold K. Ho. (2009, 5
        Jan). Fear Extinction to an Out-Group Face: The Role of
        Target Gender. *Psychological Science, 20*(2), 155–158.
        (Http://www3.interscience.wiley.com/cgi-
        bin/fulltext/121641572/PDFSTART)
49.   Carlson, J., Muthaly, S., & Rosenberger, P. (2002). GOAL!
        An exploratory study of the information content in the
        Australian National Soccer League websites. In *Marketing and
        Market Research (350204).* Swinburne University of
        Technology.

(Http://search.arrow.edu.au/main/redirect_to_title?identifier
=oai%3Aarrow.nla.gov.au%3A1209122445219151)

50.   Carpenter, A. F., Georgopoulos, A. P., & Pellizzer, G.
       (1999, 12 Mar). Motor Cortical Encoding of Serial Order in a
       Context-Recall Task. *Science, 283*(5408), 1752–1757.
       (Http://www.sciencemag.org/cgi/reprint/sci;283/5408/1752.
       pdf)

51.   Carrabis, J., Bratton, S., & Evans, D. (2008, 9 Jun). *Guest
       Blogger Joseph Carrabis Answers Dave Evans, CEO of Digital
       Voodoo's Question About Male Executives Weilding Social
       Media Influence on Par with Female Executives.*
       PersonalLifeMedia.
       (Http://blogs.personallifemedia.com/dishymix/guest-blogger-
       joseph-carrabis-answers-dave-evans-ceo-of-digital-voodoos-
       question-about-male-executives-weilding-social-media-
       influence-on-par-with-female-executives/2008/06/09/)

52.   Carrabis, J., & Carrabis, S. (2009). *Designing Information
       for Automatic Memorization (Branding).* Scotsburn, NS:
       NextStage Evolution.

53.   Carrabis, J. (1997). *Information Driven Web Systems.*
       NextStage Evolution Research Paper. Scotsburn, NS:
       Northern Lights Publishing.
       (Http://www.nextstagevolution.com/membership.cfm)

54.   Carrabis, J. (1999–2005). *Information Mechanics.*
       NextStage Evolution Research Paper. Scotsburn, NS:
       Northern Lights Publishing.
       (Http://www.nextstagevolution.com/membership.cfm)

55.   Carrabis, J. (2001). Can Autonomous Entities Act on Non-
       Conscious Meaning in Human Applications? (Theory and
       Applications of Evolution Technology). IIAS.

56.   Carrabis, J. (2001). *Internal Experience and the Web.*
       Scotsburn, NS: NextStage Evolution Research Paper.
       (Http://www.nextstagevolution.com/membership.cfm)

57.   Carrabis, J. (2001, Jul). *Utilizing Visitor "Goal-Seeking" in
       eCommerce.* BizMediaScience.
       (Http://bizmediascience.hungrypeasant.com/2015/01/02/utili
       zing-visitor-goal-seeking-in-ecommerce/)

58.   Carrabis, J. (2002). *Signatures and the Identity Matrix, Part 2: Psychomotor Behavioral Activity as an Indicator of Personal Identity.* NextStage Evolution Research Paper.
59.   Carrabis, J. (2003). *Evolution Technology as an Adjunct to Homeland Defense and Security.* Scotsburn, NS: NextStage Evolution.
        (Http://www.nextstagevolution.com/membership.cfm)
60.   Carrabis, J. (2003). *Evolution Technology: Proof of Concept* [Whitepaper]. Scotsburn, NS: NextStage Evolution.
61.   Carrabis, J. (2004). *What We're Learning About Visitors From Websites.* NextStage Evolution. Scotsburn, NS: Northern Lights Publishing.
        (Http://www.nextstagevolution.com/membership.cfm)
62.   Carrabis, J. (2005). *Defining the Visitor Action Metric* [NSE Marketing Paper]. NextStage Evolution.
        (Http://www.nextstagevolution.com/pdfdownload.cfm?thison e=nsempvam.pdf)
63.   Carrabis, J. (2005, 3 June). *Usability Studies 101: Barriers to Entry.* ImediaConnections.
        (Http://www.imediaconnection.com/content/6046.asp)
64.   Carrabis, J. (2005, 8 Apr). *Usability Studies 101: Brand Loyalty.* IMediaConnections.
        (Http://www.imediaconnection.com/content/5440.asp)
65.   Carrabis, J. (2005, 15 July). *Usability Studies 101: Defining Visitor Action.* ImediaConnections.
        (Http://www.imediaconnection.com//content//6330.asp)
66.   Carrabis, J. (2005, 16 November). *Usability Studies 101: Design Questions.* ImediaConnections.
        (Http://www.imediaconnection.com/content/7321.asp)
67.   Carrabis, J. (2005, 7 Oct). *Usability Studies 101: Landmarks Ahead?.* ImediaConnections.
        (Http://www.imediaconnection.com/content/6913.asp)
68.   Carrabis, J. (2005, 23 Dec). *Usability Studies 101: Making Cookies from Breadcrumbs.* ImediaConnections.
        (Http://www.imediaconnection.com/content/7675.asp)

69.   Carrabis, J. (2005, 28 Oct). *Usability Studies 101: Redesign Timing.* ImediaConnections. (Http://www.imediaconnection.com/content/7083.asp)

70.   Carrabis, J. (2005, Dec). *Working with Prediction Markets via NextStage's Evolution Technology.* BizMediaScience. (Http://bizmediascience.hungrypeasant.com/2014/12/22/working-with-prediction-markets-via-nextstages-evolution-technology/)

71.   Carrabis, J. (2006–8, 28 Nov - 30 May). *BizMediaScience Search Engine Archive.* BizMediaScience. (Http://bizmediascience.hungrypeasant.com/category/search/)

72.   Carrabis, J. (2006, Dec). *The Answer Is "What's the Optimal Length of Spaghetti?".* BizMediaScience. (Http://bizmediascience.hungrypeasant.com/2015/03/14/the-answer-is-whats-the-optimal-length-of-spaghetti/)

73.   Carrabis, J. (2006). *Author's Foreword, Reading Virtual Minds Volume I: Science and History.* Nashua, NH: Northern Lights Publishing. (Http://www.amazon.com/Reading-Virtual-Minds-Joseph-Carrabis/dp/0984140301)

74.   Carrabis, J. (2006-). *BizMediaScience Attention Entries.* BizMediaScience. (Http://bizmediascience.hungrypeasant.com/tag/attention/)

75.   Carrabis, J. (2006-). *BizMediaScience Rich Media Archive.* BizMediaScience. (Http://bizmediascience.hungrypeasant.com/category/analytics/rich-media/)

76.   Carrabis, J. (2006, 24 Mar). *Can Customers See Your Information?.* ImediaConnections. (Http://www.imediaconnection.com/content/8797.asp)

77.   Carrabis, J. (2006). *Chapter 3 "Behaviors, Offline to On," Reading Virtual Minds Volume I: Science and History.* Nashua, NH: Northern Lights Publishing. (Http://www.amazon.com/Reading-Virtual-Minds-Joseph-Carrabis/dp/0984140301)

78.   Carrabis, J. (2006). *Chapter 4 "Anecdotes of Learning," Reading Virtual Minds Volume I: Science and History.*

Nashua, NH: Northern Lights Publishing.
(Http://www.amazon.com/Reading-Virtual-Minds-Joseph-
Carrabis/dp/0984140301)
79.   Carrabis, J. (2006). *Chapter 5, "The Science Behind
Reading Virtual Minds," Reading Virtual Minds Volume I:
Science and History.* Nashua, NH: Northern Lights Publishing.
(Http://www.amazon.com/Reading-Virtual-Minds-Joseph-
Carrabis/dp/0984140301)
80.   Carrabis, J. (2006). *Determining Prior Knowledge of
Information via PsychoMotor Behavioral Cuing.* Scotsburn,
NS: NextStage Evolution.
81.   Carrabis, J. (2006, 10 Mar). *Directing Your Customer's
Gaze.* ImediaConnections.
(Http://www.imediaconnection.com/content/8601.asp)
82.   Carrabis, J. (2006, 8 Dec). *Eric Braden's Intelligent
Carpets.* BizMediaScience.
(Http://bizmediascience.hungrypeasant.com/2015/03/14/eric
-bradens-intelligent-carpets/)
83.   Carrabis, J. (2006, 24 Feb). *Focusing Your Customer's
Attention.* ImediaConnections.
(Http://www.imediaconnection.com/content/8412.asp)
84.   Carrabis, J. (2006-). *Gender Based Marketing Blog Entries.*
BizMediaScience.
(Http://bizmediascience.hungrypeasant.com/category/market
ing/gender-marketing/)
85.   Carrabis, J. (2006, 22 Sept). *Gender Marketing Web
Design Differences.* ImediaConnections.
(Http://www.imediaconnection.com/content/11359.asp)
86.   Carrabis, J. (2006, 5 Dec). *Gender Specific Marketing
Discoveries Presentation Podcast.* IMediaConnection: 2006
Agency Summit.
(Http://www.imediaconnection.com/content/12684.asp)
87.   Carrabis, J. (2006, 15 Nov). *How to Create a Super-Sticky
Homepage.* ImediaConnections.
(Http://www.imediaconnection.com/content/12444.asp)

88.   Carrabis, J. (2006, 11 Aug). *Know Your Audience, and Reach It.* ImediaConnections. (Http://www.imediaconnection.com/content/10732.asp)

89.   Carrabis, J. (2006, 9 Jun). *Listening to and Seeing Searches.* IMediaConnection. (Http://www.imediaconnection.com//content//9898.asp)

90.   Carrabis, J. (2006, 10 Nov). *Mapping Personae to Outcomes.* (Http://www.imediaconnection.com/content/12358.asp)

91.   Carrabis, J. (2006, 8 Dec). *Paid Search Delivers Magic.* IMediaConnection. (Http://www.imediaconnection.com//content//12737.asp)

92.   Carrabis, J. (2006, May). *"Predicting Election Outcomes via NextStage's TargetTrack" or "Why Dean Led, Kerry was Droll and Lieberman Foundered in 2004.".* BizMediaScience. (Http://bizmediascience.hungrypeasant.com/2014/12/22/predicting-election-outcomes-via-nextstages-targettrack-or-why-dean-led-kerry-was-droll-and-lieberman-foundered-in-2004/)

93.   Carrabis, J. (2006). *Reading Virtual Minds Volume I: Science and History.* Nashua, NH: Northern Lights Publishing. (Http://www.amazon.com/Reading-Virtual-Minds-Joseph-Carrabis/dp/0984140301)

94.   Carrabis, J. (2006, 25 Aug). Shared Traits of Great Web Design. *ImediaConnections, http://www.imediaconnection.com/content/10876.asp.*

95.   Carrabis, J. (2006, 6 Jan). *Usability Studies 101: Design by Groups.* ImediaConnections. (Http://www.imediaconnection.com/content/7513.asp)

96.   Carrabis, J. (2006). *Use of Eye Images as Navigation and Action Cues on Websites* [NSE WhitePaper]. NextStage Evolution. Scotsburn, NS: Northern Lights Publishing. (Http://www.nextstagevolution.com/membership.cfm)

97.   Carrabis, J. (2007, 15 Jan). *6 Ways to Make Your Ads Sticky.* IMediaConnection. (Http://www.imediaconnection.com/content/13220.asp)

98.   Carrabis, J. (2007–9, 11 Sept - 3 Mar). *BizMediaScience Politics Archive.* BizMediaScience. (Http://bizmediascience.hungrypeasant.com/category/scienc es/sociology/politics/)

99.   Carrabis, J. (2007, 29 Nov). *Adding sound to your brand website.* ImediaConnections. (Http://www.imediaconnection.com//content//17473.asp)

100.   Carrabis, J. (2007, 28 March). *Alarming Results.* (Http://www.bizmediascience.com/2007/03/alarming_results .html)

101.   Carrabis, J. (2007). *Attention, Engagement and Trust: The Internet Trinity and Websites.* TriQuatroTriteCale. (Http://triquatrotritecale.hungrypeasant.com/index.php/2013 /06/18/attention-engagement-and-trust-the-internet-trinity- and-websites/)

102.   Carrabis, J. (2007-). *BizMediaScience Engagement Archive.* BizMediaScience. (Http://bizmediascience.hungrypeasant.com/tag/engagement /)

103.   Carrabis, J. (2007, 8 Sep). *The Complete "NextStage Evolution's Evolution Technology, Web Analytics, Behavioral Analytics and Marketing Analytics Reports for the BizMediaScience Blog, 7 day Cycle" Arc.* BizMediaScience. (Http://bizmediascience.hungrypeasant.com/2015/01/08/the -complete-nextstage-evolutions-evolution-technology-web- analytics-behavioral-analytics-and-marketing-analytics- reports-for-the-bizmediascience-blog-7-day-cycle-arc/)

104.   Carrabis, J. (2007, 20 April). *Defining Attention on Websites & Blogs.* IMediaConnection. (Http://www.imediaconnection.com//content//14568.asp)

105.   Carrabis, J. (2007, 25 Sept). *Expertise - Who Decides?.* BizMediaScience. (Http://bizmediascience.hungrypeasant.com/2014/12/28/exp ertise-who-decides/)

106.   Carrabis, J. (2007, 9 Nov). *God, Satan and your brand website.* ImediaConnections. (Http://www.imediaconnection.com//content//17287.asp)

107.   Carrabis, J. (2007, 7 Sept). *Help visitors focus and reap the rewards.* ImediaConnections.
(Http://www.imediaconnection.com//content//16533.asp)

108.   Carrabis, J. (2007). *Impact (The Use of Colors and Color Imagery in Direct Response Marketing and eBranding).* Scotsburn, NS: NextStage Evolution.
(Http://www.nextstagevolution.com/membership.cfm)

109.   Carrabis, J. (2007, 6 Jul). *Intelligent Website Design: Expand Your Market.* ImediaConnections.
(Http://www.imediaconnection.com//content//15697.asp)

110.   Carrabis, J. (2007, 21 Dec). *Males 3.0.* AllBusiness.com.
(Http://www.allbusiness.com/electronics/computer-electronics-manufacturing/5004089–1.html)

111.   Carrabis, J. (2007, 5 Oct). *Using Images to Create Visitor Rapport or "That Little Look..".* AllBusiness.com.
(Http://www.allbusiness.com/marketing-advertising/internet-marketing/4968229–1.html)

112.   Carrabis, J. (2007, Jan). *Using NextStage's TargetTrack in Political Campaigns.* BizMediaScience.
(Http://bizmediascience.hungrypeasant.com/2014/12/24/using-nextstages-targettrack-in-political-campaigns/)

113.   Carrabis, J. (2007, 5 Jan). *Using Sound and Music on Websites.* IMediaConnection.
(Http://www.imediaconnection.com/content/13098.asp)

114.   Carrabis, J. (2007, 20 Jul). *Websites: The Secret to Landing Pages and Shopping Carts.* IMediaConnection.
(Http://www.imediaconnection.com//content//15839.asp)

115.   Carrabis, J. (2007, 23 Mar). *Websites: You've Only Got 3 Seconds.* ImediaConnections.
(Http://www.imediaconnection.com/content/7513.asp)

116.   Carrabis, J. (2008–9, 3 Jul/11 Jul). *From TheFutureOf (10 Jul 08): Back into the fray.* The Analytics Ecology.
(Http://analyticsecology.hungrypeasant.com/index.php/2009/07/03/from-thefutureof-10-jul-08-back-into-the-fray/)

117.   Carrabis, J. (2008/9, 18 Jul/7 Jul). *From TheFutureOf (16 Jul 08): Responses to Geertz, Papadakis and others, 5 Feb*

08. The Analytics Ecology.
(Http://www.theanalyticsecology.com/?p=106)

118.   Carrabis, J. (2008/9, 18 Jul/7 Jul). *From TheFutureOf (16 Jul 08): Responses to Papadakis 7 Feb 08.* The Analytics Ecology. (Http://www.theanalyticsecology.com/?p=104)

119.   Carrabis, J. (2008/9, 28 Jan/1 Jul). *From TheFutureOf (22 Jan 08): Starting the discussion: Attention, Engagement, Authority, Influence, ….* The Analytics Ecology. (Http://www.theanalyticsecology.com/?p=13)

120.   Carrabis, J. (2008/9, 29 Aug/9 Jul). *From TheFutureOf (28 Aug 08): Response to Jim Novo's 12 Jul 08 9:40am comment.* The Analytics Ecology. (Http://www.theanalyticsecology.com/?p=127)

121.   Carrabis, J. (2008/9, 10 Nov/15 Jul). *From TheFutureOf (7 Nov 08): Debbie Pascoe asked me to pontificate on "What are we measuring when we measure 'engagement'?".* The Analytics Ecology. (Http://www.theanalyticsecology.com/?p=137)

122.   Carrabis, J. (2008, 26 Jun). *The Complete "Canadian Based Business Differences -- Responding to June Li, Christopher Berry and Jaques Warren" Arc (also known as "Responding to Christopher Berry's 'A Vexing Problem.." and incorporating "The Language of Web Analytics - The Hard(er) Sell in Canada").* BizMediaScience. (Http://bizmediascience.hungrypeasant.com/2015/01/28/the-complete-canadian-based-business-differences-responding-to-june-li-christopher-berry-and-jaques-warren-arc-also-known-as-responding-to-christopher-berrys-a-vexing-problem-and-incorpo/)

123.   Carrabis, J. (2008, 27 May). *The Complete "TS Eliot, Ezekiel, Beehives and Mighty Mouse – Why 'Whispering to Be Heard'?" Arc.* BizMediaScience. (Http://bizmediascience.hungrypeasant.com/2015/03/14/the-complete-ts-eliot-ezekiel-beehives-and-mighty-mouse-why-whispering-to-be-heard-arc/)

124.   Carrabis, J. (2008, 30 Oct). *The Complete "What is an A6 or A11 or V6 or V21, etc. decision style?" Arc (Originally "Do*

McCain, Biden, Palin and Obama Think the Way We Do? (Part...)". BizMediaScience. (Http://bizmediascience.hungrypeasant.com/2015/01/28/the-complete-what-is-an-a6-or-a11-or-v6-or-v21-etc-decision-style-arc-originally-do-mccain-biden-palin-and-obama-think-the-way-we-do-part/)

125.   Carrabis, J. (2008). *Designing an Email Newsletter for Maximum ROI*. Scotsburn, NS: NextStage Evolution. (Http://www.nextstagevolution.com/membership.cfm)

126.   Carrabis, J. (2008, 1 Oct). *Do McCain, Biden, Palin and Obama Think the Way We Do? (Part 1)The Complete "What is an A6 or A11 or V6 or V21, etc. decision style?" Arc (Originally "Do McCain, Biden, Palin and Obama Think the Way We Do? (Part...)"*. BizMediaScience. (Http://bizmediascience.hungrypeasant.com/2015/01/28/the-complete-what-is-an-a6-or-a11-or-v6-or-v21-etc-decision-style-arc-originally-do-mccain-biden-palin-and-obama-think-the-way-we-do-part/)

127.   Carrabis, J. (2008, 31 Oct). *Governor Palin's (and everybody else's) Popularity*. BizMediaScience. (Http://bizmediascience.hungrypeasant.com/2015/03/14/governor-palins-and-everybody-elses-popularity/)

128.   Carrabis, J. (2008, 21 May). *Meet Online Engagement's Little Friend, Satisfaction*. AllBusiness.com. (Http://www.allbusiness.com/marketing-advertising/marketing-advertising/10174308–1.html)

129.   Carrabis, J. (2008, 15 Aug). *NextStage's Token Republican Calls McCain a Raging Duopolist!*. BizMediaScience. (Http://bizmediascience.hungrypeasant.com/2015/01/23/nextstages-token-republican-calls-mccain-a-raging-duopolist/)

130.   Carrabis, J. (2008, 17 Mar). *SEO/SEM Formulas, Whitehats in Black Clothing and Predicting Search Engine Placement and Outcomes*. AllBusiness.com. (Http://www.allbusiness.com/technology/software-services-applications-search-engines/7389826–1.html)

131.   Carrabis, J. (2008, 17 Mar). *Situational Awareness, Too Much Information Too Fast, and Voting v Voting with your*

Feet. BizMediaScience.
(Http://bizmediascience.hungrypeasant.com/2015/01/29/situ
ational-awareness-too-much-information-too-fast-and-
voting-v-voting-with-your-feet/)

132.   Carrabis, J. (2008, 29 Feb). *Troublesome Targets: Where
Analytics and Audiences.* AllBusiness.com.
(Http://www.allbusiness.com/retail/retailers-nonstore-
retailers-mail-order-internet/7065845–1.html)

133.   Carrabis, J. (2008, 14 Mar). *Website marketing across
genders.* IMediaConnection.
(Http://www.imediaconnection.com/content/18685.imc)

134.   Carrabis, J. (2009, 12 Jun). *Canoeing with Stephane
(Sentiment Analysis, Anyone? (Part 2)).* BizMediaScience.
(Http://bizmediascience.hungrypeasant.com/2015/01/29/can
oeing-with-stephane-sentiment-analysis-anyone-part-2/)

135.   Carrabis, J. (2009). *A Demonstration of Professional Test-
Taker Bias in Web-Based Panels and Applications.* San
Francisco, CA: Society for New Communications Research.

136.   Carrabis, J. (2009). *A Demonstration of Professional Test-
Taker Bias in Web-Based Panels and Applications.* Nashua,
NH: NextStage Evolution.
(Http://www.nextstagevolution.com/membership.cfm)

137.   Carrabis, J. (2009). *Frequency of Blog Posts is Best
Determined by Audience Size and Psychological Distance from
the Author.* Scotsburn, NS: NextStage Evolution.
(Http://www.nextstagevolution.com/membership.cfm)

138.   Carrabis, J. (2009). Machine Detection of and Response to
User Non-Conscious Thought Processes to Increase Usability,
Experience and Satisfaction - Case Studies and Examples. In
*The 2nd International Multi-Conference on Engineering and
Technological Innovation* (Vol. 3, pp. 69–74). Orlando, FL:
International Institute of Informatics and Systemics.

139.   Carrabis, J. (2009, 17 Jun). *Relevancy, or "Oh, gosh.
Joseph's been at it again.".* BizMediaScience.
(Http://bizmediascience.hungrypeasant.com/2015/01/30/rele
vancy-or-oh-gosh-josephs-been-at-it-again/)

140.   Carrabis, J. (2009, 5 Jun). *Sentiment Analysis, Anyone? (Part 1).* BizMediaScience. (Http://bizmediascience.hungrypeasant.com/2015/01/08/sen timent-analysis-anyone-part-1/)

141.   Carrabis, J. (2009, 29 Jan). *Tripping the Light Fantastic.* Personal Life Media. (Http://think.personallifemedia.com/?p=36)

142.   Carrabis, J. (2013, 9 Oct). *Digital Divisivity.* An Economy of Meanings. (Http://aneconomyofmeaning.wordpress.com/2013/10/09/di gital-divisivity/)

143.   Carrabis, J. (2013). *"Fair-Exchange, or 'You Have to Give as Good as You Get'," Reading Virtual Minds Volume II: Experience and Expectation.* Scotsburn, NS: Northern Lights Publishing. (Http://www.amazon.com/Reading-Virtual-Minds-Joseph-Carrabis/dp/0984140301)

144.   Carrabis, J. (2013, 23 Oct). *Joseph Carrabis' Under the Influence: Customer Service, Acquisition and Retention in the Age of Digital Divisivity.* IMediaConnection. (Http://blogs.imediaconnection.com/blog/2013/10/23/joseph -carrabis-under-the-influence-customer-service-acquisition- and-retention-in-the-age-of-digital-divisivity/)

145.   Carrabis, J. (2013). *Reading Virtual Minds Volume II: Experience and Expectation.* Nashua. NH: Northern Lights Publishing. (Http://www.amazon.com/Reading-Virtual-Minds-Joseph-Carrabis/dp/0984140301)

146.   Carrabis, J. (2014, 4 Jun). *This puts a whole new meaning on impatience, doesn't it?.* LinkedIn. (Https://www.linkedin.com/today/post/article/201406041959 42–112718-this-puts-a-whole-new-meaning-on-impatience- doesn-t-it?trk=mp-author-card)

147.   Casey, B. (2002, 24 May). Windows into the Human Brain. *Science, 296*(5572), 1408–1409. (Http://www.sciencemag.org/cgi/reprint/296/5572/1408.pdf)

148.   Chabris, C. F., & Glickman, M. E. (2006, Dec). Sex Differences in Intellectual Performance: Analysis of a Large Cohort of Competitive Chess Players. *Psychological*

Science, 12, 1040–1046.
(Http://www.psychologicalscience.org/members/goToSynerg
y.cfm?issn=0956–7976&date=2006&article=01828)
149.   Chalmers, D. J. (1995). Facing Up to the Problem of
Consciousness. *Journal of Consciousness Studies, 2*(3), 212.
150.   Chambon, M. (2008, Jan). Embodied perception with
others' bodies in mind: Stereotype priming influence on the
perception of spatial environment. *Journal of Experimental
Social Psychology, 45*(1), 283–287.
(Http://www.sciencedirect.com/science?_ob=MImg&_imagek
ey=B6WJB-4TDK70V-3-
5&_cdi=6874&_user=10&_orig=search&_coverDate=01%2F3
1%2F2009&_sk=999549998&view=c&wchp=dGLbVzW-
zSkWA&md5=b1a78bae30578615af294c5e1ca517d5&ie=/sd
article.pdf)
151.   Chandler, D. (2007). *Semiotics: The Basics.* Routledge.
152.   Changeux, J.-P. (2004). *The physiology of truth:
Neuroscience and human knowledge.* Cambridge, Mass.:
Belknap Press of Harvard University Press.
153.   Chaparro, B. S. (2008, Oct). Usability Evaluation of a
University Portal Website. *Usability News (Software Usability
Research Laboratory (SURL) at Wichita State
University), 10*(2).
(Http://surl.org/usabilitynews/102/portal_usability.asp)
154.   Check, E. (2005, 27 Oct). Trial aims to measure social
effects of choosing babies' sex. *Nature, 437*(7063), 1214–
1215.
(Http://www.nature.com/nature/journal/v437/n7063/pdf/437
1214b.pdf)
155.   Chicurel, M. (2002, 15 Mar). Neurons Weigh Options,
Come to a Decision. *Science, 295*(5562), 1995b-1997.
(Http://www.sciencemag.org/cgi/reprint/sci;295/5562/1995b
.pdf)
156.   Chisholm, R., & Karrer, R. (1983). Movement-related brain
potentials during hand squeezing in children and adults.
International Journal of Neuroscience, 19, 243–58.

157.   Churchland, P. S. (1995, 25 Sept). Can Neurobiology
       Teach Us Anything about Consciousness? University of
       California, San Diego, Salk Institute.
       (Http://www.ecs.soton.ac.uk/~harnad/Papers/Py104/church.
       neuro.html)
158.   Claxton G. (1999, Feb/Mar). Moving the cursor of
       consciousness: Cognitive science and human welfare. *Journal
       of Consciousness Studies, 6*(s 2–3), 219–222.
159.   Cole, J. (1997). On 'being faceless': Selfhood and facial
       embodiment. *Journal of Consciousness Studies, 4*(5–6), 467–
       484.
       (Http://www.ingentaconnect.com/content/imp/jcs/1997/000
       00004/F0020005/805)
160.   Crain, S., & Thornton, R. (1998). *Investigations in
       Universal Grammar.* MIT Press.
161.   Crary, J. (1999). *Suspensions of Perception: Attention,
       Spectacle, and Modern Culture.* MIT: MIT Press.
162.   Crick, F., & Koch, C. (1990). Toward a Neurobiological
       Theory of Consciousness. *Seminars in the
       Neurosciences, 2,* 263–275.
163.   Crinion, J., Turner, R., Grogan, A., Hanakawa, T.,
       Noppeney, U., Devlin, J. T., et al. (2006, 9 Jun). Language
       Control in the Bilingual Brain. *Science, 312*(5779), 1537–
       1540.
       (Http://www.sciencemag.org/cgi/reprint/312/5779/1537.pdf)
164.   Crisp, R. J., Farrow, C. V., Rosenthal, H. E., Walsh, J.,
       Blisset, J., & Penn, N. M. (2008, Jan). Interpersonal
       attachment predicts identification with groups. *Journal of
       Experimental Social Psychology, 45*(1), 115–122.
       (Http://www.sciencedirect.com/science?_ob=ArticleURL&_udi
       =B6WJB-4TJTXDC-
       2&_user=10&_coverDate=01%2F31%2F2009&_alid=912434
       385&_rdoc=4&_fmt=high&_orig=search&_cdi=6874&_sort=d
       &_docanchor=&view=c&_ct=11&_acct=C000050221&_versio
       n=1&_urlVersion=0&_userid=10&md5=f93edcd7378d30f4fc1
       548b955c548ec)

165.   Daw, N. D., & Dayan, P. (2004, 18 Jun). Matchmaking. *Science, 304*(5678), 1753–1754.
(Http://www.sciencemag.org/cgi/reprint/304/5678/1753.pdf)

166.   Daw, N. D., O'Doherty, J. P., Dayan, P., Seymour, B., & Dolan, R. J. (2006, 15 Jun). Cortical substrates for exploratory decisions in humans. *Nature, 441*(7095), 876–879.
(Http://www.nature.com/nature/journal/v441/n7095/pdf/nature04766.pdf)

167.   Deborah A. Prentice, D. T. M. (2006, Feb). Essentializing Differences Between Women and Men. *Psychological Science, 17*(2), 129–135.
(Http://www3.interscience.wiley.com/cgi-bin/fulltext/118597330/PDFSTART)

168.   Decety, J., Grezes, J., Costes, N., Perani, D., Jeannerod, M., Procyk, E., et al. (1997). Brain activity during observation of actions (Influence of action content and subject's strategy). *Brain, 120,* 1763–1777.

169.   Dede, C. Immersive Interfaces for Engagement and Learning. *Science, 323*(5910), 66–69.
(Http://www.sciencemag.org/cgi/reprint/323/5910/66.pdf)

170.   Dedre Gentner, L. L. N. (2006). Analogical Processes in Language Learning. *Current Directions in Psychological Science, 15*(6), 297–301.
(Http://www3.interscience.wiley.com/cgi-bin/fulltext/118584118/PDFSTART)

171.   Deecke, L. (1980). Influence of age on human cerebral potentials associated with voluntary movement. In D. G. Stein (Ed.), *The Psychobiology of Aging: Problems and Perspectives.* Elsevier.

172.   Dennis, C. (2004, 29 Jan). The most important sexual organ. *Nature, 427*(6973), 390–392.
(Http://www.nature.com/nature/journal/v427/n6973/pdf/427390a.pdf)

173.   Deron, M. (2000, Jan). How Important is Visual Feedback When Using a TouchScreen? *Usability News, 2*(1).

174.   Dreger, A. (2008–06–01). The Controversy Surrounding 'The Man Who Would Be Queen': A Case History of the Politics of Science, Identity, and Sex in the Internet Age. *Archives of Sexual Behavior, 37*(3), 366–421. Springer Netherlands.

175.   *Education, Employment, and Everything: The triple layers of a woman's life* (M. (. Albion & P. (. Collins). University of Southern Queensland, Toowoomba, Queensland, Australia: IWC (International Women's Conference) 2007.

176.   Eisenberger, N. I., Lieberman, M. D., & Williams, K. D. (2003, 10 Oct). Does Rejection Hurt? An fMRI Study of Social Exclusion. *Science, 302*(5643), 290–292. (Http://www.sciencemag.org/cgi/reprint/sci;302/5643/290.pdf)

177.   Erard, M. (2015, 27 Feb). What's in a name? *Science, 347*(6225), 941–943. (Http://www.sciencemag.org/content/347/6225/941.full.pdf)

178.   Ethofer, T., Van De Ville, D., Scherer, K., & Vuilleumier, P. (2009, 23 Jun). Decoding of Emotional Information in Voice-Sensitive Cortices. *Current Biology, 19*(12), 1028–1033. (Http://www.sciencedirect.com/science?_ob=ArticleURL&_udi=B6VRT-4W929HC-4&_user=10&_coverDate=06%2F23%2F2009&_rdoc=1&_fmt=high&_orig=browse&_sort=d&view=c&_acct=C000050221&_version=1&_urlVersion=0&_userid=10&md5=a57e07a3255950cfe2327d7f453d588e)

179.   Faris, R., & Felmlee, D. (2011, Feb). Network Centrality and Gender Segregation in Same- and Cross-Gender Aggression. *American Sociological Review.* (Http://www.asanet.org/images/journals/docs/pdf/Faris_FelmleeASRFeb11.pdf)

180.   Fehr, E., Bernhard, H., & Rockenbach, B. (2008, 28 Aug). Egalitarianism in young children. *Nature, 454*(7208), 1079–1083. (Http://www.nature.com/nature/journal/v454/n7208/pdf/nature07155.pdf)

181.   Fenske, M. J., Raymond, J. E., Kessler, K., Westoby, N., &
Tipper, S. E. (2005, Oct). Attentional Inhibition Has Social-
Emotional Consequences for Unfamiliar Faces. *Psychological
Science, 16*(10), 753–758.
(Http://www3.interscience.wiley.com/cgi-
bin/fulltext/118661655/PDFSTART)
182.   Fernandez-Duque, D., & Posner, M. (1997, 28 Feb).
Relating the mechanisms of orienting and alerting.
Neuropsychologia, 35(4), 477–486.
183.   Fogg, B., Marshall, J., Laraki, O., Osipovich, A., Varma, C.,
Fang, N., et al. (2001, 31 Mar - 5 Apr). What Makes Web
Sites Credible? A Report on a Large Quantitative Study.
CHI, 3(1), 8. (Www.webcredibility.org)
184.   Franks, N. R., Dornhaus, A., Fitzsimmons, J. P., & Stevens,
M. (2003, 7 Dec). Speed versus accuracy in collective
decision making. *Proceedings of the Royal Society of London.
Series B: Biological Sciences, 270*(1532), 2457–2463.
(Http://rspb.royalsocietypublishing.org/content/270/1532/24
57.full.pdf+html)
185.   Friesen, N. (2010, 6 Dec). Education and the social Web:
Connective learning and the commercial imperative. *First
Monday, 15*(12).
(Http://firstmonday.org/htbin/cgiwrap/bin/ojs/index.php/fm/
article/view/3149/2718)
186.   Gabora L.[1]. (2002). Amplifying Phenomenal Information
Toward a Fundamental Theory of Consciousness. *Journal of
Consciousness Studies, 9*(8), 3–29.
187.   Gaffan, D. (2005, 30 Sep). Widespread Cortical Networks
Underlie Memory and Attention. *Science, 309*(5744), 2172–
2173.
(Http://www.sciencemag.org/cgi/reprint/309/5744/2172.pdf)
188.   Galin D. (1999, Feb/Mar). Separating first-personness
from the other problems of consciousness or 'you had to have
been there!'. *Journal of Consciousness Studies, 6*(s 2–
3), 222–229.

189.   Gallagher, S. (2001). The Practice of Mind (Theory, Simulation or Primary Interaction). *Journal of Consciousness Studies, 8*(5–7), 83–108.
190.   Geertz, C. (1977). *The Interpretation of Cultures.* Basic Books.
191.   Geertz, C. (1983). *Local knowledge: Further essays in interpretive anthropology.* New York: Basic Books.
192.   Gendlin E.T. (1999, Feb/Mar). A new model. *Journal of Consciousness Studies, 6*(s 2–3), 232–237.
193.   Gernsbacher, M. A. (2007, March). Neural Diversity. *Psychological Science Observer, 20*(3), 3. (Http://www.psychologicalscience.org/observer/getArticle.cfm?id=2134)
194.   Giles, J. (2005, 14 Dec). Internet encyclopaedias go head to head. *Nature.* (Http://www.nature.com/nature/journal/v438/n7070/pdf/438900a.pdf)
195.   Ginsberg, J., Mohebbi, M. H., Patel, R. S., Brammer, L., Smolinski, M. S., & Brilliant, L. (2009, 19 Feb). Detecting influenza epidemics using search engine query data. *Nature, 457*(7232), 1012–1014. (Http://www.nature.com/nature/journal/v457/n7232/pdf/nature07634.pdf)
196.   Ginsburg, C. (2005). First Person Experiments. *Journal of Consciousness Studies, 12*(2), 29. (Http://www.ingentaconnect.com/content/imp/jcs/2005/00000012/00000002/art00002)
197.   Glanville R. (2002). A (Cybernetic) Musing: Cybernetics and Human Knowing. *Cybernetics & Human Knowing, 9*(1), 75–82. (Http://www.ingentaconnect.com/content/imp/chk/2002/00000009/00000001/109)
198.   Goldfarb, L., & Henik, A. (2006, Feb). New Data Analysis of the Stroop Matching Task Calls for a Reevaluation of Theory. *Psychological Science, 17*(2), 96–100. (Http://www3.interscience.wiley.com/cgi-bin/fulltext/118597325/PDFSTART)

199.   Goldstein, M. H., Schwade, J. A., & Bornstein, M. H. (2009). The Value of Vocalizing: Five-Month-Old Infants Associate Their Own Noncry Vocalizations With Responses From Caregivers. *Child Development, 80*(3), 636–644.

200.   Graddol, D. (2004, 27 Feb). The Future of Language. *Science, 303*(5662), 1329–1331. (Http://www.sciencemag.org/cgi/reprint/sci;303/5662/1329. pdf)

201.   Gray, N. S., MacCulloch, M. J., Smith, J., Morris, M., & Snowden, R. J. (2003, 29 May). Violence viewed by psychopathic murderers. *Nature, 423*(6939), 497–498. (Http://www.nature.com/nature/journal/v423/n6939/pdf/423 497a.pdf)

202.   Green, C. S., & Bavelier, D. (2003, 29 May). Action video game modifies visual selective attention. *Nature, 423*(6939), 534–537. (Http://www.nature.com/nature/journal/v423/n6939/pdf/nat ure01647.pdf)

203.   Greenfield, P. M. (2009, 2 Jan). Technology and Informal Education: What Is Taught, What Is Learned. *Science, 323*(5910), 69–71. (Http://www.sciencemag.org/cgi/reprint/323/5910/69.pdf)

204.   Guiso, L., Monte, F., Sapienza, P., & Zingales, L. (2008, 30 May). Culture, Gender, and Math. *Science, 320*(5880), 1164–1165. (Http://www.sciencemag.org/cgi/reprint/320/5880/1164.pd)

205.   Gutfreund, Y., Zheng, W., & Knudsen, E. I. (2002, 30 Aug). Gated Visual Input to the Central Auditory System. *Science, 297*(5586), 1556–1559. (Http://www.sciencemag.org/cgi/reprint/sci;297/5586/1556. pdf)

206.   Haarmeier, T., Bunjes, F., Lindner, A., Berret, E., & Thier, P. (2001, 8 Nov). Optimizing Visual Motion Perception during Eye Movements. *Neuron, 32*(3), 527–535. (Http://download.cell.com/neuron/pdf/PIIS08966273010048 6X.pdf)

207.   Hall, E. T. (1959). *The Silent Language.* Anchor.

208.   Hartelius, G. (2007). Quantitative Somatic
        Phenomenology: Toward and Epistemology of Subjective.
        Journal of Consciousness Studies, 14(12), 24–56.
        (Http://www.ingentaconnect.com/search/article?title=Quantit
        ative+Somatic+Phenomenology&title_type=tka&year_from=
        1998&year_to=2009&database=1&pageSize=20&index=1)
209.   Hauser, M. D., Chomsky, N., & Fitch, W. T. (2002, 22
        November). The Faculty of Language: What Is It, Who Has It
        and How Did It Evolve? *Science, 298,* 1569–1579.
        (Http://www.sciencemag.org/cgi/reprint/298/5598/1569.pdf)
210.   Hawkley, L. C., Browne, M. W., & Caciopo, J. T. (2005,
        Oct). How Can I Connect With Thee? *Psychological
        Science, 16*(10), 798–804.
        (Http://www3.interscience.wiley.com/cgi-
        bin/fulltext/118661663/PDFSTART)
211.   Hendry, J. (2005). E-Gender or Agenda: Are Women
        Getting What They Want? [Monash University] (p. 5).
212.   Hernández, A., Zainos, A., & Romo, R. (2002, 14 Mar).
        Temporal Evolution of a Decision-Making Process in Medial
        Premotor Cortex. *Neuron, 33*(6), 959–972.
        (Http://www.sciencedirect.com/science?_ob=MImg&_imagek
        ey=B6WSS-47MC579-D-
        3&_cdi=7054&_user=10&_orig=search&_coverDate=03%2F1
        4%2F2002&_sk=999669993&view=c&wchp=dGLzVtb-
        zSkzk&md5=213a3365b29e25dcb74f5a9307df5ef5&ie=/sdart
        icle.pdf)
213.   Heylighen, F. (1993/2002, 8 Jul/31 Oct). *Principia
        Cybernetica Web.* (Http://pespmc1.vub.ac.be/Default.html)
214.   Heyman, K. (2006, 5 May). The Map in the Brain: Grid
        Cells May Help Us Navigate. *Science, 312*(5774), 680–681.
        (Http://www.sciencemag.org/cgi/reprint/312/5774/680.pdf)
215.   Hodkinson, C., & Kiel, G. (2006). WWW Consumer
        External Information Search: Do Traditional Predictors of
        Search Apply in this New Information Environment?
        University of Queensland.

216.   Holden, C. (1995, 12 May). Sex and the Granular Layer.
        Science, 5212, 807.
        (Http://www.sciencemag.org/cgi/reprint/268/5212/807.pdf)
217.   Holden, C. (2001, 2 Nov). 'Behavioral' Addictions: Do They
        Exist? *Science, 294*(5544), 980–982.
        (Http://www.sciencemag.org/cgi/reprint/294/5544/980.pdf)
218.   Holden, C. (2001, 27 Apr). How the Brain Understands
        Music. *Science, 292*(5517), 623.
        (Http://www.sciencemag.org/cgi/content/full/sci;292/5517/6
        23)
219.   Holden, C. (2004, 27 Feb). The Origin of Speech.
        Science, 303(5662), 1316–1319.
        (Http://www.sciencemag.org/cgi/reprint/sci;303/5662/1316.
        pdf)
220.   Horst, P. (1966). *Psychological measurement and
        prediction.* Belmont, Calif.: Wadsworth Pub. Co.
221.   Hut P. (1999, Feb/Mar). Theory and experiment in
        philosophy. *Journal of Consciousness Studies, 6*(s 2–3), 241–
        244.
222.   Hyunkyu Lee, S. P. V. (2005, Oct). Visual Cognition
        Influences Early Vision. *Psychological Science, 16*(10), 763–
        768. (Http://www3.interscience.wiley.com/cgi-
        bin/fulltext/118661657/PDFSTART)
223.   In the Eye of the Beholder (Color)? (2005, 3 June).
        Science, 308(5727), 1406.
        (Http://www.sciencemag.org/content/308/5727/1406.2.full.p
        df)
224.   Isalan, M., & Morrison, M. (2009, 23 Apr). This title is
        false. *Nature, 458*(7241), 969–969.
        (Http://www.nature.com/nature/journal/v458/n7241/full/458
        969a.html)
225.   Johansson, P., Hall, L., Sikstrom, S., & Olsson, A. (2005, 7
        Oct). Failure to Detect Mismatches Between Intention and
        Outcome in a Simple Decision Task.
        Science, 310(5745), 116–119.
        (Http://www.sciencemag.org/cgi/reprint/310/5745/116.pdf)

226.   Joliveau, E., Smith, J., & Wolfe, J. (2004, 8 Jan). Tuning of vocal tract resonance by sopranos. *Nature, 427*(6970), 116–116.
(Http://www.nature.com/nature/journal/v427/n6970/pdf/427116a.pdf)

227.   Joyce F. Benenson, H. M., Caitlin Fitzgerald. (2009, 5 Jan). Males' Greater Tolerance of Same-Sex Peers. *Psychological Science, 20*(2), 184–190.
(Http://www3.interscience.wiley.com/cgi-bin/fulltext/121615904/PDFSTART)

228.   Kara, P., & Boyd, J. D. (2009, 2 Apr). A micro-architecture for binocular disparity and ocular dominance in visual cortex. *Nature, 458*(7238), 627–631.
(Http://www.nature.com/nature/journal/v458/n7238/pdf/nature07721.pdf)

229.   Kearney, H. (1971). *Science and Change: 1500–1700.* McGraw-Hill.

230.   Kinsley, C. H., Madonia, L., Gifford, G. W., Tureski, K., Griffin, G. R., Lowry, C., et al. (1999, 11 Nov). Motherhood improves learning and memory. *Nature, 401*(6758), 137–138.
(Http://www.nature.com/nature/journal/v402/n6758/pdf/402137a0.pdf)

231.   Kitagawa, N., & Ichihara, S. (2002, 14 Mar). Hearing visual motion in depth. *Nature, 416*(6877), 172–174.
(Http://www.nature.com/nature/journal/v416/n6877/pdf/416172a.pdf)

232.   Kohler, E., Keysers, C., Umilta, M. A., Fogassi, L., Gallese, V., & Rizzolatti, G. (2002, 2 Aug). Hearing Sounds, Understanding Actions: Action Representation in Mirror Neurons. *Science, 297*(5582), 846–848.
(Http://www.sciencemag.org/cgi/reprint/sci;297/5582/846.pdf)

233.   Konttinen, N., & Lyytinen, H. (1993). Brain slow waves preceding time-locked visuo-motor performance. *Journal of Sport Sciences, 11,* 257–66.

234.   Kovics, Ã. M., & Mehler, J. (2009, 21 Apr). Cognitive gains in 7-month-old bilingual infants. *Proceedings of the National Academy of Sciences, 106*(16), 6556–6560. (Http://www.pnas.org/content/106/16/6556.full.pdf+html)

235.   Kozlowski, S. W., & Ilgen, D. R. (2006, Dec). Enhancing the Effectiveness of Work Groups and Teams. *Psychological Science in the Public Interest, 7*(3), 77–124. (Http://www3.interscience.wiley.com/cgi-bin/fulltext/118600272/PDFSTART)

236.   Kramer, A. F., & Jacobson, A. (1991). Perceptual organization and focused attention: The role of objects and proximity in visual processing. *Perception and Psychophysics, 50,* 267–284.

237.   Kristan, W. B. (2007, 19 Jan). A Push-Me Pull-You Neural Design. *Science, 315,* 339–340. (Http://www.sciencemag.org/cgi/content/full/315/5810/339)

238.   Kuhn L. (2002). Complexity, Cybernetics and Human Knowing. *Cybernetics & Human Knowing, 9*(1), 39–50. (Http://www.ingentaconnect.com/content/imp/chk/2002/000 00009/00000001/107)

239.   Kuo, W.-J., Sjostrom, T., Chen, Y.-P., Wang, Y.-H., & Huang, C.-Y. (2009, 24 Apr). Intuition and Deliberation: Two Systems for Strategizing in the Brain. *Science, 324*(5926), 519–522. (Http://www.sciencemag.org/cgi/reprint/324/5926/519.pdf)

240.   Lau, H. C., Rogers, R. D., Haggard, P., & Passingham, R. E. (2004, 20 Feb). Attention to Intention. *Science, 303*(5661), 1208–1210. (Http://www.sciencemag.org/cgi/reprint/sci;303/5661/1208.pdf)

241.   Lazer, D., Pentland, A., Adamic, L., Aral, S., Barabasi, A.-L., Brewer, D., et al. (2009, 6 Feb). Computational Social Science. *Science, 323*(5915), 721–723. (Http://www.sciencemag.org/cgi/reprint/sci;323/5915/721.pdf)

242.   Lee, N. R. (2002). *Colour as a tool for e-branding.* (Eun-Seon). MA Design Futures.
(Http://www.colormatters.com/research/nrl_ebrand3.pdf)

243.   Levine, J. A., Weisell, R., Chevassus, S., Martinez, C. D., Burlingame, B., & Coward, W. A. (2001, 26 Oct). The Work Burden of Women. *Science, 294*(5543), 812.
(Http://www.sciencemag.org/cgi/reprint/sci;294/5543/812.pdf)

244.   Liberman, N., & Trope, Y. (2008, 21 Nov). The Psychology of Transcending the Here and Now.
Science, 322(5905), 1201–1205.
(Http://www.sciencemag.org/cgi/reprint/sci;322/5905/1201.pdf)

245.   Libet, B., Wright Jr., E., Feinstein, B., & Pearl, D. (1979). Subjective referral of the timing for a conscious experience: A functional role for the somatosensory specific projection system in man. *Brain, 102,* 193–224.
(Http://www.idemployee.id.tue.nl/g.w.m.rauterberg/lecturenotes/DGB01%20ADD/libet-et-al-1979.pdf)

246.   Libet, B. (1985). Unconscious cerebral initiative and the role of conscious will in the initiation of action. *Behavioral and Brain Sciences, 8,* 529–66.

247.   Libet, B. (2003). Can Conscious Experience Affect Brain Activity? *Journal of Consciousness Studies, 10*(12), 26.
(Http://docserver.ingentaconnect.com/deliver/connect/imp/13558250/v10n12/s2.pdf?expires=1417389027&id=80052408&titleid=3956&accname=Joseph+Carrabis&checksum=A8F7E49703B1F4A64AB16C33444F4C22)

248.   Lida, B. (2002, Jul). Can Personality Be Used to Predict How We Use the Internet? *Usability News (Software Usability Research Laboratory (SURL) at Wichita State University), 4*(2). (Http://www.surl.org/usabilitynews/42/e-shopping_personality.asp)

249.   Loewenstein, G. (2006, 5 May). The Pleasures and Pains of Information. *Science, 312*(5774), 704–706.
(Http://www.sciencemag.org/cgi/reprint/312/5774/704.pdf)

250.   Lynch, A. (1996). *Thought Contagion: How Belief Spreads Through Society (The New Science of Memes).* Basic Books.
251.   Mack, A., & Rock, I. (1998). *Inattentional Blindness.* Cambridge, MA: MIT Press.
252.   Macpherson Fiona. (2002). The Power of Natural Selection. *Journal of Consciousness Studies, 9*(8), 30–35. (Http://www.ingentaconnect.com/search/article?title=%22Th e+Power+of+Natural+Selection%22&title_type=tka&journal =Journal+of+Consciousness+Studies&journal_type=exact&v olume=9&issue=8&year_from=1998&year_to=2009&databas e=1&pageSize=20&index=1)
253.   Mamassian, P. (2008). Overconfidence in an Objective Anticipatory Motor Task. *Psychological Science, 19*(6), 601–606.
254.   Marc H. Bornstein, C.-S. H., Clare Bell. (2006, Feb). Stability in Cognition Across Early Childhood. *Psychological Science, 17*(2), 151–158.
255.   Mark L. Howe. (2007). Children's Emotional False Memories. *Psychological Science, 18*(10), 856–860. (Http://www3.interscience.wiley.com/cgi-bin/fulltext/118505435/PDFSTART)
256.   Marsh, R. L., Ellerby, D. J., Carr, J. A., Henry, H. T., & Buchanan, C. I. (2004, 2 Jan). Partitioning the Energetics of Walking and Running: Swinging the Limbs Is Expensive. *Science, 303*(5654), 80–83. (Http://www.sciencemag.org/cgi/reprint/sci;303/5654/80.pdf)
257.   McCabe, K., Houser, D., Ryan, L., Smith, V., & Trouard, T. (2001, 25 Sep). A functional imaging study of cooperation in two-person reciprocal exchange. *Proceedings of the National Academy of Sciences of the United States of America, 98*(20), 11832–11835. (Http://www.pnas.org/content/98/20/11832.full.pdf+html)
258.   McMains, S. A., & Somers, D. C. (2005, 12 Oct). Processing Efficiency of Divided Spatial Attention Mechanisms in Human Visual Cortex. *Journal of*

Neuroscience, 25(41), 9444–9448.
(Http://www.jneurosci.org/cgi/reprint/25/41/9444)

259.   McNeil, D. (Ed.). (2000). *Language and Gesture.*
Cambridge: Cambridge University Press.

260.   Mehta, R., & Zhu, R. (. (2009, 27 Feb). Blue or Red?
Exploring the Effect of Color on Cognitive Task Performances.
Science, 323(5918), 1226–1229.
(Http://www.sciencemag.org/cgi/reprint/sci;323/5918/1226.
pdf)

261.   Miller, J. (1991). The flanker compatibility effect as a
function of visual angle, attentional focus,visual transients,
and perceptual load: A search for boundary conditions.
Perception and Psychophysics, 49, 270–288.
(Http://www.psychonomic.org/search/view.cgi?id=5499)

262.   Mitchell, J. F., Stoner, G. R., & Reynolds, J. H. (2004, 27
May). Object-based attention determines dominance in
binocular rivalry. *Nature, 429*(6990), 410–413.
(Http://www.nature.com/nature/journal/v429/n6990/pdf/nat
ure02584.pdf)

263.   Montgomery, S. (2004, 27 Feb). Of Towers, Walls, and
Fields: Perspectives on Language in Science.
Science, 303(5662), 1333–1335.
(Http://www.sciencemag.org/cgi/reprint/sci;303/5662/1333.
pdf)

264.   Murphy, J., Hofacker, C., & Mizerski, R. (2006). Primacy
and recency effects on clicking behavior. *Journal of
Computer-Mediated Communication, 11*(2).
(Http://jcmc.indiana.edu/vol11/issue2/murphy.html)

265.   Murray, J. (1998). Information, Communication and
Technology. *Cybernetics&Human Knowing, 5*(2), 45.

266.   Nichols, M. J., & Newsome, W. T. (1999, 15 Jul). Monkeys
play the odds. *Nature, 400*(6741), 217–218.
(Http://www.nature.com/nature/journal/v400/n6741/pdf/400
217a0.pdf)

267.   Offer, S., & Schneider, B. (2011, Dec). Revisiting the
Gender Gap in Time-Use Patterns: Multitasking and Well-
Being among Mothers and Fathers in Dual-Earner Families.

American Sociological Review.
(Http://www.asanet.org/images/journals/docs/pdf/asr/Dec11
ASRFeature.pdf)

268.   Otamendi, R. D., Carrabis, J., & Carrabis, S. (2009).
Predicting Age & Gender Online. Brussels, Belgium:
NextStage Analytics.

269.   Otamendi, R. D. (2009, 26 May). *NextStage Analytics
predicts age & gender: The proof.* NextStage Analytics.
(Http://makingmarketingactionable.com/2009/05/26/nextsta
ge-analytics-predicts-age-gender-the-proof/)

270.   Overgaard, M., & Sorensen, T. A. (2004, 2004).
Introspection Distinct From First-Order Experiences. *Journal
of Consciousness Studies, 11*(7–8), 79–95.

271.   Pascalis, O., de Haan, M., & Nelson, C. A. (2002, 17 May).
Is Face Processing Species-Specific During the First Year of
Life? *Science, 296*(5571), 1321–1323.
(Http://www.sciencemag.org/cgi/reprint/296/5571/1321.pdf)

272.   Patston, L. L., Corballis, M. C., Hogg, S. L., & Tippett, L. J.
(2006, Dec). The Neglect of Musicians: Line Bisection Reveals
an Opposite Bias. *Psychological Science, 12,* 1029–1031.
(Http://www.psychologicalscience.org/members/goToSynerg
y.cfm?issn=0956–7976&date=2006&article=01823)

273.   Paul E. Dux, V. C. (2005, Oct). The Meaning of the Mask
Matters. *Psychological Science, 16*(10), 775–779.
(Http://www3.interscience.wiley.com/cgi-
bin/fulltext/118661659/PDFSTART)

274.   Paynter, J., & Satitkit, S. (2002, 3 Dec). User Perceptions
of Travel Industry Websites. ANZMAC.
(Http://smib.vuw.ac.nz:8081/WWW/ANZMAC2001/anzmac/A
UTHORS/pdfs/Paynter.pdf)

275.   Pelli, D. G. (1999, 6 Aug). Close Encounters--An Artist
Shows that Size Affects Shape. *Science, 285*(5429), 844–
846.
(Http://www.sciencemag.org/cgi/content/full/285/5429/844)

276.   Pennisi, E. (2004, 27 Feb). The First Language?
Science, 303(5662), 1319–1320.

(Http://www.sciencemag.org/cgi/reprint/sci;303/5662/1319.
pdf)

277.   Pennisi, E. (2004, 27 Feb). Speaking in Tongues.
        Science, 303(5662), 1321–1323.
        (Http://www.sciencemag.org/cgi/reprint/sci;303/5662/1321.
        pdf)

278.   Perviz, A. (2006). Narcissistic Sensations and Intentional
        Directedness: How Second-Order Cybernetics Helps Dissolve
        the Tension Between the Egocentric Character of Sensory
        Information and the (Seemingly) World-Centered Character
        of Cognitive Representations. *Cybernetics And Human
        Knowing., 13*(3–4), 74–86.
        (Http://www.ingentaconnect.com/search/article?journal=Cyb
        ernetics++Human+Knowing&journal_type=words&year_from
        =2006&year_to=2006&database=1&pageSize=20&index=6)

279.   Peta Marcela, Maki, A., Kovacic, A. D., Dehaene-Lambertz,
        G., Koizumi, H., Bouquet, F., et al. (2003, 30 Sep). Sounds
        and silence: An optical topography study of language
        recognition at birth. *Proceedings of the National Academy of
        Sciences of the United States of America, 100*(20), 11702–
        11705.
        (Http://www.pnas.org/content/100/20/11702.full.pdf+html)

280.   Petitmengin-Peugeot C. (1999, Feb/March). The intuitive
        experience. *Journal of Consciousness Studies, 6*(s 2–3), 43–
        77.

281.   Petranker, J. (2003). Inhabiting Conscious Experience.
        Journal of Consciousness Studies, 10(12), 3–23.
        (Http://docserver.ingentaconnect.com/deliver/connect/imp/1
        3558250/v10n12/s1.pdf?expires=1417388603&id=80052364
        &titleid=3956&accname=Joseph+Carrabis&checksum=265FC
        200995D7F31F7B4FB285CE5E13E)

282.   Platt, M. L., & Glimcher, P. W. (1999, 15 Jul). Neural
        correlates of decision variables in parietal cortex.
        Nature, 400(6741), 233–238.
        (Http://www.nature.com/nature/journal/v400/n6741/pdf/400
        233a0.pdf)

283.   Pocket, S. (2002, June). On Subjective Back-Referral and
        How Long It Takes to Become Conscious of a Stimulus: A
        Reinterpretation of Libet's Data. *Consciousness and
        Cognition, 11*(2), 144–161.
284.   Poggio, T., Rifkin, R., Mukherjee, S., & Niyogi, P. (2004,
        25 Mar). General conditions for predictivity in learning
        theory. *Nature, 428*(6981), 419–422.
        (Http://www.nature.com/nature/journal/v428/n6981/pdf/nat
        ure02341.pdf)
285.   Polanyi, M. (1962). *Personal Knowledge.* Chicago:
        University of Chicago Press.
286.   Powell, R. M. Using Traditional Gender Norms to Expand
        Gender: A Qualitative Study of Old Time Dance Communities.
        Journal of Mundane Behavior, 3(1).
287.   Prinzmetal, W., Amiri, H., Allen, K., & Edwards, T. (1998,
        subjective experience;). Phenomenology of Attention: 1.
        Color, Location, Orientation, and Spatial Frequency. *Journal
        of Experimental Psychology, 24*(1), 261–282.
288.   Prinzmetal, W., Nwachuku, I., Bodanski, L., Blumenfeld,
        L., & Shimizu, N. (1997). The Phenomenology of Attention: 2.
        Brightness and Contrast. *Consciousness and
        Cognition, 6,* 372–412.
289.   Prinzmetal, W., & Wilson, A. (1997). The Effect of
        Attention on Phenomenal Length. UCal Berkeley, U Oregon.
        (Http://socrates.berkeley.edu/~wprinz/research/Length.pdf)
290.   Quirke, L. (2006, 1 Nov). "Keeping young minds sharp":
        Children's cognitive stimulation and the rise of parenting
        magazines, 1959–2003. *The Canadian Review of Sociology
        and Anthropology.*
291.   R. Sprengelmeyer, D. P., E.C. Fagan. (2009, 5 Jan). The
        Cutest Little Baby Face: A Hormonal Link to Sensitivity to
        Cuteness in Infant Faces. *Psychological Science, 20*(2), 149–
        154. (Http://www3.interscience.wiley.com/cgi-
        bin/fulltext/121641571/PDFSTART)
292.   Raz, A., Kirsch, I., Pollard, J., & Nitkin-Kaner, Y. (2006,
        Feb). Suggestion Reduces the Stroop Effect. *Psychological
        Science, 17*(2), 91–95.

(Http://www3.interscience.wiley.com/cgi-bin/fulltext/118597324/PDFSTART)

293.   Rees, G., Russell, C., Frith, C. D., & Driver, J. (1999, 24 Dec). Inattentional Blindness Versus Inattentional Amnesia for Fixated But Ignored Words. *Science, 286*(5449), 2504–2507.
(Http://www.sciencemag.org/content/286/5449/2504.full.pdf)

294.   Rothwell, N. (2004, 19 Feb). One more thing.. *Nature, 427*(6976), 683–683.
(Http://www.nature.com/nature/journal/v427/n6976/pdf/427683a.pdf)

295.   Rowe, M. L., & Goldin-Meadow, S. (2009, 13 Feb). Differences in Early Gesture Explain SES Disparities in Child Vocabulary Size at School Entry. *Science, 323*(5916), 951–953.
(Http://www.sciencemag.org/cgi/reprint/323/5916/951.pdf)

296.   Sanes, J., Donoghue, J., Thangaraj, V., Edelman, R., & Warach, S. (1995, 23 Jun). Shared neural substrates controlling hand movements in human motor cortex. *Science, 268*(5218), 1775–1777.
(Http://www.sciencemag.org/cgi/reprint/sci;268/5218/1775.pdf)

297.   Sapolsky, R. (1995). Ego Boundaries, or the Fit of My Father's Shirt. *Discover, 16,* 62–67.
(Http://discovermagazine.com/1995/nov/egoboundariesort586/?searchterm=ego%20boundaries,%20or%20the%20fit%20of%20my%20father's%20shirt)

298.   Sargolini, F., Fyhn, M., Hafting, T., McNaughton, B. L., Witter, M. P., Moser, M.-B., et al. (2006, 5 May). Conjunctive Representation of Position, Direction, and Velocity in Entorhinal Cortex. *Science, 312*(5774), 758–762.
(Http://www.sciencemag.org/cgi/reprint/312/5774/758.pdf)

299.   Satitkit, S., & Everett, A. (2001). Strategies for developing web sites for the travel industry. In *Bridging Marketing Theory and Practice.* Wellington: Massey University.

300.   Schlaggar, B. L., Brown, T. T., Lugar, H. M., Visscher, K.
        M., Miezin, F. M., & Petersen, S. E. (2002, 24 May).
        Functional Neuroanatomical Differences Between Adults and
        School-Age Children in the Processing of Single Words.
        Science, 296(5572), 1476–1479.
        (Http://www.sciencemag.org/cgi/reprint/sci;296/5572/1476.
        pdf)
301.   Schnupp, J. W. H., Mrsic-Flogel, T. D., & King, A. J. (2001,
        8 Nov). Linear processing of spatial cues in primary auditory
        cortex. *Nature, 414*(6860), 200–204.
        (Http://www.nature.com/nature/journal/v414/n6860/pdf/414
        200a0.pdf)
302.   Schooler, J. W., & Schrieber, C. A. (2004, 2004).
        Experience, Meta-consciousness, and the Paradox of
        Introspection. *Journal of Consciouness Studies, 11*(7–8), 17–
        39.
303.   Schraefel, M. (2007). What is an analogue for the
        semantic web and why is having one important? In
        *Proceedings of the eighteenth conference on Hypertext and
        hypermedia* (pp. 123–132). Manchester, UK: ACM (NYC).
        (Http://portal.acm.org/ft_gateway.cfm?id=1286271&type=p
        df&coll=GUIDE&dl=GUIDE&CFID=47214215&CFTOKEN=6735
        1009)
304.   Schwartz, H., Eichstaedt, J., Dziurzynski, L., & Ramones,
        S. (2013, 25 Sep). Personality, Gender, and Age in the
        Language of Social Media: The Open-Vocabulary Approach.
        PLoS One, 8(9).
        (Http://www.plosone.org/article/fetchObject.action;jsessionid
        =5374E28E1A87A4693F166ACB2915DD41?uri=info%3Adoi%
        2F10.1371%2Fjournal.pone.0073791&representation=PDF)
305.   Seifritz, E., Esposito, F., Hennel, F., Mustovic, H., Neuhoff,
        J. G., Bilecen, D., et al. (2002, 6 Sep). Spatiotemporal
        Pattern of Neural Processing in the Human Auditory Cortex.
        Science, 297(5587), 1706–1708.
        (Http://www.sciencemag.org/cgi/reprint/sci;297/5587/1706.
        pdf)

306.   Selvidge, P. (2003, Oct). Examining Tolerance for Online Delays. *Usability News (Software Usability Research Laboratory (SURL) at Wichita State University), 5*(1). (Http://surl.org/usabilitynews/51/delaytime.htm)

307.   Shaikh, A. D., Chaparro, B. S., & Fox, D. (2006, Feb). Perception of Fonts: Perceived Personality Traits and Uses. *Usability News (Software Usability Research Laboratory (SURL) at Wichita State University), 8*(1). (Http://www.surl.org/usabilitynews/81/PersonalityofFonts.asp)

308.   Shaikh, A. D., Fox, D., & Chaparro, B. S. (2007, Jan). The Effect of Typeface on the Perception of Email. *Usability News (Software Usability Research Laboratory (SURL) at Wichita State University), 9*(1). (Http://www.surl.org/usabilitynews/91/POF2.asp)

309.   Shaikh, A. D. (2007, June). The Effect of Website Typeface Appropriateness on the Perception of a Company's Ethos. *Usability News (Software Usability Research Laboratory (SURL) at Wichita State University), 9*(2). (Http://www.surl.org/usabilitynews/92/POF.asp)

310.   Shani, I. (2007). Consciousness and the First Person. *Journal of Consciousness Studies, 14*(12), 57–91.

311.   Shapiro, B. J. (2000). *A Culture of Fact; England, 1550–1720.* Cornell University: Cornell University Press.

312.   Shear J., & Jevning R. (1999, Feb/Mar). Pure consciousness: Scientific exploration of meditation techniques. *Journal of Consciousness Studies, 6*(s 2–3), 189–210.

313.   Shear, J. (1995). Editor's Introduction. *Journal of Consciousness Studies, 2*(3), 195.

314.   Shena Lu. (2006, Feb). Cue Duration and Parvocellular Guidance of Visual Attention. *Psychological Science, 17*(2), 101–102. (Http://www3.interscience.wiley.com/cgi-bin/fulltext/118597326/PDFSTART)

315.   Shettleworth, S. J. (1998). *Cognition, Evolution and Behavior.* Oxford: Oxford.

316.   Shettleworth, S. J. (2007, 22 Feb). Planning for Breakfast. *Nature, 445,* 825–826. (Http://www.nature.com/nature/journal/v445/n7130/pdf/445 825a.pdf)

317.   Shouse, B. (2001, 11 Sep). Reality TV Puts Group Behavior to the Test. *Science, 294*(5545), 1262b-1263. (Http://www.sciencemag.org/cgi/reprint/sci;294/5545/1262b .pdf)

318.   Sirotin, Y. B., & Das, A. (2009, 22 Jan). Anticipatory haemodynamic signals in sensory cortex not predicted by local neuronal activity. *Nature, 457*(7228), 475–479.

319.   Sloman, A., & Chrisley, R. (2003). Virtual Machines and Consciousness. *Journal of Consciousness Studies, 10*(4–5), 133–172. (Http://www.ingentaconnect.com/search/article?title=%22Vir tual+Machines+and+Consciousness%22&title_type=tka&aut hor=Sloman&journal=Journal+of+Consciousness+Studies&jo urnal_type=exact&year_from=1998&year_to=2009&databas e=1&pageSize=20&index=1)

320.   Strogatz, S. H., Abrams, D. M., McRobie, A., Eckhardt, B., & Ott, E. (2005, 3 Nov). Theoretical mechanics: Crowd synchrony on the Millennium Bridge. *Nature, 438*(7064), 43–44. (Http://www.nature.com/nature/journal/v438/n7064/pdf/438 043a.pdf)

321.   Sundberg, K. A., Mitchell, J. F., & Reynolds, J. H. (2009, 26 Mar). Spatial Attention Modulates Center-Surround Interactions in Macaque Visual Area V4. *Neuron, 61*(6), 952–963. (Http://download.cell.com/neuron/pdf/PIIS08966273090016 9X.pdf)

322.   Tanenhaus, M. K., Spivey-Knowlton, M. J., Eberhard, K. M., & Sedivy, J. C. (1995, 16 June). Integration of Visual and Linguistic Information in Spoken Language Comprehension. *Science, 268,* 1632–1634. (Http://www.sciencemag.org/cgi/reprint/268/5217/1632.pdf)

323.   Thompson, K. G., Biscoe, K. L., & Sato, T. R. (2005, 12
       Oct). Neuronal Basis of Covert Spatial Attention in the Frontal
       Eye Field. *Journal of Neuroscience, 25*(41), 9479–9487.
       (Http://www.jneurosci.org/cgi/reprint/25/41/9479)
324.   Travis, J. (1999, 15 May). Battle of the Sexes. *Science
       News, 155,* 312–314.
       (Http://www.articlearchives.com/science-
       technology/biochemistry-genetic-biochemistry/607404–
       1.html)
325.   Tyler, C. W. (1999, 30 Jul). Is Art Lawful?
       Science, 285(5428), 673–674.
       (Http://www.sciencemag.org/cgi/content/full/sci;285/5428/6
       73)
326.   Vaina, L. M., Solomon, J., Chowdhury, S., Sinha, P., &
       Belliveau, J. W. (2001, 25 Sep). Functional neuroanatomy of
       biological motion perception in humans. *Proceedings of the
       National Academy of Sciences of the United States of
       America, 98*(20), 11656–11661.
       (Http://www.pnas.org/content/98/20/11656.full.pdf+html)
327.   Varela F.J. (1999, Feb/Mar). Present-time consciousness.
       Journal of Consciousness Studies, 6(s 2–3), 111–140.
328.   Varela, F. J., & Shear, J. (1999, Feb/March). First-person
       Methodologies: What, Why, How? *Journal of Consciousness
       Studies, 6*(s 2–3), 1–14.
329.   Velmans, M. (2003). Preconscious Free Will. *Journal of
       Consciousness Studies, 10*(12), 42–61.
330.   Vergassola, M., Villermaux, E., & Shraiman, B. I. (2007,
       25 Jan). 'Infotaxis' as a strategy for searching without
       gradients. *Nature, 445,* 406–409.
       (Http://www.nature.com/nature/journal/v445/n7126/pdf/nat
       ure05464.pdf)
331.   Vermersch P. (1999, Feb/March). Introspection as
       practice. *Journal of Consciousness Studies, 6*(s 2–3), 17–42.
332.   Vieceli, J., & Sharp, B. (2005). The Inhibiting Effect of
       Brand Salience on Brand Name Recall (p. 6). Deakin
       University, University of South Australia.

333.   Vlok, D. (2005). An Assessment of the Knowledge
       Processing Environment in an Organisation - A Case Study.
       Rhodes Investec Business School: Rhodes University.
       (Www.macroinnovation.com/Assessment_of_Knowledge_Proc
       essing.pdf)
334.   Vohs, K. D., Baumesiter, R. F., Schmeichel, B. J., Twenge,
       J. M., Nelson, n. M., & Tice, D. M. (2008). Making Choices
       Impairs Subsequent Self-Control: A Limited-Resource
       Account of Decision Making, Self-Regulation, and Active
       Initiative. *Journal of Personality and Social
       Psychology, 94*(5), 883–898.
       (Http://www.apa.org/journals/releases/psp945883.pdf)
335.   Ward, M. (2015, Feb). Careless Responding on Internet-
       Based Surveys. *APS Observer, 28,* 2.
       (Http://www.psychologicalscience.org/index.php/publications
       /observer/2015/february-15/careless-responding-on-internet-
       based-surveys.html)
336.   Wargo, E. (2008, May). Talk to the Hand: New Insights
       into the Evolution of Language and Gesture. *APS
       Observer, 21*(5), 16–22.
       (Http://www.psychologicalscience.org/observer/getArticle.cf
       m?id=2340)
337.   Warren, C., & Karrer, R. (1984). Movement-related
       potentials during development: A replication and extension of
       relationships to age, motor control, mental status and IQ
       [Brain and information: Event Related Potentials].
       International Journal of Neuroscience, 24, 81–96.
338.   Warren, C., & Karrer, R. (1984). Movement-related
       potentials in children: A replication of waveforms and their
       relationships to age, performance, and cognitive development
       [Brain and information: Event Related Potentials].
       *International Journal of Neuroscience, 425.*R. Karrer, J.
       Cohen & P. Tueting (Eds.).
339.   Watts, D. J., Dodds, P. S., & Newman, M. E. J. (2002, 17
       May). Identity and Search in Social Networks.
       Science, 296(5571), 1302–1305.
       (Http://www.sciencemag.org/cgi/reprint/296/5571/1302.pdf)

340.   Waxman, S. R., & Lidz, J. Early Word learning. In
       Handbook of Child Psychology.
341.   Webb, E. J., Campbell, D. T., Schwartz, R. D., & Sechrest,
       L. (1966). *Unobtrusive Measures: Nonreactive Research in
       the Social Sciences.* Chicago: Rand McNally & Co.
342.   Weikum, W. M., Vouloumanos, A., Navarra, J., Soto-
       Faraco, S., Sebastian-Galles, N., & Werker, J. F. (2007, 25
       May). Visual Language Discrimination in Infancy.
       Science, 316, 1159.
       (Http://www.sciencemag.org/cgi/reprint/316/5828/1159.pdf)
343.   Wellman, H. M., Fang, F., Liu, D., Zhu, L., & Liu, G. (2006,
       Dec). Scaling of Theory-of-Mind Understandings in Chinese
       Children. *Psychological Science, 12,* 1075–1081.
       (Http://www.psychologicalscience.org/members/goToSynerg
       y.cfm?issn=0956–7976&date=2006&article=01830)
344.   Wentworth, C. (1995). *Sample Size and Sampling Error.*
       (Http://www.msearch.com/pdfs/SampleSizeError.pdf)
345.   Whitfield, J. (2006, 22 June). An MRI Scanner Darkly.
       Nature, 441, 922.
346.   Wolfe, J. M., Horowitz, T. S., & Kenner, N. M. (2005, 26
       May). Rare items often missed in visual searches.
       Nature, 435, 439–40.
       (Http://www.nature.com/nature/journal/v435/n7041/pdf/435
       439a.pdf)
347.   Wynne, C. D. L. (2004, 8 Apr). The Perils of
       Anthropomorphism. *Nature, 428,* 606.
       (Http://www.nature.com/nature/journal/v428/n6983/pdf/428
       606a.pdf)
348.   Yair Bar-Haim, T. Z., Dominique Lamy. (2006, Feb).
       Nature and Nurture in Own-Race Face Processing.
       Psychological Science, 17(2), 159–163.
       (Http://www3.interscience.wiley.com/cgi-
       bin/fulltext/118597334/PDFSTART)
349.   Yeshurun, Y., Rotshtein, P., Fried, I., Ben-Bashat, D., &
       Hendler, T. (2002, 14 Mar). The Role of the Amygdala in
       Signaling Prospective Outcome of Choice.
       Neuron, 33(6), 983–994.

(Http://download.cell.com/neuron/pdf/PIIS08966273020062
68.pdf)
350.   Yuri Miyamoto, R. E. N., Takahiko Masuda. (2006, Feb).
Culture and the Physical Environment. *Psychological
Science, 17*(2), 113–119.
(Http://www3.interscience.wiley.com/cgi-
bin/fulltext/118597328/PDFSTART)
351.   Zeki, S. (2001, 6 Jul). Artistic Creativity and the Brain.
Science, 293(5527), 51–52.
(Http://www.sciencemag.org/cgi/content/full/293/5527/51)

Index[a]

---

[a] – with many thanks to Jennifer "The Editress" Day

About the Author

Back twenty-five years ago when I wrote regularly for several publishers, we would eventually get to the "About the Author" section and I would pull a blank. I think of myself as a fairly boring person and I've never been able to write about things that bore me. Over the intervening years five people have written author bios for me as the need arose.[a] Here they are, chronologically, 1, 2, 3, 4 and 5, and all modality engineered because it's so much fun!

1 – From 1995

Joseph Carrabis was once called, "a cross between the Dalai Lama and Disneyland." That unlikely starting point is adequate so long as it doesn't end there. It is a convenient container for that which cannot be contained.

For the listmakers, there is a drawer somewhere holding degrees, credentials, certifications — pieces of paper that are important symbols for some. For the chronologists, there is a verifiable timeline of travels, teachers, studies, events, and contacts with people — if timelines are important. For the categorizers, there is only disappointment, as Carrabis is impossible to pigeonhole.

The facts of the matter can be laid out plainly, when it is possible to extract them. Blind until the age of five, Carrabis was raised by his grandparents. His grandfather, who died when Carrabis was ten, is obviously the most important influence on his life, but remains only the first in a long line of teachers whose guidance shaped and continues to shape who he is at this particular moment and how he does himself.

---

[a] *– Note to the 4th Edition* — We were going to remove the first four of these and then thought "Why don't we do an "Intersection of Four Statements" (page 223) style analysis of these. Obviously the people who wrote these biographs thought well of Joseph. I wonder how well they would have gotten along with each other?" and so you have it, at the end of this section, *Linguistic Intersections* (page 290).

In what might be called a polychromatic career, he has had published books and papers on subjects ranging from database programming to psychoneuroimmunology to Native American mythologies. Over two hundred published articles have dipped into dozens of specialties, from chaos theory to neurolinguistic programming to psychopomp. For labeling purposes, he can be called psychotherapist, computer programming consultant, author, healer, raconteur — all are true and none are the truth, which is why labels should only be applied to prescription bottles.

But these are the clichés of dust jacket biography, the conventional phrases used to delineate the life of an author for the casual reader.

Cultural Anthropology studies shamanism, and within shamanism there is a discipline called Storyteller. Carrabis swears this is not his discipline, though he has studied it. And I will believe that he believes that.

I don't. You must draw your own conclusions.

The above biograph mathematizes to figure 1 (page 282).

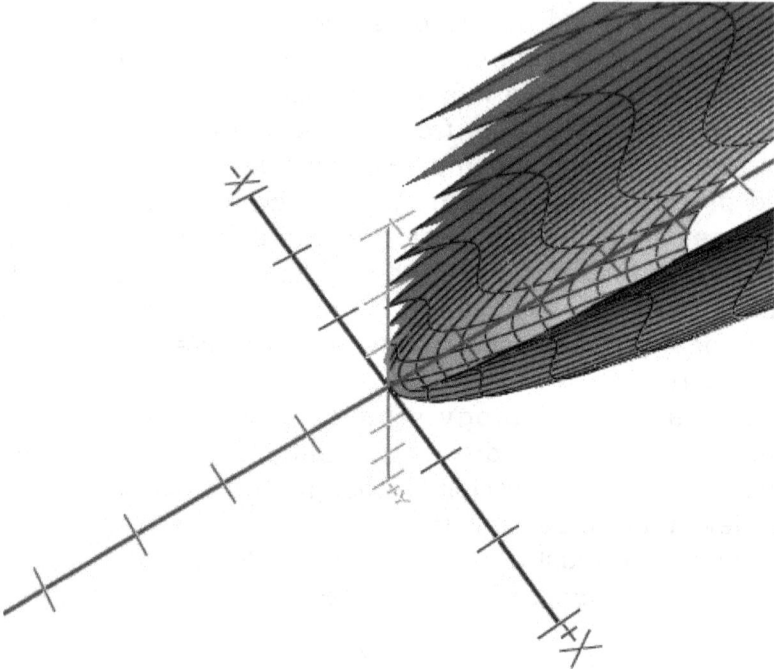

Figure 1 - My 1995 biographer conceived of me as someone ever reaching, ever exploring, with very distinct opinions and with boundaries I wouldn't cross.

2 – From 1997

Joseph "Je broussé ma chein sur la bouche" Carrabis has blended studies of physics, mathematics, linguistics, psychology, and anthropology to author multidisciplinary books and papers on database design and theory, mathematical linguistics, psycholinguistics, cultural anthropology, psychodymanics, neurolinguistics, gravitational physics, and creativity. His work has been noted, referenced, cited, and reprinted internationally, most recently in Italy's *Sacre Radici*. He's also a Certified HypnoTherapist and Therapist/Practitioner whose work with adolescents and personal mythologies has received national recognition. He's taught and been a guest lecturer at the university level, most recently as an adjunct professor at NECHAS, and continues to lecture on various topics internationally. He's also available for lectures and consulting on the topics presented in this paper. Joseph has also been nominated for several fiction and poetry prizes for his non-technical and non-academic writing. Hasn't won any yet, but he's working on it. In his spare time, he sleeps with his dog, kisses his cat, and walks his wife, or some permutation of that. He also plays lots of musical instruments just to keep his fingers quick, nimble, and free.

The above biograph mathematizes to figure 2 (page 283).

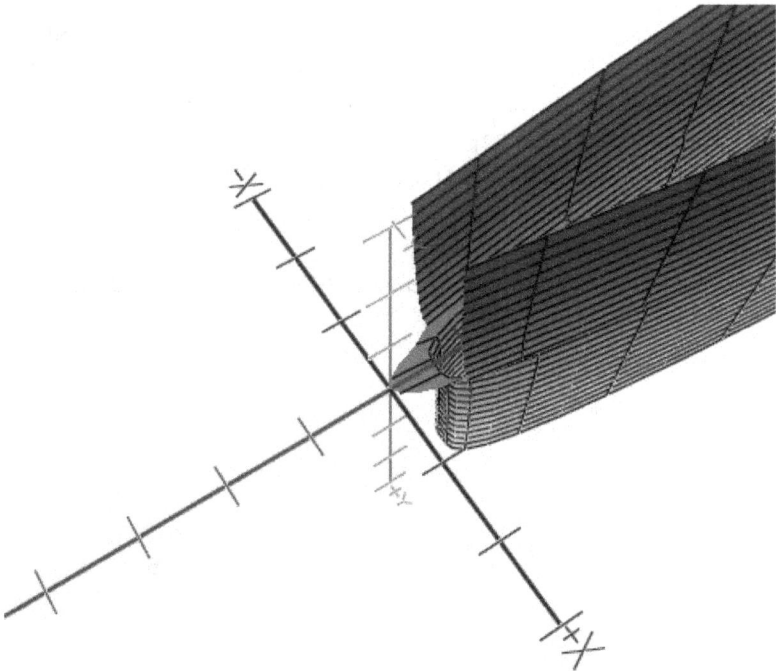

Figure 2 - In 1997 I'd lost some of my edginess but there were still boundaries I wouldn't cross, at least according to this biographer

3 – From 2000

Joseph Carrabis, Chief Research Scientist, applies studies of physics, mathematics, linguistics, psychology and anthropology to create high technology business solutions. He has authored multidisciplinary books and papers on database design and theory, mathematical linguistics and neurolinguistics. Joseph will utilize his multi-disciplinary skills to help AscendantOne create and enhance x-Commerce and B2x solutions for targeted and broader audiences such as P&C carriers, affinity groups and new economy financial services organizations. His contacts within the insurance industry include working with the research division of Arkwright Insurance, developing risk models and test procedures. Joseph's overall work has received national recognition, and he is referenced, cited and reprinted internationally, most recently in Italy's *Sacre Radici*. He has taught at the university level, most recently as an adjunct professor at NECHAS, and continues to lecture on various topics internationally. Joseph, who plays a number of musical instruments, has also been nominated for several fiction and poetry prizes for his non-technical and non-academic writing.

The above biograph mathematizes to figure 3 (page 285).

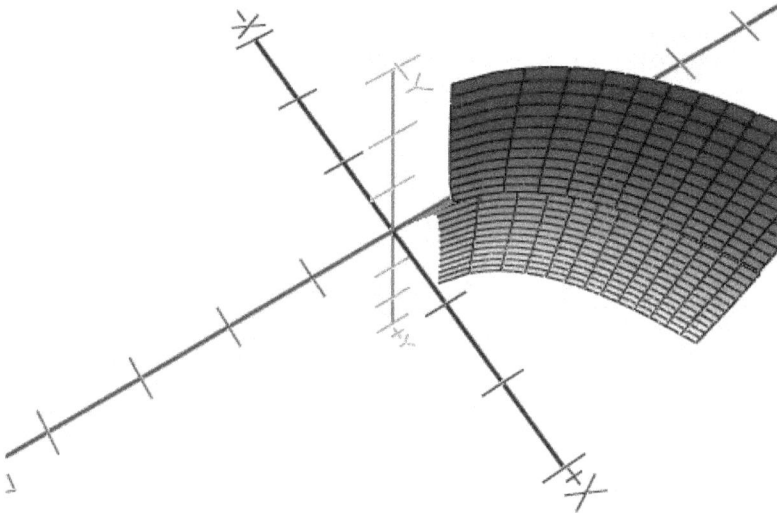

Figure 3 - I started off the norm and went way off the norm in 2000

4 – From 2003

Joseph Carrabis has authored 22 books and 225 articles in five areas of expertise. His books have covered cultural anthropology, database technology and methods, information mechanics, language acquisition, learning and education theory, mathematics, network topologies, and psycholinguistic modeling. His articles have covered computer technology, cultural-knowledge modeling, equine management, knowledge studies and applications, library science, martial arts, myth and folklore, neurolinguistic, psychodynamic and psychosocial modeling, studies of group and tribal behavior, studies of social interactions in NYC and more. In 2001 his paper and presentation, *Can Autonomous Entities Act on Non-Conscious Meaning in Human Communication?*, was the lead paper at the Baden-Baden IIAS conference. His knowledge and data designs have been used by Caltech, Citibank, DOD, IBM, NASA, Owens-Corning and Smith-Barney among others. He's been everything from butcher to truckdriver to Senior Knowledge Architect to Chief Research Scientist. Currently, Carrabis is Chairman and Chief Research Officer of NextStage Evolution, LLC, and its business subsidiary, NextStage Analytics, and founder of KnowledgeNH and NH Business Development Network. He's inventor and developer of Evolution Technology. You can reach him at jcarrabis@nextstagevolution.com.

The above biograph mathematizes to figure 4 (page 286).

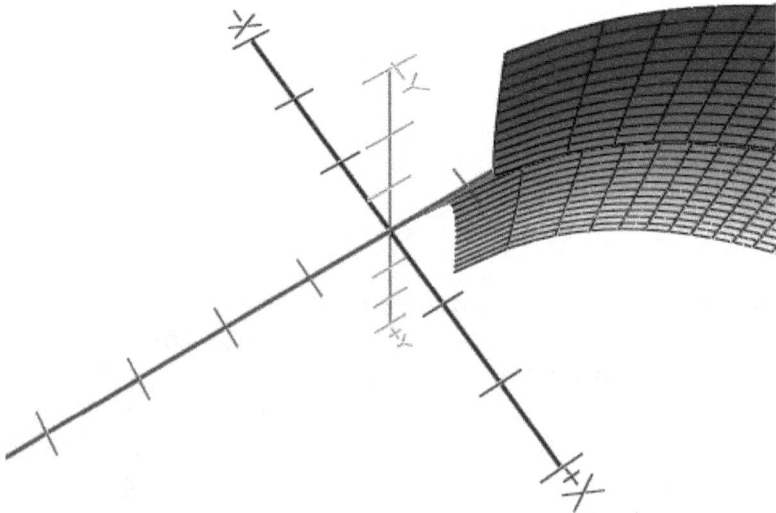

Figure 4 - In 2003, this biographer thought they understood me but only in certain ways (in a private conversation this person said, "I've known you twenty years and still feel I've only seen the surface of the ocean.")

5 – From 2008

Joseph Carrabis has been programming computers and other programmable systems since programming satellites for NASA in the 1970s. Since working with NASA, Joseph has served extensively as a consultant and computer solutions developer assisting the US DoD, Citibank, Merrill Lynch, Caltech, and Owens-Corning, among others. During the 1980s and early 1990s, Joseph authored a couple dozen computer science texts that raised him to the ranks of the top selling international non-fiction authors for years. Joseph has also authored numerous articles on cultural anthropology, mathematics, and linguistics for various publications. While consulting, Joseph cultivated his personal interest in anthropology and behavioral studies with extensive reading and personal study. That personal interest blossomed into an expertise that has led to many speaking engagements over the past five years, national recognition, and an appointment to the Society for New Communication Research board. In the past decade, utilizing his long-standing programming knowledge and anthropological studies, Joseph unveiled a patented disruptive technology that recognizes behavioral elements of human interactions with machines, behaviors that cue gender, age, financial status, buying interest, and other rich data opportunities previously unavailable to the online marketing world.

The above biograph mathematizes to figure 5 (page 288).

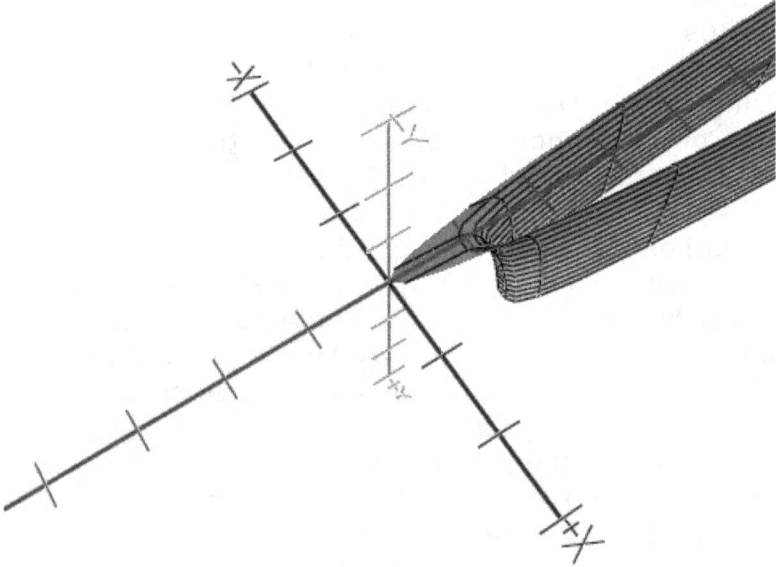

Figure 5 - I'm back where I was in the 1990s except there are areas I'd never address or consider.

6 – From later in 2008

Joseph Carrabis is a loyal husband, one of his few characteristics that fills him with pride. He is a stalwart friend, willing to support anyone in a time of need with only their request for help as remuneration. Joseph is a respected, open-minded researcher, happily devoting time, energy and thought to any intellectual pursuit that piques his interest (the more esoteric the better). He is a romantic, a free-spirit that refuses to be pigeon-holed, a spiritual man without faith in religion. Joseph has the scientific curiosity to challenge accepted ideas and the logical discipline to resolve those challenges. Over his lifetime, Joseph has enjoyed a wide range of experiences and walked a mile in many different pairs of shoes, frequently changing them lest he be defined by one pair. The thesis project of his lifelong educational pursuits is Evolution Technology, a tool with a myriad of uses across a broad expanse of technologies and environments. Joseph's desire to share Evolutionary Technology with others to solve problems and unlock doors has forced him to learn the skills of a marketer and business owner, roles that he loathes, but handles admirably while concurrently, nimbly gaining recognition within the field of media technology. Through it all, Joseph's ambitions have been limited to gathering the requisite resources to allow himself to share tranquility and solitude with his wife, the comradery of a close circle of friends and peers, and ample time for research and other intellectual endeavors.

The above biograph mathematizes to figure 6 (page 289).

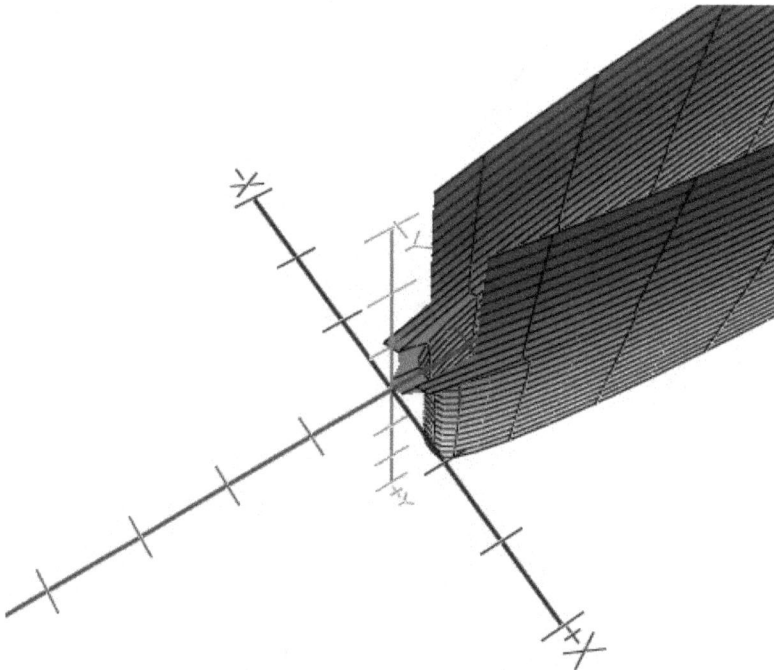

Figure 6 - Like Joseph Campbell's Hero's Journey, I return to myself...more or less. And it only took about ten years to do it!

7 – Linguistic Intersections

Figure 7 (page 290) is the intersection of the above biographies with the following color codings:

1995 – green
1997 – aqua
2000 – yellow
2003 – blue
2008(1) – red
2008(2) – orange

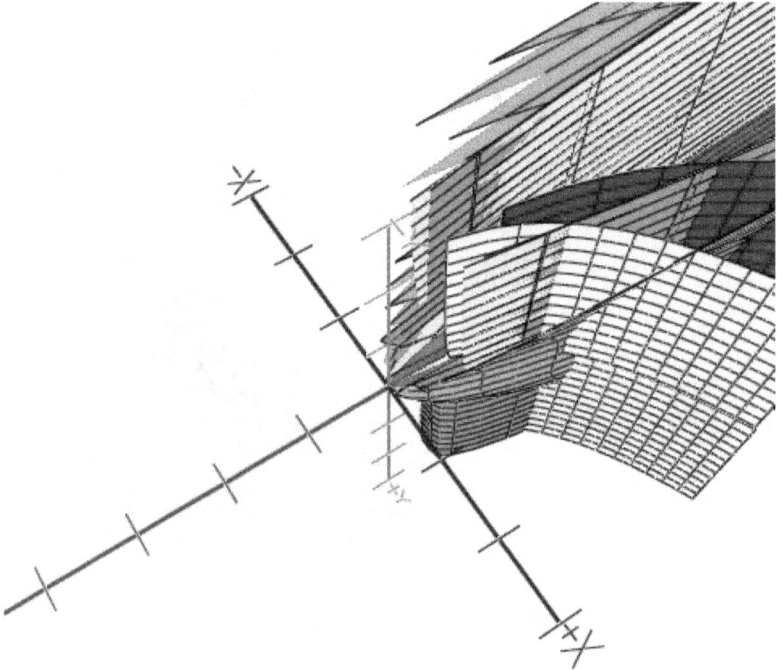

Figure 7 - Aside from a brief period from 2000-2003, people's concepts of me haven't changed all that much despite the differences in language used or topics referenced when they define me

It is fascinating in how well it demonstrates my mental states from 1995 to late in 2008 and that, even if these different biographers didn't recognize it, each were memorializing my changing self:

> 1995 – I was teaching, pushing students to work themselves, expand themselves and in doing so, expand me
>
> 1997– The original ET is fully operational and producing results. Susan and I are wondering what to do with it
>
> 2000 – I'm working for an online company. Susan and I decide to start NextStage Evolution although I have no idea what's involved in that so I go into an almost pure learning mode. My first lessons are from those in the online company whom I interact with daily. I struggle to be like them because (de facto due to ignorance) "Isn't that how people running a business are suppose to be?"
>
> 2003 – We've been at it for three years. We (I) come to the conclusion that these people (business folk, investors, others who call themselves "entrepreneurs", etc) are a bunch of idiots and I won't be like them because taking on their attitudes, beliefs and agendas is a) too painful and b) much of what they do is defined psychologically as "crazy-making behavior"
>
> 2008(1) – I've gotten rid of the last of the CEO-not's who was draining the company and am returning to my "arrogant, obnoxious and disliked" state of mind while keeping what I'd learned from the crazies easily accessible
>
> 2008(2) – As they say in 12-Step programs, I took what I liked and left the rest. I'm back to me with more knowledge, more ability...and I'm sure others would say "Definitely more of an attitude."

NextStage Evolution Live and Webinar Trainings

Much of the material covered in this book is available as both live and webinar trainings and classes. For that matter, there's a whole lot of stuff not covered in this book that's available as live and webinar trainings and classes.

Seriously, contact us at 603-791-4925 or info@nextstagevolution.com. Tell us what you want to learn. Chances are we already have a training on it, can modify an existing training to suit your exact needs or design a new training specific to your goals and desires.

Most frequently requested trainings can be found at http://nlb.pub/G. A training schedule is available at http://nlb.pub/l.

Comments from Live and Web Training Participants

"A MAGICAL TRIP! ... a phantasmagoric rollercoaster ride through our neural networks, showing us places we didn't know existed. And leaving us limp, giddy and exhilarated. ... push you to the wild fringe of your imagination and beyond. Race. Race. Race. Push your mind as far as it can go. MORE! We all wanted more." – Vienna, VA

"Put down your guard, stop thinking you know what you're doing, keep quiet, watch, learn, listen. Carrabis gave us 500 things if he gave us five and each one paid off a million fold." – St. John, NB

"...someone whose insights, talent and generosity with their time turned out to make a big difference in the quality of our work. ... You were a real find...and I wanted you to know that we are grateful to you." – Bedford, NH

"Carrabis is a wonderfully articulate speaker who draws on a lot of different images to makes things clear to people of many backgrounds." – Waltham, MA

"We didn't know what we didn't know until working with NextStage." – Bedford, MA

"I was unprepared for the amount of learning Carrabis packed into a one-day session." – Rothesay, NB

"Of all the tips and tricks that I learned, none proved more effective than the many I received from Mr. Carrabis in regards to the tone, inflection and proper nomenclature to be used in my pitch to the client. In fact, after one specific sitting with him I was able to improve my results 500%." – Burlington, MA

"Taking a NextStage seminar is rather like having the top of your skull surgically removed, turned around backwards and reattached. It's like trying to tell someone all the things you always believed were true, then finding those things sound silly even to you. It's like taking what you know and turning it inside out and upside down and backwards, and suddenly realizing it looks better that way. Taking a NextStage seminar will stretch your mind if your mind is capable of stretching without breaking. What are Carrabis' methods? I can't tell you, because the methods used in the seminars I attended probably won't be the ones he uses in yours. Carrabis suits the method to his current purpose, as far as I can tell, and you never know exactly what's going to happen until it already has, (believe me, I saw it time after time) you end all of a sudden with a clear understanding of something you didn't even know existed before you started. And it turns out to be something that's important to you! Amazing." – Columbia, SC

"I am not exaggerating: Everybody who has trained me has been excellent, but you are the best, really." – Burlington, MA

"I've worked with Joseph for three years and still find myself surprised by his truly unique perspective and insight. At the recent iMedia Brand Summit, his workshop was a big hit— both enlightening and entertaining the participants." – Los Angeles, CA

"...seeing your insights in action (especially with the relationship website and some of your ideas on how to present copy, deal with someone who is in pain, remove blame by replacing 'your relationship' with 'the relationship' – that was really cool. ... my favorite part of the time was discussing male versus female humor. ... Considering so many advertisers use humor in their ads, this is a super relevant subject." – NYC

"Ever since I met Joseph several years ago I was always fascinated by his ability to be so attentive to one's thoughts, emotions and physical messages. Since I do more speaking appearances and often meet with executives, I asked if he could coach me a little. The experience was revealing - it allowed me to uncover little things that will help me improve my verbal and non-verbal communication skills and even become more aware of others." – Stephane Hamel, Director of Innovation, Cardinal Path

"I've been lucky enough to have experienced one of the intensive individual trainings and it was simply mind-blowing/life-altering/universe-opening." – Dan Linton, Group Director Analytics at MRM // McCann

"An excellent investment of time. Joseph not only provided "how to interpret" but also gives actionable advice on 'how to respond'." – June Li, Managing Director, ClickInsight - Online Marketing Optimization Consulting

"This was a fabulous session with Joseph and the team on the moves that matter." – Dr. Amy Price, CEO at Empower2Go

"WOW, what an impressive webinar, thanks so much for opening the door, the cheek and the conversation. If you haven't had the pleasure of spending sometime with Joseph, you should start today. Different levels of information that fit just about every level of interaction. Take some time out and see if there is any room in his future classes well worth the time and energy plus you walk away ready to take on every level of interaction with a new approach. A must for business people wanting to better understand the emotions and subliminal references from their perspective business relationships." – Spencer Wade, Trusted Digital Media Adviser, Google Partner, Google Partners Ambassador, City Expert

"Impressive, informative content presented to our group of volunteers in an interactive approach. Each attendee brought a different perspective on how we were reading Joseph's facial expressions and hand gestures while exhibiting traits of our personality.
"By interpreting and better understanding the behavioral patterns encountered in business settings, we learned how to generate better outcomes by counteracting with different measures overseen in the training session.
"Joseph was great! We had lots of fun practicing in real time using a new set of tools to influence whoever we were interacting with by modifying our hand gestures and facial expressions. We all enjoyed our time together sharing thoughts and perceptions on issues encountered in our everyday life.
"Each of us will definitely perform and achieve better results. Thanks Joseph and each participant in our training session." – Lyn Demers, Business Development, Product Development, E-Marketing Strategies, CHINA LOGISTICS

"My 'Know how someone is thinking' training with Joseph and Susan was life altering. A year ago, I embarked on 'the journey' with them for two days in a conference room in New Hampshire. The training focused on them observing me, me observing them, and me observing myself. Through the repetition of observations they put the information into my 'deep memory'. After which, and for about two weeks, my brain underwent a process that literally 'hurt'. Thankfully, after that period, my brain continued to work on it subconsciously and with no pain.

"I was initially concerned I wouldn't remember what I'd learned, but to my delight, a year later, I've noticed that I'm even more skilled at reading people's micro-expressions than I was immediately after the training. I have used the knowledge and new brain wiring I have in various circumstances to my advantage; be it new business pitches, presentations to large and small audiences, negotiations with clients, management of my staff, as well as general interpersonal relationships.

"Knowing what they are thinking allows me to tailor myself and my communication to the needs of the situation be it putting someone at ease, or putting myself in a position of authority. I would and have, recommended this to anyone in a leadership, management or a sales position." – Shaina Boone, Managing Director, Marketing Decision Sciences at OMD USA

Contact Northern Lights Publishing

Did you enjoy Joseph Carrabis' ***Reading Virtual Minds Volume I: Science and History***? We hope so and would be interested in your thoughts on what worked and what didn't, and if you'd be interested in reading anything else by Joseph Carrabis or some of our other authors.

You can email us with your comments at feedback@northernlightspublishing.com.

Reading Virtual Minds Volume 2: Experience and Expectation Preview

Reading Virtual Minds Volume 2: Experience and Expectation is a big book that covers the following material and more:

> Experience versus Expectation
> Expectation versus Satisfaction
> You Have to Get As Good As You Give
> Digital Altruism
> Privacy, Identity and Digital Divisivity
> Floor-to-Ceiling Studies and Concept Price
> The New Cost of Information
> Getting as Good as You Give
> The Differences Between Use, Usable, Usability and Usage,
>   and how to design so each is maximized
> Case Studies
> (and more)

Perhaps the real benefit of Volume 2 is that each section has highlighted TakeAways. Each takeaway demonstrates a quick win for interface developers and designers.

From "Experience and Expectation"

People over a certain age, regardless of who they are or what they're doing, expect certain things to occur in certain ways. This process of expecting what has been experienced starts with birth and continues throughout life. The more varied someone's experiences are the less static their expectations, the less varied their experiences the more static their expectations. Someone who's never traveled beyond their town or neighborhood, is poorly-read and -educated, can only respond to new situations based on their neighborhood experiences. The individual who is well-traveled and/or well-read, who has opened themselves up to new experiences, is much more flexible in how they respond to new and novel situations.

What is the same in both the highly experienced and poorly experienced individuals' cases is that they will respond with tools first from their Personality, then from their Identity and lastly from their Core. They will go deeper inside themselves to get a desired outcome – to have their expectation fulfilled – based on how any given immediate experience escalates. This is why some people, when they're involved in some kind of negotiation (it can be with a partner, a peer, their family and sometimes in business) and are repeatedly not getting what they want, resort to childhood personae; they are literally going back through their life to find the right emotional key for this experiential lock and when maturity fails, out comes the child. This can be anything from the obstreperous, annoying child to the coy, cloying child. Basically whatever worked with their parents and siblings, that's what they'll resort to when all else fails. Ever see a grown man pout because his partner said "No!"? Congratulations, you've seen their inner child (oy, what an overused term!) coming out.

The poorly experienced person exhausts their Personality and Identity store fairly rapidly in new situations and, if they survive, this new experience modifies the last used element in that store. The individual who exhausts their Personality and Identity store and survives a new experience with tools from their Core will have their Identity and Personality stores modified by the new experiential information. This appears in language as "they've learned to expect it" or "they've learned what to expect". The individual who exhausts their Core and survives has their Core changed. Core change occurs when people go through "remission" from major disease, faith or spiritual upheaval and the like. The Apostle Paul's falling off his ass on the road to Damascus is an example of Core change. Literally, their life has acquired a new perceptual (cognitive) basis, new motivational drivers, new behavior patterns and ways of expressing their behaviors (effects) and if you've intuited that this means they've radically changed their {C,B/e,M} matrices, you're spot on and congratulations! Whatever their previous "mission" was in life – to have a family, to gain wisdom, to get rich – they've acquired a new "mission", hence we use the term "*re*mission" and in language this becomes "He's not the person he used to be" or "She's got a new lease on life", etc.

Long ago I knew a young Christian woman who had an amazing faith in her god. People loved to hear her testimony because she had such strong faith, always had a positive, uplifting attitude, always a smile, always a kind warming word for those around her. Her tag line was "I'm a Little Princess and my Daddy owns the Universe" and, forgive the marketing speak, she actually used that phrase to describe herself, time and time again, and you could hear the capitalization in the way she said it.

Her faith was based on a belief that god always answered her prayers and not in a general, god answers everybody's prayers sense. Her faith came from a belief in a genuine two-way communication between parent and child. I questioned her about this once and realized she had never really asked god for anything in her prayers, they were always psalmic odes for god's will or statements of acceptance of immediate situations as demonstrations of god's will. Somehow she had redefined this general bottom-up prayer into a genuine bidirectional communication.

One day I noticed she was agitated. She was flushed, her normally bright eyes were fearful, her breathing shallow and oral, almost panting, her voice quiet and anxious. In short, a major conflict between Identity and Core, and Personality was the casualty.

What had caused this?

God hadn't answered one of her prayers.

But god always answered her prayers. That was the basis of her faith.

This time her prayer was different. She asked god to act in someone else's benefit. Her prayer was no longer psalmic. She had, in gambling lingo, upped the ante believing her bet –her prayer – was a sure thing because god always answered her prayers.

Besides, this prayer wasn't for herself, it was for someone else. I didn't ask what the prayer was and whatever it was, god's silence demonstrated to her a broken covenant, a lost bet. For the first time in her life, her gamble hadn't paid off. She'd played old odds without realizing she'd changed how the odds were calculated and the result was that the god she worshipped was not the god she now knew. Several people spoke to her about this. God was testing her faith, so on and so forth. She responded, "But God doesn't test us beyond what we can endure." and this was beyond her endurance. Because god had never failed her, she promised a response to this other person and when none came, experience, a Core experience that was fueling her Identity and Personality, failed.

Experience had trained her to have certain expectations and now expectation-realized – what neuromathematicians and QBists know as "immediate experience" or "experience of the *Now*" – was not matching experience. Her agitation, fear, anxiety and especially frustration were all outward demonstrations of Personality, Identity and especially Core in chaos. The level of frustration, especially, was a demonstration of her Core in a high state of flux.

Frustration (as I use the term here) occurs when we've exhausted our repertoire of learned responses to a situation, when our solutions no longer work, when things aren't going as planned.

Children demonstrate frustration when their problem solving skills aren't up to the challenge at hand. Give a child a puzzle beyond their solving ability and, based on other factors in their environment, they'll either rise to the challenge or start repeating their known problem solving methods and continue failing. Good teachers watch for such things and intervene, demonstrating new problem solving skills or encouraging the child to explore alternatives. Bad teachers will set students up for failure, demonstrating weaknesses in the teacher's own Personality, Identity and Core.

Users demonstrate frustration when their problem solving skills aren't up to the challenge at hand. Give a user a new or modified interface without warning during an otherwise mundane upgrade and, based on other factors in their environment, they'll either rise to the challenge or start looking for elements of the old interface (which usually no longer exist) and continue failing. Good designers watch for such things and offer migration paths from old to new designs. Good designers create migration paths that demonstrate new problem solving skills or encourage the user to explore alternatives. Bad designers set users up for failure, demonstrating weaknesses in the designer's own Personality, Identity and Core.[a]

Notice how little those last two paragraphs are changed? Hopefully it's making you think.

TAKE-AWAY #1: PEOPLE WILL USE A NEW INTERFACE WHEN THEY BELIEVE IT REWARDS THEM MORE THAN THE OLD INTERFACE REWARDS THEM.

---

[a] – Here's a bit of psychology for you. People set up other people to fail when they fear them. They may fear them as individuals, as group members, they may fear what they will or won't do. It takes a bit of digging to determine what the fear is about and you'll always find it there. So bad designers set up users to fail because they fear...what? There is no greater group with imposter syndrome than digital property designers, it seems. I've had more web/digital designers have emotional blow ups because nobody could use their interfaces than in any other field I know.

www.ingramcontent.com/pod-product-compliance
Lightning Source LLC
Chambersburg PA
CBHW060329200326
41519CB00011BA/1883